The Making of Energy and Telecommunications Policy

Georgia A. Persons

PRAEGER

Westport, Connecticut
London

Library of Congress Cataloging-in-Publication Data

Persons, Georgia Anne.
   The making of energy and telecommunications policy / Georgia A.
   Persons.
        p.   cm.
   Includes bibliographical references and index.
   ISBN 0–275–95039–5
   1. Energy policy—United States.   2. Telecommunication policy—
   United States.   I. Title.
   HD9502.U52P467   1995
   333.7'0973—dc20   94–34318

British Library Cataloguing in Publication Data is available.

Library of Congress Catalog Card Number: 94–34318
ISBN: 0–275–95039–5

First published in 1995

Praeger Publishers, 88 Post Road West, Westport, CT 06881
An imprint of Greenwood Publishing Group, Inc.

Printed in the United States of America

The paper used in this book complies with the
Permanent Paper Standard issued by the National
Information Standards Organization (Z39.48–1984).

10 9 8 7 6 5 4 3 2 1

For
Bertha, Marshall, Michael,
Hattie, Milton, and Norman,
who share special places in my heart

Contents

Preface

This book grew out of a continuing interest in the activities of policymaking. As an observer of American politics, one notices that, like perpetual motion machines, two processes are always underway. Individuals and groups are always pressing Congress to give focused attention to particular problems, and Congress is always in the business of making policy to address some particular problem. These processes are rather visible thanks to continual updates by the national media. What is less visible from a public perch is the process by which the content of specific policy responses is determined. What happens when a group goes forth to enter the policymaking thicket to press Congress for a response to its problems? How are decisions made about which aspects of a problem are addressed in policy responses and which aspects are neglected? What happens to a group's idea of what would be an ideal or preferred response to its problems? What factors structure the policy debate on a particular problem? These are the kinds of questions which provoked the research and writing of this book.

The policy debates presented in this book come from the congressional legislative record, and some explanation of its contents and use are in order. The congressional legislative record is an invaluable source for tracking policy debates and other activities of the Congress and other federal agencies. It is comprised of four major parts, which were used extensively in this study.

1. *The Committee hearings record* is the most extensive and detailed record of congressional activities. Most hearings are held by subcommittees in each house, and the records are published by the subcommittee and the parent full committee. Select committees and joint committees also hold hearings and publish their records.
2. *Committee prints* are often continuing-interest reports prepared as follow-up on key issues raised in committee hearings. They provide background on issues and some analysis as well. Committee prints are usually prepared by committee staff and published on behalf of select, standing, and joint committees.

3. *Committee reports* are sometimes published to accompany a favorable or adverse report on a bill by the full committee. They not only provide background and discussion on a specific bill but frequently provide a summary discussion of prior hearings and legislation on a given topic.
4. *House and Senate Documents* are published by the Congress but are often reports prepared by other agencies as required by legislation or as otherwise requested. They are valuable in tracking implementation of component policy initiatives. Similar information can be found in the annual reports published by major federal agencies.

Access to the congressional legislative record is provided by way of the Congressional Information Service, which publishes both an index of topics covered in congressional hearings and an annual of summary data on hearings, reports, and legislation enacted into law.

The policy debate at the committee level is recorded in real time as it occurs at an identifiable place. The words of all participants are recorded by stenographers in the manner found in most courts of law. Each participant is identified by name and affiliation. Hearings usually begin with an opening statement by the chair of the sponsoring committee, followed by opening statements by each committee member desiring to speak. Some committee members and others not attending submit written statements for the official record, and such statements are so identified. Individuals appearing before the committee give oral testimony in accord with a preset time limit. Most participants provide a longer written statement, which is included in the official record immediately following their oral testimony. Participants may be questioned by members of the committee, and this question-and-answer exchange is recorded as well. In reporting on positions expressed by an individual, reference may be made to oral testimony, the written statement, responses to questions, or some combination of these.

The hearings record also contains reports of a great variety submitted by individual participants, correspondence between committee members and other governmental officials, newspaper clippings, etc. A few reports are referenced as being held in committee files and are not a part of the public record. Many hearings involve hundreds of witnesses, span several weeks, and yield multiple volumes of record totaling thousands of pages each. Some hearings records can make for tedious reading, but the overall effect of each hearing is that of witnessing a segment of a major drama. Collectively, the congressional hearings record reveals that annually we engage in what amounts to a national debate on a broad range of policy issues. The public does participate in this national debate, though not always in an optimally effective manner.

Utilization of the congressional legislative record to track policy debates makes for presentation of the policy debate in a relatively clear, chronological order as developments unfold over time. Reliance on this record also facilitates a desired containment of the debates. I have deliberately not reviewed coverage and interpretations of the policy debates as reported in trade journals and newspapers. The debates are largely told in the words of the participants. The interpretations, commentary, assessments, and analysis are those of the author. So, too, are the errors.

Research for this book was supported in part by the Georgia Tech Foundation, which provided salary for a summer of research and writing. Barbara Walker and Richard Leacy of the Government Documents Section of the Georgia Tech Library were always willing to be helpful beyond the call of duty. They demonstrated a friendship which provided much needed inspiration. Jane Holly Wilson, former administrative assistant in the School of Public Policy (and now retired), patiently typed the first draft of this book and was the first to declare it worthy of publication. I am indebted to the late Richelieu Richardson, who was my friend and constant companion during the research and first draft of this book. The legacy of that friendship remains a source of support.

Georgia A. Persons
Atlanta, Georgia

Part I

THE DYNAMICS OF POLICYMAKING

Chapter 1

Introduction: Policy Ideas and the Policy Debate

One of the most important things that government does in a democracy is to develop public policies in response to societal problems. Indeed the open and deliberate process of policymaking is a hallmark of a democratic society. Yet we have questions about how government responds, how it is that a decision is made to pursue one purposive course of action over another. Part of the answer to such questions is that what government decides to do, which purposive course of action it decides to pursue, is in part a function of how a particular problem gets defined. This factor is more significant than one might assume. As the chapters in this book reveal, in policymaking there is little about the process of problem definition that is self-evident, automatic, or eminently rational. Problems lend themselves to diverse definitions, only some of which are compelling enough to evoke formal policy responses.

This book is about how policy gets made and the role of policy ideas in the policymaking process. A policy idea is a concept designed to capture the essence of both a general definition of a problem and a preferred policy response. A policy idea captures that critical nexus between the definition of a problem and the formulation of a policy response which anticipates resolution of the problem via its implementation. When proffered in a policy debate, policy ideas capture the policymaking process whole—from identification of a societal problem to its resolution—and frame that process (Reich 1988).

Questions regarding the utility and fate of policy ideas are only part of the focus in this book. The assessments in the two case studies are intended to illuminate other questions pertinent to policy formulation, such as (1) how problems or issues get defined in the policy debate; (2) how policy responses emerge as solutions to specific definitions of problems; (3) how specific policy ideas structure the policy debate and under what circumstances; and (4) how bias mobilizes in favor of or against a particular policy idea.

Because they have responsibility for explaining how public policy gets made, analysts have responded by offering explanations which seek to simplify and make understandable that which is a veritable swamp of unpredictable processes and contradictory relationships. The conventional model of policymaking is that of a linear process comprised of identifiable and relatively distinct stages through which an issue evolves as it engages the attention of decisionmakers. In this model, an issue is given a formal definition, which is captured in an authoritative response in the form of a statute or other policy formation. The policy is implemented, evaluated, refined, and so on (Anderson 1990). Although analysts have never argued that Congress explicitly focuses on problem definition as a distinct phase to agree on a precise definition of a problem before proceeding further in policymaking, the notion of a policy process implies a certain degree of analytical rigor and deliberate thinking and acting. The model suggests that policymaking should be comprehensive in terms of the breadth of assessment of a particular problem, deliberative in terms of consideration of a range of solutions suggested by this assessment, and rational in terms of the course of action decided on. We know that in practice the policymaking process is far less deliberate and focused than the model of the process implies. One of the questions which provoked the analyses presented in this book is whether policy ideas, which by their definition and apparent purpose imply a rational linkage between problem definition and policy response, in actuality bring structure and focus to the policymaking process.

This book explores the role of policy ideas in policy formulation. The specific context is the policy debate carried out at the level of congressional committees in the formal congressional hearings process. Congressional hearings at the subcommittee and full committee levels provide a forum for the primary policy debate in Congress, in which both authoritative decisionmakers and the public participate. It is at the level of committee hearings that the parameters which bound future debate on the House and Senate floor are set. It is also at this level that problem definition takes place, albeit in an undirected and somewhat muddled process. Indeed, one observes an informal process of problem definition. Early legislative proposals basically serve as trial balloons. They help to structure the debate but have little chance of passage. Among these are legislative proposals dedicated to responding to a single definition of a problem. Many subsequent legislative proposals represent synthesis of and responses to the concerns raised in the debate on the early round of proposals. Thus these latter proposals usually define and embrace a larger set of related problems. These latter proposals are also more often accorded major consideration as the policy debate fully develops. Dedicated or single-idea proposals usually receive considerably less consideration in the policy debate and are relegated to a secondary status. Sometimes major shifts occur in the policy debate in which an ongoing debate gets enveloped within the context of an emergent, overarching policy theme that has significant political currency (such as the policy themes of energy conservation and deregulation). The sometimes short-lived but potent currency of overarching policy themes can affect the saliency of specific policy ideas, spawn new policy ideas, and generally provide a new context for problem definition. If particular policy ideas are to hold sway in the policy debate, it is in this informal process of problem definition that they must do so.

In this study, the fate of a specific policy idea—that of lifeline rates—is examined in policy debates in two areas: (1) reform of electric utility ratemaking, and (2) efforts to rewrite telecommunications policy. In the first case, lifeline rates were proposed as a policy response to the severe and adverse impacts of rapidly rising utilty costs on elderly citizens in the aftermath of the Arab oil embargo of the early 1970s. The idea of lifeline rates was to provide a basic amount of electric energy sufficient to sustain the basic essentials of living—cooking, refrigeration, heating and cooling, clothes washing—and to guarantee electric energy at a fixed rate affordable to elderly citizens and others on low and fixed incomes. Thus, lifeline rates were an idea which incorporated a policy response deemed appropriate given the nature and definition of the problem as initially perceived. In the debate on telecommunications policy, the idea of lifeline rates emerged as a response to anticipated rapid increases in the costs of basic telephone service due to the introduction of competition in a formerly monopoly service. The restructuring of the telecommunications industry was expected to result in a problem of "drop-off" as many subscribers would be unable to afford the costs of retaining basic telephone service and many others would be rendered unable to afford the costs of having telephone service installed. In this case, lifeline rates were advanced as a policy solution to a practical problem and as an embodiment of the public interest. It was posited that the public interest would be served by retaining the maximum number of subscribers on the national telecommunications network, thus enhancing the value of what had become a utility service essential to life in modern society.

In the case of the policy debate to develop a response to the impact of high electric energy costs on the elderly/low-income consumer, the idea of lifeline rates emerged early. The debate initially drove a series of emergency, bureaucratic responses utilizing preexisting policy mandates. The public law that eventually emerged from the debate, the Public Utilities Regulatory Policies Act, reformed electric utility ratemaking and incorporated the idea of lifeline rates in what was largely a symbolic gesture. However, in the end, the problem of high energy costs causing further impoverishment of elderly/low-income citizens was dealt with in a separate and dedicated policy response. In the case of the debate on rewriting telecommunications policy, the issue of lifeline policy emerged early as well but was set aside as an explicit focus of the debate. However, the issue that provoked the idea of telephone lifeline—higher rates for basic service—remained at the center of the debate over whether and how the public interest would beserved by competition in telecommunications. In the end, telecommunications policy was not altered through the legislative process despite an extended policy debate focusing on such an effort. Lifeline policy was adopted in administrative rulings by the Federal Communications Commission (FCC).

This, then, is a story of two policy debates joined by a focus on the policy idea of lifeline rates. The two debates are similar in that they also involve major issues of social policy in conflict with pressures to develop policies to maximize the use of new technologies in the pursuit of economic efficiency. Both debates are about major areas of regulatory policy which involve utility services vital to a quality lifestyle as defined by modern American society.

Although policy ideas embrace both problem definition and solutions in ways which can potentially simplify the tasks of policymaking, these constructs encounter the difficulty of bridging the chasm which divides considerations of technical issues and issues of social policy.

Just as problems are interwined, with one problem being part of a matrix of other problems, one might argue or assume that policy responses would be intertwined as well. Such is frequently the case, but there appear to be critical exceptions. The policy debates presented here involve policymaking in the broad areas of energy policy and telecommunications policy, both of which lie within the analytical category of regulatory policy. However, both debates involve major issues of social policy—how to mitigate severe impacts of rising prices for basic utility services on the elderly and low income—in conflict with arguments in support of maximizing the use of new technologies in pursuit of economic efficiency. The goals were in conflict because the argument and reasoning of major participants in the debate viewed them as mutually exclusive. In both cases, the argument for maximizing economic efficiency was an argument against the idea of lifeline rates and was not otherwise an integral element of preferred problem definitions or policy options. In the case for reforming electric utility ratemaking, the early argument, which favored abandoning declining block rates (a pricing scheme which favored high- volume users at the expense of low-volume users), lost priority to a value of greater suasion, that of energy conservation. The issue of affordability was set adrift. Although the debate on telecommunications policy focused extended attention on the question of whether long-distance revenues subsidized local telephone service under the AT&T monopoly, the primary concern was not one of maximizing economic efficiency. Rather, the larger issue which drove the debate was that of facilitating or mandating competition. In other words, the basic issue was one of opening up access to the telecommunications industry to a host of new entrants, who sought to exploit the availability of new technologies in the pursuit of handsome profits.

This study reveals that policy ideas which attempt to bridge the conventional dichotomy between technical issues and social problems must first obtain legitimacy in the policy debate, survive a protracted debate and policymaking activities to develop responses to the technical issues, and then await a policy response based on chance and political indulgence.

The two case studies presented here also provide insights into an interesting contrast in policymaking activities. In the first case of electric utility reform, the policy debate pivots around the search for a solution to a particular problem or set of related problems as defined by the debate. The problem was initially defined as a seasonal crisis of economic hardships due to rapidly rising energy costs and physical hardships due to an inability to pay to heat poorly insulated homes. This provoked an interim response of a major weatherization effort supported by supplemental funding of an existing statutory mandate and implemented by existing bureaucratic structures. Subsequent legislative proposals seeking long-term policy responses presented varying definitions of the problem. For example, for the problem of affordability of basic energy requirements for residential consumers, a special lifeline rate for basic energy usage was proposed. For the problem of closed, nonparticipatory ratemaking proceedings by state public service commissions (PSCs), proposals were offered which mandated enhanced citizen participation. For the problem of wasteful usage of electric energy encouraged by declining block rates, proposals were made to structure electricity rates to encourage energy conservation. These were, comparatively speaking, more routine aspects of policymaking in which problems are defined and solutions proposed.

In the case of rewriting telecommunications policy, the core issue of the debate was much more profound. The debate pivoted around the primary question of whether to abandon monopoly and permit competition in telecomunications. The monopoly arrangement was coupled in both public perceptions and settled regulatory policies and practices with the goal of universal service as an embodiment of the public interest in telecommunications policy. It is frequently the case that statutory delegations of authority to regulatory agencies contain broad statements of the public interest which constitute standards for establishing derivative administrative rulings of enormous consequence. Such was the case with the FCC and the Communications Act of 1934. Thus any consideration of rewriting telecommunications policy entailed the crucial question of whether and how to redefine the public interest in this major area of public policy. That question made this debate a far less routine exercise in policymaking.

Another area of illumination yielded by this study are the differing roles of Congress in policymaking and the variable relationships beween Congress and other institutions in policymaking activities. Congress has constitutional and institutional rank over other institutional players in the policy process. In other words, Congress has superordinate authority but not exclusive authority in policymaking. Congress has the prerogative of being the major initiator of policy and, in effect, has legislative veto power in that it can pass laws to undo the actions of other branches and agencies of government. This superordinate authority of the Congress can have a singular effect on the policy debate and on influencing the policy initiatives of other institutions. However, the superordinate authority of Congress is sometimes of greater significance in potential than in actuality.

In the case of electric utility rate reform, Congress was the driving force behind policy considerations and bureaucratic responses by other agencies of government. Congress defined the problems, decided on the appropriate solutions, and enacted long-term policies via legislative statutes. Although there was considerable influence by the executive branch over the course of the debate, Congress retained the lead role. Such was not the case in the debate over telecommunications policy.

In the debate on telecommunications policy, Congress's main opponent in the contest for lead policymaker was the FCC. This occurred despite the fact that Congress makes the foundational policy which sets the anchors and parameters for the FCC and other regulatory agencies. Although regulatory agencies may exercise a broad reach in policymaking activities, such initiatives are expected to be in accord with the statutory mandate granted by Congress. Regulatory agencies, in particular, are expected to make what we might call derivative policies. In this study, we observe how a regulatory agency can extend the reach of its original enabling legislation in unexpected and probably unintended ways. In its derivative policymaking role, the FCC adopted and implemented over time a major new policy of competition in telecommunications. The FCC had two major advantages over Congress in this effort. First, the FCC had the advantage of specialized expertise and institutional memory in an area of arcane and technical policy issues. This constituted an essentially insurmountable hurdle for Congress. Second, Congress was faced with the challenge of legislating major changes in an area of settled policy in which underlying definitions, standards, and administrative rulings have cumulative and interlocking meanings which have also been reinforced by judicial rulings. To attempt to supplant an enormous body of settled policy with new policy would have risked economic and legal havoc in a vast and vital national industry. Although the FCC had incentives to be responsive to congressional concerns and pleadings, the FCC also held some critical advantages and thus never abandoned its policy course. Congress's significant power potential was difficult, perhaps even impossible, to realize.

One major observation made in this book about the policymaking process is that it is indeed a protracted one. We observe a seven-year policy cycle in both cases presented from the time at which an issue is raised to the enactment of a definitive policy response. Seven years is a long time. However, one might choose to be impressed by the fact that issues can be retained on the policy agenda for such an extended period of relatively sustained attention. In the case of telecommunications policy, the policy debate was propelled along by FCC rulings, Department of Justice antitrust proceedings, and AT&T's reactions to these. However, over the course of the debate on electric utility ratemaking and low-income energy assistance, we observe Congress as a major participant in and facilitator of an extended process of national energy planning.

Another major observation is that although there is an absence of predictability in the policymaking process, one should not rush to conclude that there is also an absence of order. What we observe is that the process of policymaking is a purposeful one, and from that process, order ensues.

REFERENCES

Anderson, James E. *Public Policymaking: An Introduction.* Boston: Houghton Mifflin Co., 1990

Reich, Robert, ed. *The Power of Public Ideas.* Boston: Ballinger Press, 1988.

Part II

THE POLICY DEBATE ON LIFELINE RATES AND ENERGY POLICY

Chapter 2

The Emergence of Lifeline Rates as an Idea in Electric Utility Ratemaking

SETTING THE STAGE: THE ROLE OF NONLEGISLATIVE COMMITTEES IN DEFINING THE POLICY DEBATE

Most formal policymaking activities are carried out by the various standing committees in each house, which have functional jurisdictions that overlap with the functions of broad segments of the executive and judicial branches. It is the standing committees which process legislation and thus exercise significant power and have received most attention from scholars and the media. Special or select committees, on the other hand, serve to investigate major issues which are not covered by the provinces of standing committees, but they do not process legislation. However, there are significant similarities between the two types of committees. For example, the Senate Special Committee on Aging (hereinafter referred to as the Special Committee) was authorized in its 1961 charter to (1) hold hearings; (2) sit and act at any time or place during the sessions, recesses, and adjournment periods of the Senate; (3) by subpoena or otherwise require the attendance of witnesses and production of correspondence, books, papers, and documents; (4) administer oaths; and (5) take testimony orally or by deposition. Thus, although less attention is given to the activities of special committees, they are not without power and are clearly in a position to provide an important forum for discussion of issues and, in turn, provide vital input into both the front-end stages of the policymaking process as well as the monitoring and feedback on policy implementation. It was within the context of its ongoing activities in monitoring the state of affairs of elderly Americans that the Special Committee first heard testimony about the severe impacts of the 1973 Arab oil embargo on the lives of the low-income elderly:

Closed gasoline stations, diminished heating fuel stocks, and soaring fuel policies began to make an impact on the lifestyles and pocketbooks of older Americans in the closing months of 1973. Travel had to be curtailed; homes became colder; and budgets already stretched by inflationary costs of food and other essential items were hard hit by rising fuel costs.[1]

The preceding quote reflects the tenor of concerns about the effects of the oil embargo on older Americans as initially expressed in hearings before the Special Committee. These concerns were raised in February 1974 hearings on the transportation problems and needs of the elderly. The impacts of the energy crisis on the elderly were felt to be greater than problems traditionally caused by inflation. The elderly were deemed hardest hit in (1) the overall cost of living, because gasoline prices had risen 12 to 15 cents per gallon in the last quarter of 1973; (2) employment, with a loss of jobs due to the energy crisis; and (3) programs serving older Americans, because gas lines had curtailed the activities of volunteers whose support was vital to many programs serving the elderly. Some elderly nutrition programs had been shut down in counties in some states due to gasoline shortages.[2] Thus the central issue of an expanding range of impacts due to the energy crisis was raised in a series of early hearings devoted primarily to other issues.

The first round of dedicated hearings by the Special Committee on "the impact of rising energy costs on older Americans" was held in late September 1974.[3] The calling of dedicated hearings reflected the severity of the problem and the growing saliency of the issue. Senator Lawton Chiles of Florida presided over the first hearing and set the context of the problem by reading excerpts of letters from his constituents attesting to electric bills which equalled the size of house payments; the deprivation of things like a telephone, newspapers, and church donations due to high energy bills; panic caused by dependency on heavy air conditioning due to health problems such as high blood pressure and heart irregularities; the substitution of proper food in order to pay energy costs; and inconveniences caused by being unable to afford to drive automobiles. Senators from northern climes reported similar stories from constituents regarding their inability to heat their homes during the preceeding winter.[4]

The hearings brought together a mix of concerned observers, representatives of various advocacy groups, federal administrators, and elected and appointed officials from state governments. This relatively small group (the numbers would swell dramatically during later congressional hearings on actual legislative proposals) formed the initial cast of characters, who would lay the foundation in this first round of hearings for the policy proposal which would eventually evolve out of the extended hearings process. The participants represented (1) The Ford Foundation, which through its energy policy project had compiled a major study of the nation's energy conditions and was seeking to influence the broad contours of a new national energy policy; (2) the chairman of the Florida Public Service Commission, who described his state's commission as one which was caught in the middle between an alarmed public and insistent utilities both of whom were concerned and sometimes overwhelmed by rising energy and fuel costs; (3) the governor of Pennsylvania, who was on the receiving end of growing citizens' complaints about rising energy costs but who was unable to exert any controls or influence the actions of his state's public utility commission; (4) the National Urban League, which was a well-established advocacy group working on behalf of the black poor; (5) the National Council of Senior Citizens, one of several advocacy groups representing the elderly; (6) the National Association of Retired Teachers and the American Association of Retired Persons (AARP and NRTA), who consistently issued joint positions throughout this policy debate; (7) the Administration on Aging, an office within the then Department of Health, Education and Welfare (HEW), responsible for administering programs established under the Older Americans Act of 1966; (8) the Consumer Federation of America (CFA), one of the oldest consumer advocacy groups noted for its empirically based analytical studies of consumer issues; (9) the Office of Economic Opportunity (OEO) which had a network of program offices throughout the nation that facilitated its contact and presence at the grassroots level; (10) and the Federal Energy Administration (FEA).[5] The FEA was a new agency with part of its mandate to recommend new or modified federal policies for alleviating the adverse effects of energy problems on consumers, the poor, the handicapped, and the elderly and to assist in the implementation of new programs.[6] It was an impressive group which assembled to develop ideas for policy responses to the energy crisis.

DEFINING THE PROBLEM AND CONTEMPLATING SOLUTIONS

All of the representatives at the hearing seemed to share some common sense of the plight of the elderly poor in regard to the energy crisis, although that shared conception was far from definitive. Part of the problem was the difficulty of defining the energy needs of the poor, elderly or otherwise. The energy needs of the poor varied according to whether they were renters or homeowners; whether they lived in extreme northern climes, southern climes, or moderate climes; how well insulated their dwellings were; and the mix of appliances to which they had access. A survey conducted by the Washington Center for Metropolitan Studies and made available to The Ford Foundation and federal agencies had provided a somewhat rigorous analysis on energy usage by the poor and had provided as well an income categorization of the poor. The poor was defined as a family with an average annual income (in 1974) of $2500, with a typical size of two to three people. A disproportionate share of the poor was said to be elderly, and 70 percent of the poor were said to have annual incomes of less than $3000. The poor was said to spend much more of its income for energy than the welloff—15 percent compared to 4 percent. Yet the poor was found to use less energy than other groups and to use it almost entirely for basic essentials such as heat and light, heating hot water, cooking, and refrigeration. More than half of the homes of the poor were found to have no insulation at all, and more than half owned no private automobile. The poor was found to pay more per unit of electricity and natural gas because of the way energy prices were structured. Electricity and natural gas were priced such that the higher the level of consumption, the lower the per unit costs. Thus the poor paid more because they used less.[7] This latter point was an oft-repeated one and would become a driving force in formulating a policy response.

During these early hearings, there was no other common database of national energy costs undergirding the committee's deliberations. The data available were reported by individual members of the Special Committee in regard to developments in their home states, or by individuals who provided similar isolated data points in their testimonies. An example of a national accounting of rising energy costs, which was referred to frequently by some participants, was contained in a newspaper column written by financial analyst Sylvia Porter for the *Idaho Statesman* on September 9, 1974; this column was entered into the formal record of the committee hearing. Porter reported that (1) in Maine the average cost of heating a home rocketed from $400 to $800 a year; (2) in South Dakota the price of propane jumped from 15 cents per gallon in January 1973 to 29 cents a year later; (3) in New England, number 2 home heating oil rose from 20 to 40 cents a gallon; (4) coal prices multiplied as much as five times in some areas where the rural poor relied on coal stoves, including Kentucky (where the price of a ton of coal jumped from $8 to $40 per ton in one year); and (5) Federal Power Commission estimates of increased demands for natural gas meant that industries would be competing with utilities, thus further driving up prices for the average individual consumer.[8] Similarly, the formal statement submitted for the record by the National Association of Retired Teachers (NRTA) and the American Association of Retired Persons (AARP) included a chart of increases in typical (average of 500 kilowat-hour, or kwh) monthly electric bills for ten cities, citing the Federal Power Commission as the source of the data.[9] However, the absence of a formal national database on rising energy costs did not mean that the participants in the hearings, who came from various parts of the country, did not have a good sense of the enormity of the problem of rising energy costs and its impact in their hometowns and nationwide.

In addition to offering varied conceptions of aspects of the problem of rising energy costs, the participants in this first round of hearings offered solutions as well. The chairman of the Florida public utility commission (PUC) depicted the position of the commission as being caught in a squeeze between two groups demanding relief from uncontrollable energy costs: consumers and the state's electric utilites. Utilities were paying increasing costs for the fuels they used to generate electricity. In addition, different utility companies in the state used different mixes of foreign oil, foreign or domestic coal, hydropower, and nuclear fuels, thus leading to different electric rates in different parts of the state. This was a situation which appeared confusing and suspect to many consumers. The most distressing factor for consumers was the steep rise in electric bills. The commissioners reported that for the typical residential consumer using the average amount of electricity of 1000 kwh per month, rates had increased from a basic charge of $20.87 and a fuel adjustment charge of $4.45 for a total of $25.32 in January 1974, to a basic charge of $22.07 and a fuel adjustment charge of $15.05 for a total monthly charge of $37.12 in September 1974.[10] The utilities were paying much higher charges for their generating fuels and were passing those charges on to customers. For many elderly Floridians who were dependent on constant air conditioning for a nine-month-long hot season, the commissioners understood that the impact was in many cases severe. Florida residential consumers were said to use an estimated 40 percent more electricity than the national average on a year-round basis. Fuel adjustment charges had risen from 0.320 cents per kwh in November 1973 to 1.560 cents in October 1974.[11] No end to the problem was foreseen. The utilities themselves faced severe problems. Overall Florida utility stock prices were down, resulting in a decline in investment, and their interest rates for borrowing were up considerably. Even after having been granted a 13 to 15 percent return on equity, Florida's utilities still faced financial difficulties. Thus, Florida's commissioners endorsed the idea of a federal "energy stamp" program to aid needy utility customers.[12]

The representative of the National Council of Senior Citizens testified that the 20 percent rise in the Consumer Price Index (CPI) since 1972 had canceled out the 20 percent increase in social security benefits received by the elderly in 1972, and the 11 percent cost of living adjustment (COLA) subsequently received had simply held the purchasing power of social security beneficiaries to their 1971 level. The Council thus called for the following: (1) that there be a semi-annual COLA; (2) that the Department of Labor (DOL) be required to compute a special CPI for the elderly which more accurately reflected their energy costs; (3) that the elderly be granted a 50 percent reduction in charges for gas, electricity, and telephone services; (4) that there be free public transportation for the elderly within their communities; (5) that mass transportation be treated as a social utility; and (6) that utilities eliminate the cash deposit requirements for connecting service for senior citizens. Interestingly, the council expressed reservations about "some kind of special grant for fuel, particularly if it would be tied with an income and means test."[13]

Another representative of the AARP and NRTA also testified about the deeply felt impacts of higher energy costs on the low-income elderly, offering real-life cases of steep increases in costs for homeowners and renters. He also testified that a report in *U.S. News and World Report* had revealed that at least five utility companies had requested rate increases to offset loss in revenues due to consumers conserving energy. The AARP and NRTA recommended that any reductions in elderly income due to high energy costs be offset by real increases in social security benefits. The AARP and NRTA also proposed that benefit increases in turn be financed by channeling funds from a windfall profits tax to be imposed on oil companies, that the Department of Housing and Urban Development (HUD) be authorized to provide low-cost loans to the aged for home insulation, and that HUD develop special energy conserving designs for HUD-assisted housing.[14]

The AARP and NRTA representative also mentioned having heard about a legislative proposal put forth by Senator Mathias of Maryland in regard to a feasibility study on a federal fuel stamp program and had implied at least a tacit AARP and NRTA endorsement of the feasibility study. Senator Mathias had submitted a statement to the Special Committee explaining the thrust of his proposal. Mathias had proposed (as an amendment to S. 3221, The Energy Supply Act of 1974) an amendment directing the Administrator of the FEA and the Secretary of HEW to jointly undertake a sixty-day study to examine the feasibility of establishing a fuel stamp program, patterned after the food stamp program, and utilizing the existing administrative machinery of local welfare offices. Mathias proposed that eligible beneficiaries include all persons existing on fixed incomes. Mathias lamented the specter of any citizens being forced to sacrifice food for fuel in the upcoming winter months.[15]

The Administrator of the Administration on Aging also expressed concern about the suitability of the CPI as a basis for social security COLAs for the elderly. The concern was that by using increases in the CPI as the basis for the automatic COLA escalator, the impact of price increases in certain inflation-prone items on which the elderly spent disproportionately was actually underestimated. The Administrator also spoke somewhat obliquely of the impact of "inverted rate schedules" adopted by utilities in which rates are reduced after an initial kilowatt-hour usage. These inverted rate schedules were deemed to pose an economic disadvantage for the elderly poor, who used less electricity than the average family.[16]

The National Urban League had issued a call for a fuel stamp program in June 1974; had submitted a proposal for a ten-city pilot program to the FEA;[17] and reiterated its recommendations in the September hearings. The Urban League recommended a means-tested energy stamp program patterned after the food stamp program. It also recommended direct cash assistance as a means of providing relief to the elderly poor. The energy stamps would be provided to eligible consumers, who would in turn use them to pay utility bills and purchase home heating oil or gasoline. The FEA had responded negatively to the Urban League proposal, arguing that the FEA did not have the staff to administer such a program, that such a program would constitute a subsidy to the petroleum industry, that the agency's funding from Congress did not include provisions for such a program, and that the agency would need requisite congressional authority to consider such a program. The Urban League argued that subsidies to the petroleum industry, in the form of tax incentives, were nothing new and pointed out the specific section of the FEA Act which gave the Administrator of FEA authority to initiate a pilot energy stamp program.[18] The National Urban League also recommended that utilities be required to notify social service agencies of impending cutoffs of service to the elderly poor for nonpayment during winter months.[19]

The idea of a national fuel stamp program was opposed by the Consumer Federation of America (CFA) because it was felt that fuel oil dealers, gasoline dealers, and others could not readily accommodate the types of transactions which would be required. Testifying for the CFA, James Feldesman argued that a fuel stamp program would also emerge from Congress with a work provision attached to it requiring that people first report to employment offices before buying fuel stamps, thus adding a burden for many would-be beneficiaries. The CFA proposed instead a cash fuel adjustment provision to be added to the payments of all persons receiving cash benefits from federal or state governments. Remarking on the lack of an extensive set of hard data to undergird any proposed remedy, the CFA proposed that the FEA be required to use some of its consultant money to support a quick study to assess the extent of those individuals needing emergency grants or loans to pay for fuel. The extent or need for emergency assistance had been deemed enormous by emergency activities undertaken by the OEO the prior winter. The CFA also called for the FEA to organize an interagency task force to explore ways in which federal agencies could coordinate assistance for energy-related problems.[20]

Concern about some of the complications which would arise from the adoption of a fuel stamp program was raised by Alvin Arnett, the former Director of the OEO. Arnett pointed out that any additional subsidies for the poor would have the effect of a loss of income from other sources. The issue was that state and federal income-support programs were tied to income and need, with a predetermined allowance for energy costs being factored into need assessment. Thus, without proper legislative or administrative authorization of exemptions, any increment in cash or in-kind income support from a new source might be offset by a corresponding loss in traditional income support. Although this was a valid issue, it was subject to easy remedy in the statutory language authorizing any new assistance program. The OEO representative also testified about a big problem of utility services being cut off to poor households, and he called for a congressional requirement that OEO have an official advocacy role for the poor in any and all FEA rulemaking that affected the poor.[21]

S. David Freeman of The Ford Foundation took the opportunity presented by the hearings to announce the forthcoming (October 1974) release of the Foundation's major report on the nation's energy condition, *A Time to Choose*. The Foundation also issued a call for a coherent, national energy policy. The thurst of Freeman's testimony was an argument to expand the policy focus beyond the elderly poor to include all low-income groups and to place a heavy emphasis on what might be characterized as a comprehensive approach to energy conservation. The argument was that the poor and everyone else would benefit from energy conservation. Specifically Freeman argued for (1) making credit available, especially to low-income families, via a specific federal loan fund to insulate existing homes; (2) an immediate action program to insulate public housing; (3) upgrading standards for federally insured mortgages to require better insulation in new homes; (4) abolishing utility promotional rates, which charge lower unit prices for greater volumes of use, unless they are clearly cost based (Freeman was referring to inverted rate structures, also called declining block rates. They were called promotional rates because electric utilities used to promote the development and purchasing of "total electric homes" by emphasizing the low energy costs associated with such homes.); (5) making mandatory the labeling of major appliances, in terms easily understood by consumers, regarding the energy costs of operating them; (6) increasing federal funding of mass transit; and (7) setting performance standards for automobiles which would require new cars to meet minimum levels of fuel economy. To alleviate the immediate burdens of high energy costs, Freeman recommended a cash grant of $10 per household per month to supplement existing support programs.[22]

Freeman's recommendations were clearly directed toward influencing the development of a national energy policy—an effort ongoing at the time—which went beyond the exigencies of the immediate crisis being experienced by the low income and went beyond the immediate focus of the hearings. However, the strong emphasis on energy conservation as a national imperative which was embodied in Freeman's testimony would later become a dominant theme in the formal public policy which eventuated from the problem identified in these hearings. Though it might not have been immediately apparent, the foundation had been laid for a major expansion and transformation of the policy debate on the energy crisis.

In addition to calling for a fuel stamp program to be funded by a windfall profits tax, Governor Milton Sharp of Pennsylvania also gave testimony which significantly expanded the range of issues to be factored into a definition of the problem of rising energy costs and the range of proposed solutions. Governor Sharp was rather blunt in asserting that the Pennsylvania PUC was woefully illequipped to deal with the situation of rapidly rising fuel costs for utilities or customers. He asserted that the PUC was poorly staffed and lacked the appropriate skilled professionals; that the staff was unable to conduct a thorough examination of utility records; that it had only recently hired a certified public accountant; that the PUC staff did not have the expertise to judge what was or was not a fair rate; that rates were being set more or less arbitrarily; that public hearings were held in the remotest parts of the state and at weird hours; and that a new Sunshine Law had been passed but that the PUC had rushed through a series of rate increases prior to the law taking effect despite a plea from the governor to delay decisions by a few days.

The governor also spoke of the restrictions imposed by Pennsylvania state law on aggrieved individuals who sought court review of PUC decisions. Governor Sharp asserted that aggrieved individuals were automatically required to hire legal counsel and experts to analyze utility records at a deliberately high cost to render individual consumers effectively bereft of any remedial action. Indeed, the governor testified that a state court had ruled that even the attorney general of the state could not intervene to represent consumers but could only represent himself as an individual. The governor testified that his attempt to force a consumer advocate onto the PUC staff as its legal counsel had been undermined by the Chairman of the PUC, who had set the salary for the legal counsel position at zero.[23]

Governor Sharp also testified that the FEA needed more consumer input because its decisionmaking was dominated by the energy industries and its professional staff was disproportionately comprised of former employees of energy companies. The FEA was an agency newly created to develop national responses to the national energy crisis and was therefore feeling enormous political pressures. It was also experiencing the frustration of significant constraints on its ability to affect the range of changes at the level of state utility regulation deemed necessary to ease aspects of the energy crisis. Furthermore, the FEA was uncomfortable with some aspects of its mission as implicitly defined by some solutions proposed to alleviate the financial burden on low-income consumers. John Sawhill, Administrator of the FEA, offered testimony explaining the actions of his agency with regard to easing energy costs, and he offered some specific proposals for short- and long-term solutions.

Sawhill began his testimony by assuring his agency's critics that he had structured the agency's organization to meet the mandate of the FEA Act to ensure that the economic impact of proposed energy regulatory and other policies did not work undue hardships on low- and middle-income groups. He announced the merger of the Office of Consumer Affairs and The Office of Special Impacts, as well as the raised status of the new office to a policymaking level within the agency. He also announced establishment of a policy analysis unit within the new office with a directive to offer input into development of the Blueprint for Energy Independence. Project Independence was the effort to develop a comprehensive national energy plan. Sawhill also informed the committee of the FEA's efforts to work with state PUCs to affect substantive change in utility rate structures, including two specific proposals. First, he recommended that PUCs adopt a Low basic rate in which the first monthly increment of electricity would be billed at a rate lower than succeeding increments. An initial increment of about 400 kwh was recommended. This provision was seen as encouraging energy conservation while assisting low-income consumers who did not use much energy.

Second, Sawhill recommended that PUCs adopt peak load pricing as a means of expanding the amount of electric generating capacity utilized on a normal basis beyond the average of 51 percent. (With peak load pricing, consumers are encouraged to shift their consumption activities away from time periods of high or peak demand-for example between 4 and 10 P.M.-to periods of low demand, such as between 1 and 5 A.M. Also called time-of-day pricing, the idea is to even out the demand for energy by drawing on and better utilizing base capacity and avoiding the development and use of reserve peaking units which are used only during times of very high demand and cause significant increases in generating costs, among other things.) It was believed that the elderly in particular could take advantage of peak load pricing, because they had more flexible schedules than working citizens. However, in later questioning, Sawhill indicated that he had no regulatory authority to compel state PUCs to adopt these measures and thus had to rely on moral suasion.

Sawhill also announced a five-city pilot program begun by FEA to assess how effectively and rapidly insulation of homes could be achieved. This effort was duplicative of a highly touted experiment launched by the OEO in the state of Maine, with the result that the OEO was seen as the sole federal agency which had mounted a direct response to the emergencies created by the energy crisis. Sawhill urged that Congress assign the FEA lead responsibility to work with other grantmaking agencies—OEO, HEW, HUD, etc.—to support responses to the energy crisis. However, at the same time, Sawhill expressed discomfort with aspects of the FEA's mandate as it was being defined:

I think in the area of human services we are really getting into an area that is somewhat outside strict energy policy. As I think of energy policy, I think of creating additional policies, or acting on the rapidly escalating energy demand, or dealing with international aspects of energy. Here we are talking about the impact of energy prices on certain groups in our society. We can identify those groups, and if the Congress feels that we should take responsibility for solving those problems, we can form interagency task forces or projects to get the job done.[24]

Sawhill proceeded to undermine somewhat the weight of his earlier call for a low basic rate in utility price structures. In response to questioning, Sawhill testified that he did not think that existing pricing policies, which resulted in the poor spending 14 percent of their income for energy in comparison to 4 percent for the well to do, discriminated against the poor; that rolling back prices for certain groups was not the answer to the problem; and that the solution probably was to be found in the tax structure or in social security and Supplemental Security Income (SSI) payment adjustments. He further testified that the plight of public utilities dictated that energy rates would continue to increase:

Utility bonds are selling at about 50 percent of their book value. Utility bonds have been lowered in their ratings so that utilities have a very difficult time now raising either equity or debt capital. . . With all of the increased costs that utilities have experienced, such as labor costs, fuel costs, construction costs, and so forth, they are going to need increased rates. Now, I think we should take steps to ameliorate the effect of these increased rates on older people and on poor people, through a plan such as I suggest, but I do not see any alternative to increasing the rates.[25]

The Energy Czar had spoken. The suggested plan to which Sawhill referred included his aforementioned recommendations that utilities adopt a low basic rate and peak load pricing.

At the end of two days of dedicated hearings on the impact of rising energy prices on the elderly, what might be characterized as a process of discovery had taken place. Perhaps the major discovery was that the problem was a multifaceted one. Accordingly, the debate shifted with each additional conception of the nature of the problem. The initial definition of the problem as one driven largely by the lack of income was quickly expanded to include a problem of energy-inefficient housing and a need to assist in insulating the homes of the low income to reduce energy consumption. The problem of energy consumption was tied to a need for electric rate reform to eliminate inverted rate structures, which penalized low consumption patterns and thus disproportionately penalized low-income consumers. There was the threat of the debate being subsumed by the broader policy concerns about energy conservation and the need to give priority to developing a national energy policy which emphasized energy conservation. The matter of the procedural fairness and political autonomy of state PUCs in setting electric rates was raised as an issue. Added to this was the issue of the lack of technical competence among state PUC professional staffs and the implications of this problem for protecting the interests of consumers.

Several policy solutions were offered. The first was to increase benefit payments to recipients of social security and SSI. This was basically a solution targeting the elderly and the initial definition of the problem. The problem extended beyond the elderly poor. However, the elderly were the constituency group of the Senate Committee on Aging. Moreover, advocacy on behalf of the aged carried more clout than advocacy on behalf of the poor as an undifferentiated group. The elderly were organized; the poor were not. Other policy solutions which incorporated concerns for the poor as a whole included (1) cash allowances to all poor who were receiving income support; (2) energy or fuel stamps to be provided to poor households; (3) utility regulatory reform to include new rate designs to benefit the low income and elderly, including a low basic rate and peakload pricing; and (4) the implied reform of PUC procedures to render them more accessible to input from residential consumers. However, in the absence of any concrete plans or recommendations to the full Congress, the hearings ended with Senator Chiles concluding that the main plan seemed to be that of praying for a mild winter.

1975: BUREAUCRATIC RESPONSES AND BUREAUCRATIC POSITIONING

The Special Committee convened again in November of 1975 for the purpose of continuing its quest for ways to ameliorate the impact of rising energy costs on the elderly. The stated purpose of the 1975 hearings, as defined by Senator Lawton Chiles of Florida, who presided, was "to update information obtained at hearings last year." Actually the committee was seeking to ascertain what administration responses had been made to deal with the problem over the past year. Although two legislative proposals had been introduced to address aspects of the problem, no new legislation had been passed establishing "a purposive course of action." However, the two legislative proposals introduced reflected the thrust of the proposed policy responses that had been developed up to that point. Senators Frank Church (Iowa) and Chiles had sponsored the Older Americans Home Repair and Winterization Act, and the administration bill had been introduced in the House as the Winterization Assistance Act. Both bills were directed at energy conservation measures with the side benefit of helping low-income households lower their energy costs.

The major substantive policy response had been one of emergency assistance, again directed toward energy conservation. In January of 1975, Congress had amended the Community Services Act, formally enabling the Community Services Administration (CSA) to conduct a program known as Emergency

Energy Conservation Services. (The OEO had been downsized and renamed the Community Services Agency.) The mandate of the new amendments had been rather broad, enabling the Director of the CSA to provide financial and other assistance for an array of programs and activities, including (but not limited to) winterization, insulation, emergency loans, grants, and revolving funds to install energy conservation technologies, to provide alternative fuel supplies, and to fund special fuel voucher or stamp programs. There were no efforts made to implement a fuel stamp program. Rather, the CSA spent its fiscal year 1975 supplemental appropriation of $6.5 million on home winterization and weatherization support. CSA funds, distributed through its state offices to its local Community Action Program (CAP) agencies, were primarily used to purchase materials. An additional $17 million in Economic Development Administration Title X job opportunities monies were utilized to provide labor for weatherization of homes. On a very limited basis, the CSA had funded utility shutoff intervention programs, making direct grants to pay delinquent energy bills of low-income consumers.[26]

Again, the committee was searching for hard data on which to base probable policy responses and against which to assess the feasibility of alternative approaches. If weatherization was to be the major policy thrust, the financial costs would be substantial. The CSA had turned to the National Bureau of Standards for assistance in developing standards for its weatherization program. The Bureau's definition of an optimal level of weatherization was "the point at which total savings exceed total cost by the greatest amount." This optimal level was expected to represent an annual return of 20 percent on the investment in weatherization. The optimal level of weatherization would vary by dwelling unit, depending on structural conditions and physical clime. In determining the costs of an optimal level of weatherization, the Bureau had selected a sample house of 1200 square feet in Indianapolis, Indiana "which had no serious infiltration problems, no broken windows, no holes in the roof, and already some insulation in the attic. The cost of weatherization of that house to the optimal level was $1200."[27] The CSA thus projected an average cost of $500 per house, not including labor and using less expensive windows than those used by the Bureau. The cost of weatherizing 2 million homes (the estimated number of poor households) would be $700 million to $1 billion depending on whether the per-unit figure was $350 or $500. The committee was using the figure of 8 million as the estimated number of poor households. Implicit in the tone of the disucssion was the assumption that all 8 million dwellings occupied by poor households needed weatherization or would benefit from weatherization. There were no distinctions made between owner-occupied and rental dwellings or detached houses and multifamily dwellings. However, the scope of the problem was slowly being defined.

In his 1974 appearance before the committee, the administrator of the FEA had spelled out the elements of a forerunner of the concept of lifeline rates in his proposal for a low basic rate. Sawhill had suggested the low basic rate as a remedy to the inequities of inverted utility rate structures. Sawhill had not labeled the concept lifeline rates, and in the end he had undermined the force of his suggestion. However, as is frequently the case with policy innovation, the principle of lifeline rates had been adopted for demonstration at the state level and the specifics of this demonstration were made available to the committee.

The state of Maine had passed the Older Citizens Lifeline Electrical Service Law which authorized the Maine PUC to establish a twelve-month demonstration of a Lifeline program. The Maine Lifeline program covered seven communities and was designed to test the feasibility of reversing utility rate structures for low-income elderly citizens. The age threshold was set at sixty-two with an annual income limitation of $4500 for an individual and $5000 for a couple. Under the Maine program, eligible households would receive the first 500 kwh of electricity at $0.03 per kilowatt-hour for a total of $15 a month, or about 5 percent less than the normal rate charged the general public.[28] Thus the first Lifeline program had been established exclusively for the low-income elderly, and it was means-tested. The discount it offered, of about 5 percent, was a modest one. However, the real question was whether the low-income elderly could reasonably restrict their consumption to 500 kwh per month.

The FEA had entered the 1974 hearings in a defensive posture, forced to develop a policy response to a problem which was defined as one of income support, an issue on which the FEA had no expertise and little interest. Although part of its mandate forced on FEA the responsibility for considering the impact of all federal energy policies on the poor—a rather vague mandate—the agency had appeared unresponsive to the hardships caused by the energy crisis because it had not addressed this part of its mandate. The agency had hastily engaged in an organizational shuffling in an effort to appease its critics but had not otherwise defined a policy response or its long-term role at the time of the 1974 hearings. However, at the 1975 hearings, the FEA had assumed a new posture and had acted to mount the issue and began to assert its lead in structuring the terms of the debate and the direction of any major new policy initiatives.

Hazel Rollins, Director of the Office of Community Affairs and Special Impact (CA/SI), represented the FEA in the 1975 hearings. Her first announcement was that her office had "conducted a review of the literature" on household energy consumption and costs, had found no hard data, and had contracted for a short-term intensive study. The reported findings yielded the same conclusions as had been attributed to the study generated earlier for The Ford Foundation: that the elderly poor consumed less energy than all other groups, utilized their consumption for only the basic essentials, and paid more per unit of energy. These findings were now presented as official, although there was no discussion of the methods used and the study's data were not submitted for the record.[29]

The FEA effectively announced its opposition to both the fuel stamp idea and the idea of lifeline rates. Rollins testified that her office had completed a feasibility study of a fuel stamp program in conjunction with the HEW and concluded that it was not the most feasible option for relieving the burden of increased energy costs on the poor. Problems with a fuel stamp program were said to be its costs, the creation of yet another bureaucracy, too little benefit to the total population of intended beneficiaries and a difficult fit between the likely criteria (if based on the food stamp program), and varying need as dictated by climatic differences.[30] Again, the record was left incomplete with regard to any of the details of the fuel stamp feasibility study.

With regard to the issue of lifeline rates, Rollins testified that her office had developed and circulated widely a paper entitled "Lifeline Concepts" in response to widespread interest in the concept. The CA/SI office had found at least two potential problems to lifeline rates: (1) that they would likely depart from a valid basis of rate design, namely costs; and (2) that they might not benefit the intended consumers in all parts of the country. The FEA position on lifeline rates was summarized as follows:

Because of the substantial interest in lifeline, we believe it is important for each regulatory commission to examine lifeline in their jurisdiction, and to get answers to the following question. What income group would benefit, and what income group would necessarily bear the burden of lifeline? What would be the departure from costs-incurred responsibility . . . . what conservation would be encouraged, and where would the inefficiencies be subsidized for such a lifeline tariff?

The Office of Utility Programs is receptive to a lifeline proposal which examines these questions. Obviously, as with all rate demonstrations, the funding of a lifeline demonstration should not be interpreted as endorsement of the concept with national application.[31]

Indeed, the FEA had initiated a set of programs which reflected the core of its interest in energy conservation and utility rate reforms. Rollins testified that the Office of Energy Conservation and Environment had funded nine utility rate demonstration projects of integrated rate structures and innovations supporting the goal of improving efficiency in generation and transmission and electricity load managment techniques. The FEA Office of Utility Programs had initiated participation in regulatory hearings in five states to advocate rate structure changes to reflect marginal costs and to advocate implementation of innovations which might prove cost effective.[32]   As a policy idea, the concept of lifeline rates was losing ground.

The only direct testimony in strong support of a lifeline policy came from the Executive Director of the Nebraska Commission on Aging.[33] The statement of the National Council on Aging (NCA) was silent on the issue of lifeline. Rather, the council advocated development of a national energy policy with equitable treatment of all citizens. Interestingly, at a hearing on energy price impacts on the elderly, the representative of the NCA did not remain at the hearings to testify in person but rather had the testimony inserted into the formal record.[34] Similarly, representatives of the NRTA and AARP did not testify in person but submitted a lengthy statement for inclusion in the record. Their statement too was silent on the issue of lifeline rates, advocating instead adjusting utility rate structures so that rates per kilo-watt hour would vary directly with consumption levels rather than inversely; establishing energy conservation standards and labeling for appliances; and increasing federal spending for mass transit.[35]

Despite the urgency of the problem of rising energy costs, the committee did not hold hearings in 1976. The winter of 1976–1977 had been an exceptionally severe one in many parts of the country, and fuel shortages had led to closings of schools and plants in some states. The opening remarks of the April 1977 hearings reflected their continuing-saga tone with the elderly being depicted as cutting energy use to the bare bones and yet were unable to pay their bills. The committee was still muddling toward a set of proposals to constitute a comprehensive response to a multifaceted problem and was having considerable difficulty moving beyond the problem definition stage. This was not because the problem had not been identified—that had effectively occurred on the first two days of the hearings in 1974. Rather, the committee (and the witnesses) essentially continued to restate the problem, or a part of it, over and over again. The drawback of this approach was that no comprehensive solution was being formulated and the core problem which the committee was addressing—rising energy costs—was indeed getting worse. The benefit of this slow process was that some new aspects of the problem were identified and clarified. The committee plodded along, apparently consoled that something, (the CSA Energy Services Program) was being done while a number of other largely piecemeal actions were beginning to gel into a more comprehensive response.

One major development was that in 1977 the committee finally had available to it hard data on the impact of rising energy costs across different age and income groups, with regional variations due to climatic differences and usage of different heating fuels at varying costs. The FEA had conducted a nationwide household energy consumption survey in the spring of 1976 to obtain data on energy usage by a range of household characteristics, including energy type, income, location, age, sex, and race of household head. Additionally the FEA had developed a household energy expenditure model (HEEM) to provide analysis of the socioeconomic impacts of energy price increases on household expenditures generally, and low-income groups in particular. The results of the survey and outputs of the model were made available to the committee, giving statistical backing to the anecdotal reports the committee had been receiving from their constituents and substantiating the reports provided by some witnesses that had appeared before the committee. John O'Leary, the new administrator of the FEA, also announced that a survey was underway of residential gas and oil users to determine the impact of the 1976-1977 winter on low-income households, and that a comprehensive human resources data sytem was being developed to evaluate the impact of proposed energy programs and policies on a variety of population subgroups.[36]

O'Leary presented the following summation of the FEA's findings regarding the impact of rising energy costs on the elderly:

1. Energy price increases from 1973 to 1976 had a disproportionate impact on

low- and fixed-income elderly households—age sixty years or older.

2. Average annual home fuel expenditures in 1976 for the low-income elderly in the northeast region were $683, a 47.8 percent increase over 1973.

3. Fuel expenditures in the northeast region were roughly two times that experienced in the western region due to two factors: larger heating requirements due to a colder climate and the widespread use of more expensive fuel oil.

4. Low-income elderly households with annual incomes of less than $5500 spent a greater proportion of their disposable income on energy than higher-income elderly, especially in the Northeast.

5. In 1976, average home fuel expenditures as a percent of disposable income for low-income elderly households were 27.3 percent in the northern Midwest, and 15.6 percent in the West. Elderly households in these regions with incomes between $15,000 and $20,000 were 4.8, 3.6, and 2.7 percent respectively.

6. Increases in retirement, social security, and income support payments, which are often tied to the CPI, did not adequately reflect the increase in energy costs.

7. The CPI as a whole increased 28.1 percent between 1973 and 1976; the indexed price of energy products rose at a greater rate: 42.2 percent for electricity, 57.1 percent for natural gas, and 83.8 percent for fuel oil.

8. Although social security and SSI benefits increased about 30 percent between 1973 and 1976, this increase did not adequately compensate low- and fixed-income elderly for rising energy costs. [37]

On the first day of the 1977 hearings, Senator Domenici (Arizona) had introduced data supplied by the Social Security Administration that showed the growth in social security benefits from 1972 to 1976. In 1972, a retired worker with no dependents had received a monthly benefit of $157; a retired worker and wife, both age sixty-two and both receiving benefits got $273; and an aged widow recieved $138. At the end of 1976, the monthly benefits were $219, $374, and $209 respectively. Thus a clearer picture of the problem was available to the committee in a form which went beyond the valid but limited evidence of particular individual cases of hardship.

Up to this point, the major substantive response to the problem of rising energy costs for the low income had been carried out by the CSA, first through a largely adhoc redirection of some of its funds; then through some emergency appropriations from Congress; and later through some funding under a formal appropriation based on special amendments to its legislative authorization. CSA activities had been directed toward emergency relief assistance largely in the form of weatherization of homes (with a much smaller amount of funds spent on crisis intervention to provide direct assistance in paying utility bills). Testimony at the 1977 hearings indicated that the CSA had weatherized a total of 150,000 homes of the poor in the three-year period from 1973 to 1976, and had spent 80 percent of its total allocation of $71.5 million for the three-year period. The remaining 20 percent was spent on education and outreach—locating, helping, and advising the aged poor—and crisis intervention activities. The CSA stated that approximately 70 percent of homes weatherized were occupied by the elderly. CSA efforts were administered by a nationwide network of some 881 CAP agencies. Although the CSA had established eligibility guidelines to determine who would be the beneficiaries of its efforts, it had no systematic means of identifying the elderly poor. For example, federal regulations placed restrictions on access to SSI records which would have permitted ready identification of the elderly poor. Thus the CSA affiliates had to seek out the eligible elderly on a one-to-one basis.[38]

Weatherization had developed as *the* policy response, but within two different contexts which embodied turf battles between the CSA and FEA, and which also reflected two different and substantially conflicting perceptions of and approaches to the problem. The CSA, as its name indicated, was a community services organization. Its main mandate was of a social services nature. The FEA, in contrast, did not see its mandate as one of social services, and although it recognized the economic limitations of the low income and their growing inability to pay the costs of energy, the agency simply saw this as a problem to be remedied through adjustments in income support systems. The matter of income support was somebody's else problem. Although the problem of energy-inefficient homes was a recognized part of the energy affordability problem for the low income, the FEA saw this problem as one of energy conservation, an issue of energy policy and not a matter of social policy. O'Leary had testified that weatherization probably meant only a 5 percent reduction in the amount of disposable income the aged poor spent on energy costs, leaving largely unaffected the underlying affordability problem.

The FEA sought to replace the CSA as the lead federal agency in weatherization activities. The FEA was strengthened in this effort by the Energy Conservation and Production Act of 1976 (ECPA; public law 94-385). The ECPA was an energy conservation measure designed to facilitate the widespread implementation of energy conservation measures in residential housing, commercial and public buildings, and industrial plants and to encourage a shift from nonrenewable to renewable sources of energy, such as solar energy. The ECPA called for the administrator of the FEA to establish rules by which states would develop energy conservation plans to meet eligibility criteria under the ECPA for the receipt of grants and loan guarantees. Title IV, Part A of the ECPA authorized a weatherization assistance program directed toward the low income, particularly the elderly and handicapped. However, the assistance would be provided primarily through grants to the states. The FEA had requested $65 million for this program for fiscal year 1978 to fund the weatherization of 460,000 homes occupied by low-income elderly and handicapped persons.

A statement by O'Leary succinctly stated the contrasts he wished to draw between the weatherization program of CSA and the FEA approach:

FEA's weatherization assistance program reflects the objective of the Energy Conservation and Production Act, which is to conserve energy. As a result, FEA has developed and is administering the weatherization program as an energy conservation effort giving consideration to social objectives, rather than as a social program giving consideration to energy conservation objectives. As such, the program is designed solely to make investments that meet long-term needs, i.e. the installation of insulation, and does not represent the combination of long-term and short-term emergency efforts sponsored by CSA.[39]

Despite the philosphical splitting of hairs by O'Leary, the Weatherization Assistance Program of ECPA duplicated the Section 222(a)(12) amendments to the Community Services Act, which were passed in January 1975 to authorize and fund energy conservation services to the low income. However the ECPA carried an amendment offered by Senator John Glenn and contained in Title II, section 205, which authorized seed money in grants to states for the purpose of establishing offices of consumer services that would assist residential customers in their presentations before state regulatory commissions. The Glenn amendment recognized the severe disadvantage of residential consumers with regard to the expertise and financial means necessary for effective participation in the highly technical and arcane proceedings of state PUCs.[40] This was a forerunner of the consumer public intervenor concept and a critical step in providing adequate representation of consumer interests in utility ratemaking proceedings.

The FEA was responsible for developing guidelines and procedures for the administration of the initial $2 million funding for these utility Consumer Services Offices. The FEA anticipated that three major areas of consumer advocacy activities would be pursued by such offices: (1) "making general factual assessments of the impact of proposed rate changes and other proposed regulatory actions on all affected consumers; (2) assisting consumers in the presentation of their positions before state and federal utility regulatory commissions; and (3) advocating, on their own behalf, a position deemed most advantageous to consumers."[41] Thus another aspect of the problem identified by the committee had emerged as a formal policy, albeit on an experimental basis.

The ECPA had also given the FEA formal authority to expand its demonstration program of innovative electric rate structures and load management techniques. The demonstrations were designed to demonstrate peak load, lifeline, flat, and inverted rate structures. On an invitational basis the FEA had expanded its participation in state utility regulatory hearings to advocate rate structure revisions and the implementation of load management techniques. Thus the hearings of the Special Committee on Aging had spawned a number of actions which were directed toward addressing aspects of a multifaceted problem.

Some aspects of the committee's activities reflected the continued uncertainty about the desired or appropriate course of action. For example, Senator Domenici continued to raise a list of possible solutions which had been discussed previously and not pursued (including energy stamps, increases in social security and SSI payments, and cash payments), and he kept alive the idea of utlility lifeline policies. Another example of continual defining of the problem was the committee's hearing of testimony from the director of the newly established National Institute of Aging (as a part of the National Institutes of Health), who testified on the elderly's susceptibility to hypothermia and hyperthermia.[42]

Although the director of the Administration on Aging (AOA) continued to press for a utility lifeline policy as a preferred means of assisting the low-income elderly and continued to call for full support of this position by the Aging Network, such support had not yet materialized.   Neither the NCA nor the NRTA and AARP had testified during the 1977 hearings. However, persuasive testimony about the sentiments of the elderly in regard to the type of assistance they found preferable and acceptable was provided by Elliott Taubman of the National Consumer Law Center. Taubman testified that the term lifeline was perceived by the elderly, and some others, as purely a social welfare measure and therefore it was better not to use the term but rather simply to speak of correcting inverted utility rate practices. Taubman spoke to the elderly's disdain for being singled out for welfare programs; their disdain for any type of program for which they had to apply; their disdain for income testing; and their opposition to an energy stamp program. He testified that the elderly wanted reformed service termination policies, installment payment plans, and adequate representation before state commissions and that they strongly supported utility regulatory reform.[43]

Taubman's testimony struck a resonant chord with many members of the committee, and although he was not a representative of an organized group representing the elderly, Taubman could lay claim to broad-based access to and interaction with state and local elderly groups through the work of the Consumer Law Center. Thus, he was a credible and persuasive witness and had brought clarity to a significant aspect of the committee's deliberations. In so doing, he had helped to determine the thrust of the major public policy which would emerge in response to the issues raised by the Senate Special Committee on Aging.

SUMMARY

The hearings of the Special Committee closed in April of 1977, with the nation anxiously awaiting the announcement of a comprehensive national energy policy. The committee's hearings had emerged in response to the aftermath of the Arab oil embargo of 1973 and proceeded over the course of four years. Its activities had overlapped two presidential administrations and concomitant changes in the leadership of the FEA and the CSA, the two agencies with major responsibility for and involvement in formulating responses to the energy crisis. Surprisingly, the position of neither agency appeared to change substantially from one administration to another. Thus, much of the tone and direction of the hearings did not change. The tone and directions of the hearings were determined primarily by the positions taken by the CSA and FEA, with the positions of a select set of witnesses—The Ford Foundation, Governor Sharp of Pennsylvania, the Florida PUC Chairman, and the representative of the National Consumer Law Center—also being influential. The FEA and CSA assumed responsive postures within the context of their perceived agency mandates. The committee itself appeared at times to play the role of providing an official forum for the presentation of viewpoints. However, several committee members did introduce formal legislative proposals through other committees in response to developments raised by the committee, and the responses of the CSA and FEA were undoubtedly influenced by the committee and other members of Congress.

In a significant sense, the Special Committee was constrained more by its jurisdictional coverage than by its inability to process legislation. Although its mandate of supporting the interests of the aged was a broad one and cut across many areas, its jurisdiction was restricted. For example, if the problem of adverse impacts of rising energy costs on the elderly was in large part due to utility rate structures and the lack of adequate representation in ratemaking procedures, then the Special Committee was effectively unable to explore these problems fully. The committee was not expected to hold hearings on utility regulatory reform because such issues were the domain of other congressional committees. The committee had served an important function of raising the debate and public consciousness on a set of interrelated issues, although it had not succeeded in formulating a comprehensive set of proposals for presentation to Congress.

The committee hearings and proddings had served to assist the FEA in defining its role and position in relationship to how the larger question of national energy policy would be perceived and defined. The FEA, by its broad mandate, had to play a major role in responding to the energy crisis of the low income. However, in doing so, it sought to define the problem in a manner which it could effectively handle, consistent with its central mandate and consistent with its wish to expand that mandate. Although the agency had entered the debate about the elderly poor and energy costs in a defensive position, it had soon positioned itself to take the lead in all aspects of the energy problem. It had done this in part by insisting on separating the policy questions of affordability and income, thus defining for itself that aspect of the problem—energy conservation—which was consonant with its central mandate.

The FEA had secured a public law giving it direct authority to develop a home weatherization assistance program as part of a broad-scope energy conservation effort. Under this legislation, it had also secured authority for regulating a consumer intervenor program as an early effort to advance the new concept of consumer advocacy in public utility rulemaking. The FEA as well had secured legislative authority to expand its electric utility demonstration projects to demonstrate a range of rate structure revisions. The FEA had effectively co-opted the core issues of the committee hearings and had garnered the lead in setting the tone and direction of any major public policy responses. If the Special Committee wished to deal with the issue of income support, it appeared that it would have to do so largely outside the context of energy policy issues.

The idea of lifeline rates had emerged and had been defined in a manner which addressed both the issues of affordability and equity as well as the need to reform utility rate structures to encourage energy conservation. However, one of the would-be strongest supporters of lifeline rates, the FEA (which had initially defined the issue) backed away from it as a major policy proposal. The strong support of the organized senior citizen interest groups had never materialized in support of lifeline policies or any other specific policy initiative. This, coupled with the impressions that the elderly did not want relief in the form of a publicly identifiable special policy, left the idea of lifeline policies in a severely weakened position in terms of formal public policy.

NOTES

1. U.S. Congress. Senate. Special Committee on Aging. *Developments in Aging: 1973 and January–March 1974.* 93rd Cong., 2nd sess., 1974. S. Rept. 846., p. 98.

2. Ibid., chap. 5.

3. U.S. Congress. Senate. Special Committee on Aging. *Hearings on the Impact of Rising Energy Costs on Older Americans.* 93rd Cong., 2nd sess., pt. 1, Sept. 24, 1974

4. Ibid., pp. 2–8.

5. This is not a complete listing of participants, but rather those participants who offered testimony deemed directly significant to the thrust of the discussion. Some testimony in congressional hearings are rambling and frequently unrelated to the topic. Some testimony is largely repetitive, and some witnesses represent the same type group or organization.

6. *Hearings on the Impact of Rising Energy Costs on Older Americans,* pt. 1, p. 63. Letter dated August 22, 1974 from John Sawhill, Administrator of the Federal Energy Administration to Honorable Frank Church, Chairman of Senate Special Committee on Aging.

7. Ibid., pt. 1, pp. 8–15. Testimony of S. David Freeman, Project Director, Ford Foundation Policy Project.

8. *Hearings on the Impact of Rising Energy Costs on Older Americans,* pt. 1, pp. 64–65.

9. Ibid., p. 70.

10. Senate. *Hearings on the Impact of Rising Energy Costs on Older Americans,* pt. 1, pp. 20–25. Testimony of William H. Bevis, Chairman Florida Public Utility Commission.

11. Ibid., pp. 74–78. Written statement submitted for the record by Willard S. Simonds, Fuels Manager, Florida Power Corporation.

12. Senate. *Hearings on the Impact of Rising Energy Costs on Older Americans,* pt. 1, p. 20–25. Testimony of William H. Bevis.

13. Ibid., pp. 41–46. Testimony and prepared statement of Rudolph T. Dawstedt, National Council of Senior Citizens.

14. Senate. *Hearings on the Impact of Rising Energy Costs on Older Americans,* pt. 1, pp. 28–30; 66–70. Testimony and prepared statement of Cyril F. Brickfield, American Association of Retired Persons and National Retired Teachers Association.

15. Ibid., pp. 30–31. Written statement submitted by Senator Charles Mathias, Jr.

16. Senate. *Hearings on the Impact of Rising Energy Costs on Older Americans,* pt. 2, pp. 107–112. Testimony and prepared statement of Honorable Arthur S. Fleming, Commissioner, Administration on Aging.

17. Senate. *Hearings on the Impact of Rising Energy Costs on Older Americans,*

pt. 1,   pp. 71-73. Written statement submitted for the record by Nadine Cooper, National Urban League.

18. Ibid., pp. 72–74. See correspondence submitted for the record between Ronald H. Brown, Director, National Urban League, and John Sawhill, Administrator, Federal Energy Administration, dated July 30 and August 6, 1974.

19. Senate. *Hearings on the Impact of Rising Energy Costs on Older Americans,* pt. 1, pp. 31–34. Testimony of Ronald H. Brown, National Urban League.

20. Ibid., pp. 47–52. Testimony and prepared statement of James Feldesman, Consumer Federation of America.

21. Senate. *Hearings on the Impact of Rising Energy Costs on Older Americans,* pt. 1, pp. 15–20. Testimony of Alvin Arnett, Former Director, Office of Economic Opportunity.

22. Ibid., pp. 8–15. Testimony of S. David Freeman, The Ford Foundation.

23. Senate. *Hearings on the Impact of Rising Energy Costs on Older Americans,* pt. 2, Sept. 25, 1974, pp. 84–100. Testimony of Honorable Milton J. Shoop, Governor, Commonwealth of Pennsylvania.

24. Ibid., pp. 100–107. Testimony of Honorable John Sawhill, Administrator, Federal Energy Administration.

25. Ibid., p. 127.

26. Senate. *Hearings on the Impact of Rising Energy Costs on Older Americans,* pt. 3, Nov. 7, 1975, pp. 157–160. Testimony of Angel Rivera, Community Services Administration.

27. Ibid., pp. 165–166.

28. Senate. *Hearings on the Impact of Rising Energy Costs on Older Americans.* pt. 3, p. 173. Testimony of Senator Edmund Muskie.

29. Ibid., pp. 147–148. Testimony of Hazel Rollins, Director, Office of Community Affairs and Special Impact, Federal Energy Administration.

30. Ibid., pp. 151, 160.

31. Ibid., pp. 151–152.

32. Ibid., p. 150.

33. Senate. *Hearings on the Impact of Rising Energy Costs on Older Americans,* pt. 3, pp. 181–187. Testimony of Glen J. Soukeep, Nebraska Commission on Aging.

34. Ibid., pp. 170–171. Testimony and written statement submitted for the record of Ollie Randall, National Council on Aging.

35. Senate. *Hearings on the Impact of Rising Energy Costs on Older Americans,* pt. 3, pp. 223–231. Letter and written statement submitted for the record by Cyril F. Brickfield, National Retired Teachers Association and American Association of Retired Persons.

36. Senate. *Hearings on the Impact of Rising Energy Costs on Older Americans,* pt. 5, April 7, 1977. pp. 308–311. Testimony and Prepared Statement of Honorable John F. O'Leary, Administrator, Federal Energy Administration.

37. Ibid., p. 307.

38. Senate. *Hearings on the Impact of Rising Energy Costs on Older Americans,* pt. 5, April 7, 1977. p. 331. Testimony of Honorable Robert Chase, Acting Director, Community Services Administration.

39. Senate. *Hearings on the Impact of Rising Energy Costs on Older Americans,* pt. 5, p. 310. Prepared Statement of Honorable John F. O'Leary.

40. Ibid., p. 305. Testimony of Honorable John Glenn, U.S. Senator from Ohio.

41. Senate. *Hearings on the Impact of Rising Energy Costs on Older Americans,* pt. 5, p. 310.

42. Senate. *Hearings on the Impact of Rising Energy Costs on Older Americans,* pt. 4, p. 264. Testimony of Dr. Robert N. Butler, Director, National Institute on Aging.

43. Ibid., pt. 4, pp. 271–277. Testimony of Elliott Taubman, Chief Counsel, Energy Project, National Consumer Law Center, Boston.

Chapter 3

Reforming Electric Utility Regulation: Policy Ideas in Conflict

THE ELECTRIC UTILITY INDUSTRY: STRUCTURE AND REGULATION

The electric power industry in the United States is large and diverse. In 1980, the greater portion of the industry—a little more than 78 percent—was comprised of privately owned or investor-owned corporations. Most of these were single corporations, although there were a few large holding companies which owned several subsidiary utilities. The Southern Company is one example of an electric utility holding company which owns, among other entities, the Georgia Power and Alabama Power companies. Publicly held utilities include federally, state, and municipally owned utilities and accounted for about 19.4 percent of the U.S. total in 1980. In that year, the breakdown was 10.48 percent, 5.07 percent, and 3.88 percent, respectively, for federally, state, and municipally owned electric generation. The largest of the federal projects include the Tennessee Valley Authority (TVA) and the Bonneville Power Authority. The largest state-owned utility is the Power Authority of the State of New York (PASNY). Municipally owned utilities are, as the title implies, owned by cities (including Los Angeles, Sacramento, and San Antonio plus some county-owned systems in Washington state). Some utilities are cooperatively owned by groups of counties in rural areas and groups of townships, primarily in the New England area. Cooperatives contributed about 2.42 percent of electric power generated in the United States in 1980 (Anderson 1981).

Regulation of the sale of electricity is divided between the federal government and the states. Interstate sales (generally wholesale, bulk power) is regulated by the federal government. At the time of the hearings under focus in this book (1974-1980), the pertinent federal regulatory body was the Federal Power Commission (FPC), later changed to the Federal Energy Regulatory Commission (FERC) under the Carter administration. Sale of electricity to end users within states is regulated by State Public Utility Commissions (PUCs), sometimes called Public Service Commissions or PSCs. PUCs consist of three to seven members, who are appointed by state governors in the majority of cases but are elected in a handful of states. Electric utilities have conventionally been seen as natural monopolies and are thus regulated in the public interest by the PUCs, with the primary objective of restricting utility profits to a fair rate of return. Other policy issues, such as setting priorities for a certain fuel usage over others, are set at the federal level (with the state PUC monitoring implementation). Many other federal regulations which affect the operations of electric power, such as environmental regulations, are also enforced at the state level by other state agencies.

Public utility regulation was once a cozy backwater of activity, with the utilities providing plentiful and cheap electricity due to their building of more and larger facilities to take advantage of economies of scale, and with the PUCs largely sanctioning the rate proposals brought in by utilities. The situation is succinctly described by Anderson:

From the end of World War II until the late 1960s, promotional campaigns urged people to "live better electrically" by purchasing electric appliances and building "all electric" homes. The declining block rate structure that utilities used to price electricity stimulated growth in demand. The more consumers used, the less per unit they paid. Everyone—utility executives, investors, state regulators, and consumers—seemed satisfied with promotional pricing because the growth in demand meant that larger generating plants could be constructed and greater economies of scale realized. Investors liked the larger plants because they promised increased profits. Utility managers were attracted to the opportunities for growth in sales. Regulators had the happy task of watching the industry become more efficient and, on occasion, of negotiating rate reduction.

In the absence of conflict, newspapers ignored the utilities except for an occasional story on the financial page noting the issuance of bonds to finance new construction. Planning and pricing decisions—how many new plants should be built, what type of plants should be built, where and when they should be built, and who should be charged for them—were largely made by the industry itself with little supervision by government regulations. (Anderson 1981:68–69)

The Arab oil embargo was primarily responsible for the economic shocks which would transform the world of PUCs and utilities. Fuel costs to the utilities spiraled due to the embargo, coupled with rising inflation in the cost of capital and in construction wages. Moreover, the number of rate cases brought before PUCs by utilities seeking rate increases greatly increased from three nationwide in 1963 to 114 in 1975. Consumers became interested in the actions of state PUCs and sought ways to make them more accountable. The organized environmental movement also focused on the electric utility industry for what it saw as a disregard by the industry of the environmental damages it caused (air pollution from the burning of fuels, water and soil pollution through waste-water discharges or runoffs from coal piles, etc.). The environmentalists in particular wanted to curb the growth of the industry and thus backed energy conservation because it served the goal of a cleaner environment. These forces combined to unveil the world of electric utility regulation, creating much controversy in the process.

Electric utilities are capital-intensive operations. The sunken investments in land and facilities are enormous, and the rates a utility charges its customers must reflect this investment. The net investment of a utility determines its rate base. The amount of profits it is allowed to make, called the rate of return, is calculated as a percentage of its rate base. Profits allow a utility to pay dividends to investors in the case of private, investor-owned utilities. Added to a utility's sunken investments are operating costs, the most expensive of which are fuel costs, followed by its labor costs. Utilities must also pay taxes and sundry fees to the state and federal governments. The sum of operating costs, depreciation on investments, taxes, plus the rate base multiplied by the rate of return determines the revenue requirements for the utility: $RR = OC + D + T + (RB)r$. The issue then is to determine how the revenue requirements will be divided across the different classes of customers—industrial, commercial, and residential—which the utility serves. This determination is the rate structure (Anderson 1981:64–65).

Revenue requirements and the rate of return are the major elements that directly affect rates. Whether and when to factor construction work in progress into the rate base is also an issue to be decided by PUCs. Because utilities must plan to accommodate new demand caused by population growth and concomitant development in their jurisdictions, and because they must retire aging facilities as well, they must construct new generating facilities. Shifting this expansion cost onto existing ratepayers is frequently a controversial matter, especially when there are questions about need and the feasibility of operating new facilities in a manner which will facilitate recouping investment costs. Nuclear power plants have been particularly controversial in this regard. Because of the long time period required to hear and conclude a rate case (a formal request for an increase in rates or a change in rate structures), which averages about eighteen months, utilities had been permitted to pass on interim increases in fuel costs through fuel adjustment charges, which also became controversial in the 1970s.

The electric power industry is also energy intensive, and this characteristic (combined with its capital requirements) made the regulation of the industry of great concern to federal lawmakers. The concerns of consumers and environmentalists converged in the mid-1970s to provoke calls for reform in the way in which states regulated electric utilities. Moreover, given the dominance of the FEA in defining the policy debate over rising energy costs, what got transferred to the standing committees were specific proposals to reform electric utilities. As part of that reform effort, there were possibilities for including issues such as lifeline rates and stronger consumer advocacy provisions. The following statement by Congressman John Dingell set the tone for the 1976 congressional hearings on electric utility regulatory reform:

The policy issues relating to the electric power industry are of particular concern because of the size of the industry, its capital intensiveness, and the amount of energy consumption which it accounts for. Energy consumed in generating electric power in this nation accounted for 26 percent of energy consumption in 1975. Estimates of capital requirements for the next 10 years for the industry have ranged as high as $490 billion. Current FEA estimates range from $215 to $322 billion.

Electric rates to ultimate consumers, after decreasing for a decade at an annual rate of almost one percent, in 1970 began a rapid increase resulting in an almost 90 percent increase in average rate per-kilowatt-hour by 1975. This reversal in price trends reflected an 80 percent increase in the cost per kilowatt of new nuclear capacity and a 100 percent increase in the cost of new coal-fired capacity between 1972 and 1975, as well as an approximate fourfold increase in fuel costs during that period.[1]

PROBLEM DEFINITIONS AND LEGISLATIVE PROPOSALS

The stakes were high. If electric utility regulation was to be reformed, many different parties would be affected. The significance of the 1976 hearings before the subcommittee on Energy and Power of the House Committee on Interstate and Foreign Commerce was reflected in the number and diversity of witnesses attending and offering testimony for the record. The witnesses represented (among others) twelve privately owned and cooperatively owned utilities, twenty-one utility industry groups representing private and cooperatively owned utilities, six state PUCs, fourteen professional experts, seven consultant and investment firms, four industrial manufacturers, two manufacturing associations, two commercial retail associations, nine citizen groups including environmentalists and consumers, two labor unions, and sixteen representatives of different entities within various federal agencies. This diversity of representation stood in sharp contrast to the representation at the hearings of the Special Committee. In the first round of almost nine consecutive days of hearings, the Subcommittee on Energy and Power compiled over 2000 pages of record.

In contrast to the hearings of the Special Committee (1973–1980), which focused on identifying and defining the problem (or rather a set of interrelated problems), the hearings of the legislative committees (1976–1978) focused on actual legislative proposals. Significantly, those legislative proposals accepted certain definitions of problems and relationships between problems and offered specific policy responses to these problems. The former hearings involved discussion and urgings which resulted in piecemeal, largely interim bureaucratic responses; the latter hearings were directed toward establishing a purposive course of action via one or more new public laws. Although the focus of the legislative hearings might not have been more sharply drawn, the prerogatives of legislative committees held a more direct promise that these hearings would end in definitive action. This too made the stakes higher.

The issues which were addressed in the legislative proposals and the legislative hearings were extensive. Some had emerged explicitly in the generic hearings of the Special Committee and others had merely been implied. The major issues included the following:

1. The extent to which electric utility rate structures created inequities in electricity costs across different classes and categories of consumers and between small-and-large volume users (this was the crux of the issue egarding declining block rates)
2. The extent to which utility rate structures discouraged energy conservation
3. The extent to which consumers were adequately represented in ratemaking proceedings before state public service commissions
4. The extent to which state public utility commissions were adequately staffed in terms of professional expertise to handle the growing complexities of utility regulation
5. The need for federal intervention in state regulation of utilities
6. The reform of federal regulation of interstate bulk sales, the siting of bulk sale facilities, and the provision of consumer representation in federal regulatory proceedings.

The issues were basically ones of utility regulatory reform that incorporated to varying degrees the issues of economic impact, which initially gave rise to this larger set of concerns.

In the first round of hearings in 1976, there were fifteen major bills introduced in the House and Senate and printed in full for the official record, focusing on varied aspects of the aforementioned issues. At least thirty-eight other bills referred to in the record as "identical, similar, and related," were not printed but were listed along with their cosponsors as also being officially considered during the House hearings. The major bills, printed for the record, can be categorized as follows: (1) comprehensive bills specifying utility rate reform, including reform of FPC regulation of interstate bulk sales of electricity and incorporating lifeline rate provisions; (2) bills dedicated exclusively to lifeline rate provisions; and (3) bills dedicated exclusively to reforming federal (FPC) regulation of interstate bulk sales of electricity.

The major legislative proposal was House Resolution (H.R.) 12461, The Electric Utility Rate Reform and Regulatory Improvement Act. This was a comprehensive bill covering state regulation of the retail sale of electricity and federal regulation of bulk or wholesale sales of electricity as well as federal regulation of bulk facility siting and facility reliability standards. H.R. 12461 was the bill of the Subcommittee on Energy and Power of the Committee on Interstate and Foreign Commerce. It was introduced by the Subcommittee Chairman, John Dingell, with four subcommittee cosponsors. It is referred to here as the committee bill. The Senate version of this bill was contained in two bills, S. 3310, The Electric Utility Rate Reform and Regulatory Improvement Act, and S. 3311, The Electric Utility Coordination Act. The (Ford) Administration bills were H.R. 2633 (Title VII) and H.R. 2650 (Title VIII), both titled The Utilities Act of 1975. Although the administration bills were considered (along with many other bills) in hearings along with the committee bill, the main focus of the hearings was clearly the committee bill. This focus is reflected in the following discussion of positions given in testimony in the formal hearings.

Legislative proposals generally begin with a title which sets forth the general provisions of the bill. The initial title also includes sections of declarations, findings, purposes, and definitions of key terms referred to in the legislation. Subsequent titles set forth the major provisions of the legislation and prohibitions and are each devoted to major areas of substantive concern. The findings and declarations are a kind of prologue which set forth the context for the major provisions and include the assumptions about the nature of the problem addressed and the presumed relationships, causal and otherwise, between different aspects of the problem. Thus one can discern from the opening title, findings, and declarations the philosophical orientation or biases represented by the bill. The findings and purposes declared in H.R. 12461 drew heavily on issues raised in the hearings of the Special Committee. Interestingly, the findings were set forth in the broadest possible terms of justification and legitimation: "The Congress finds and declares that the continued generation and transmission of an adequate supply of electrical energy at reasonable rates is critical to the nation's defense, a sound and stable economy, and the general health and welfare of the people of the United States."

In regard to state-level regulation of retail sale of electricity, H.R. 12461 set forth national minimum standards affecting all utilities equally so that those states which adopted innovations in rates and consumer representation would not be placed at a competitive economic disadvantage. In regard to concerns about PUCs granting rate increases virtually in response to utilities' requests and in the absence of formal hearings or competent assessments, the bill required that all rate increases be granted only after a full evidentiary hearing. The bill defined an evidentiary hearing as "a proceeding (a) which includes notice to, and an opportunity for, participants to present direct and rebuttal evidence and to cross-examine witnesses, and a written decision based upon evidence appearing in a written record of the proceeding, and (b) which is subject to judicial review." The bill went further to specify in detail those elements to be included in the analysis underlying a determination of cost of service.

In regard to the concern that the residential class of electric consumers might have been subsidizing high-volume industrial users (through the use of declining block rates), the bill required that state PUCs ensure that the rates charged to each class of consumers reflect the cost of providing electric service to that class of consumers. In this same vein of concern, inverted or declining block rates were prohibited unless it could be shown that costs actually decreased as consumption increased. Declining block rates had been widely alleged, and shown (by FEA analysis) to impose an inequity on very low volume residential consumers and had been alleged to discourage energy conservation. Under the proposed legislation, PUCs were directed to ensure that rates were to be based on the marginal cost of service. The legislation defined "marginal cost" to mean "the change in total cost which results if (A) additional capacity is added to meet demand at the peak, (B) additional kilowatt-hours of electric energy are delivered to users, or (C) additional electric consumers are connected to the electric utility." Additionally, a lifeline rate for a subsistence quantity of electricity was required to be established by all utilities at a rate not to exceed the lowest kilowatt hour charge to any consumer. State PUCs were given authority to determine what constituted a subsistence quantity of energy. This flexibility reflected variations in regional climatic and seasonal conditions and energy demands.

A major consumer protection measure was the requirement that utilities notify consumers of a utility's application for a rate increase. Consumers were also to be notified at least annually of all rate schedules (charges) for all classes of consumers. On a monthly basis, utilities were required to provide consumers with information on past-year comparative consumption amounts. Utilities were prohibited from spending for poltical, promotional, or institutional advertisement except to explain rates, provide other information about rate schedules, or promote energy conservation. The baneful automatic fuel adjustment increases were permitted, but with a cap on the amount of increase and only if such increases had been approved in a prior evidentiary hearing. Title VII, initially introduced as a separate bill, would have permitted approval of monthly increases due to fuel adjustment charges (FACs) (with advance notice to the PUC) but would have subjected them to rollback if the PUC found that such increases had been unlawful. Up to 66 2/3 percent of construction work in progress (CWIP) could be included in a utility's rate base after an evidentiary hearing. These last two standards would force utilities to better anticipate their costs, document and justify their costs, and submit their costs to public scrutiny and formal challenge in an evidentiary hearing.

To ensure that utilities moved to adopt conservation measures (and measures which would contribute to stabilizing costs), the legislation required state PUCs to hold evidentiary hearings on alternative load management techniques within one year of enactment of the Act and at least biennially thereafter. PUCs were directed to require prompt implementation of any load management techniques determined to be cost effective. Applications for rate increases filed subsequent to a one year grace period were to include an analysis of the cost effectiveness of load management techniques identified as feasible by the FEA Office of Electric Utility Ratemaking Assistance. Load management techniques were defined as "any technique to reduce maximum kilowatt demand on the electric utility. Such techniques could include [but were not limited to] time-of-use peak load pricing structures based on marginal cost determination, ripple or radio control mechanisms, energy storage devices, interrupted or interruptible electrical services, customer-owned meters or load-limiting devices, elimination of master metering, and techniques to minimize inefficient end use of electric energy." Thus the legislation took a forceful position on the issue of energy conservation and firmly placed federal officials in the role of prompter and enforcer.

The legislation proposed the establishment within the FEA of the Office of Electric Utility Ratemaking Assistance to intervene in evidentiary hearings upon request of the state PUC, any state agency, or any party to the hearing. The Office would have full standing and rights, including the right to obtain judicial review. The Office was also authorized to make grants to state PUCs to enable them to increase their staff capabilities to better respond to the demands of an increasingly complex and open ratemaking environment. Grants were also authorized to support the demonstration of load management techniques and to support the establishment of offices of public intervenor to represent consumer interests in ratemaking proceedings. The legislation also gave full standing and rights to any consumer or state agency to intervene in evidentiary hearings. If such parties prevailed, the legislation required that they be compensated for all legal and expert witness costs by the utility if no alternative means of consumer representation was adopted. PUCs were required under Title VII to give prompt consideration to utility applications for rate increases, and they were prohibited from disallowing capital costs of environmental controls in calculation of a utility's rate base.

Although the federal government could not directly regulate privately and cooperatively owned electric utilities, it could, in effect, regulate the state regulators of these utilities. The thrust of the proposed legislation was to assert a major, new federal role in the activities of state PUCs. Federal objectives had been decided on, and few things were left to the discretion of state PUCs. The formerly cozy backwater of utility ratemaking proceedings was opened up. A stronger consumer role in ratemaking proceedings was established. State PUCs were challenged to strengthen their staff resources. The elements of analyses underlying cost-of-service determination (the foundation of all utility rates) were dictated, as was a requirement that certain rate schedules and load management techniques be adopted. The FEA could intervene directly as a party in ratemaking proceedings to challenge all aspects of ratemaking and to ensure compliance with the objectives of the Law.

Title III of H.R. 12461 was devoted to the regulation of bulk power supply (as an amendment to the Federal Power Act). The legislation defined "bulk power generating facilities" as "generating equipment and associated facilities designed for, or capable of operation at a single site with an aggregated capacity of 200 megawatts or more." For transmission facilities, the capacity was defined as 200 kilovolts or more. Regulation of bulk power sales was primarily the domain of the FPC. Although some large, publicly owned generated facilities such at the TVA and the Bonneville Power Authority engaged only in bulk sales, any utility could own bulk power facilities or engage in bulk power sales. For the latter, most bulk power sales were interstate sales through the national power grid. All such sales were at wholesale rates. The objectives of the new legislation in regard to bulk power were to enhance competition in production of bulk power and to maximize the utilization of existing capacity for the production of bulk power. There was also the goal of getting a handle on energy costs at the wholesale level. "Pancaking" or the submission of multiple requests for rate increases prior to final determination of a pending request, was prohibited; automatic fuel adjustment charges were slowed; and the inclusion of CWIP in the rate base for determining bulk sale prices was prohibited.

Title III also created area planning councils to coordinate the siting and licensing of bulk power facilities. The FPC was authorized to establish and enforce compliance with minimum utility reliability standards for all bulk power facilities to ensure the reliability of an adequate national supply of electric energy. The Office of Public Counsel was to be established within the FPC to support consumer representation in FPC hearings.The effect of this amendment to the Federal Power Act was ι_ have all aspects of electric energy generation, sale, and regulation more accountable to the federal regulators and presumably to the public. The proposed reforms would constitute a clean sweep.

The dedicated lifeline proposals (H.R. 10869, and substantively identical H.R. 11449) were short and to the point. They required all utilities to provide a susbsistence level of electric energy at a rate not to exceed the lowest rate charged to any consumer. Lifeline rates were to apply to a consumer's principal place of residence; to entail an amount to be determined by the PUC (or the utility) to sustain heating, lighting, cooking, cooling, and food refrigeration, and to allow for seasonal fluctuations in climate and consumption patterns. These dedicated lifeline proposals were different from the lifeline provision of H.R. 12461 mainly in that they offered a more detailed discussion of the specifics of a basic lifeline policy.

The (Ford) administration proposals were introduced as H.R. 2633 and H.R. 2650, which were identical bills, each with Title VII being devoted to state regulation of electric utility retail sales and Title VIII being devoted to streamlining the processes for facility siting and approval. Both titles had been previously introduced as part of the Energy Independence Act, a major administration initiative introduced in January 1975. The administration proposals were very different from the committee bill in objectives, directives, and contents. The findings of Title VII focused on the need for regulatory authorities to make adaptations in ways which would enhance the total revenues of utilities and their return on capital. The findings asserted that utilities were canceling or deferring planned plant expansions because their full operating costs were not being recovered, leading to an inability to attract sufficient capital to meet current and expected demand. These financial problems were said to cause energy shortages and the unreliability of electric energy supply. Although the administration proposal sought federal intervention in regard to state regulation of retail electric generation and sales, it sought to do so in the direction of removing constraints as opposed to imposing requirements on utilities and their regulators. The language was written as directives to state regulatory agencies forbidding them to:

1. Suspend or defer the operation of a properly filed and documented rate schedule for longer than five months (otherwise the proposed change or rate would go into effect and continue until a final order was given by the regulatory authority)
2. Prohibit as part of any rate schedule, without further proceedings, monthly fuel adjustment charges upon notice being given to the regulatory authority by the utility
3. Prohibit sale of energy produced offpeak at lower rates than sales made during periods of peak consumption
4. Prohibit inclusion in the rate base of reasonable expenditures associated with construction work in progress (CWIP)

5. Prohibit inclusion in the rate base of capital costs for environmental control
   facilities and equipment.

The stated objectives of Title VIII of the administration proposal were to
enhance the efficiency of planning for the necessary nationwide production
capacity to meet projected energy demands, and to streamline and expedite the
state and federal approach processes for the siting and licensing of new energy
facilities. To realize these objectives, the proposal included certain requirements
of federal and state agencies. The first major requirement was for the administrator of the FEA to prepare and submit to the President and Congress a National
Energy Site and Facility Report. The report was to include an inventory of the
location, type, size, and production capacity of all existing energy facilities
nationwide; a list of those facilities likely to be removed from production; and
a report of the present or projected status of all applications for siting or
operation of energy facilities pending at federal, regional, or state levels.

The report was also to provide information on present and projected long-
range energy needs and demands on a national, regional, and market area basis
and the projected availability and shortfall of suitable energy facilities and facility
sites to meet that demand. Within a year of the issuance of the FEA report, the
states were each to submit to the administrator of the FEA for approval an
Energy Facility Management Plan for long-term energy facility planning, and a
plan for the expedited processing of application to site, construct, and operate
energy facilities. In the case of requirements for federal approval for siting (in
regard to nuclear power plants, consideration of environmental regulations
including those in coastal zones, etc.) the administrator of the FEA was to
consult with other agencies and develop a single composite application and
approval process. Both requirements for the FEA report and the state plans
included admonitions for considering environmental impacts and assuring public
participation in the facility planning process and the administrative procedures
for facility siting and approval.

The contrast between the administration bill and the committee bill was
pointed. The administration bill was far from a comprehensive reform of electric
utilities regulation. There was no conjoining of regulatory reform and energy
conservation. Indeed, missing from the administration proposal was the
overarching concern for energy conservation, which had otherwise become a
consensual ethic in regard to developing energy policy. Instead, there was simply
the assumption that utilities would adopt energy conservation measures.
Although there was an allusion in the findings to pricing practices that did not
reflect the full costs of service, there was no requirement for prohibiting
declining block rates. There was no mention of the adverse impacts of energy
price increases on the elderly and poor and no provision for lifeline rates.
Although there was a nod in the direction of time-of-day or peak load pricing,
there was no requirement for the adoption of cost-based pricing. There was no
requirement for evidentiary hearings on utility rate increase requests, and there
was a prohibition on any delays in regard to requested FACs. There were no

requirements for guaranteed consumer representation or improving staff resources of PUCs. The provision for including cost of work in progress in the electric rate base represented a major break for utilities and a major departure from the committee bill which had forbidden its inclusion in retail rates.

The vast differences between the contents of the committee bill and the administration bill reflected very different perceptions or definitions of the problem. The committee's perception was that electric utilities had to be required to make certain changes in regard to pricing and energy conservation, and thus state regulators had to be required to make certain changes; and that state PUC procedures should be opened up and the public given a viable participatory role. The administration's position was that electric utilities needed to be unfettered by regulations and restrictions on earnings to allow them to meet the nation's future energy demands.

IDEAS IN CONFLICT

The Official Administration Position

In the actual hearings, the administration position was presented by several top administrators, whose testimonies varied somewhat in terms of the issues they addressed and somewhat in terms of the specificity of their remarks. Generally those administrators who were more directly responsible for analytical staff functions provided the more specific and detailed testimony. Overall, these administrators articulated positions which were somewhat more expansive than those taken in the administration bill. However, the thrust of their testimony was to oppose H.R. 12461, the committee bill.

Frank Zarb, the administrator of the FEA, complimented the committee on its work and its examination of the utility question in a comprehensive way. However, in his written testimony, Zarb characterized the committee bill as embodying "a series of general remedies for an undefined problem. . . . [It is] a complex, unfocused proposal for sweeping regulatory reform."[2] Zarb acknowledged that there was a serious problem of high energy costs, but he saw the more immediate problem as one in which utility executives and state regulators had begun to deny the truth of what would be required in the future. This unusual behavior, Zarb held, was because utility executives had recently been beseiged by outraged consumers and outraged environmentalists and, feeling pressure from state regulators, were deciding to postpone planning for future energy needs. The administration thus was concerned with whether future energy demands would be met, especially because its position was to discourage the use of residual oil (heavy-grade crude oil) and natural gas to generate electricity, in favor of the use of coal and nuclear fuel as the best, but considerably more costly, energy options.[3] Thus for the FEA, the driving question was one of how to ensure that sufficient generating capacity would be on line in time to meet future energy demand.

Zarb opposed the imposition of national standards for ratemaking in favor of permitting state regulators to define their own needs and to develop strategies to meet those needs. He argued against a separate office of Electric Utility Ratemaking Assistance within the FEA. The FEA favored limited intervention in state PUC ratemaking proceedings generally and a specifically limited role in urging the adoption of certain ratemaking practices. Zarb cited and listed for the record a number of formal invitations declined by the FEA from private parties (individuals, consumer and FEA public interest groups) urging their intervention in state ratemaking proceedings. Zarb cited a recognition of the need to preserve the jurisdictional boundaries between state and federal roles in public utility regulation as the reason for the declination. The FEA had intervened in a number of state ratemaking cases (a practice initiated and touted with some zeal under the preceding FEA administrator) but, according to Zarb, only at the invitation of state regulatory commissions. The FEA role had been that of a full party (an intervenor) and in an amicus curiae ("friend of the court") capacity in which written testimony is filed in a case.[4] These interventions had been handled by the FEA Office of Utility Programs, a component of the Office of Energy Conservation and Environment, which was at that time a major administrative component of FEA. The written description of the FEA Regulatory Intervention Program submitted for the record differed somewhat from Zarb's oral testimony in regard to FEA nonadvocacy of specific ratemaking practices:

The purpose of those program activities is to articulate national energy policy as it relates to utility load management and conservation practices. FEA testimony advocates the implementation of time-of-day rates (based on marginal costs), load control systems, and improved end-use conservation practices. In particular, FEA testimony focuses on improving the capacity utilization of electric utilities through the practical application of load management pricing and control tools.[5]

The FEA position was clarified somewhat in testimony provided by Roger W. Sant, Assistant Administrator, Energy Conservation and Environment. In response to questioning by members of the committee, Sant explained that the administration favored the principles of marginal cost pricing and peak pricing but did not advocate a particular rate structure. Sant submitted for the record a formal, written statement of the FEA position on marginal cost pricing. Basically the FEA position acknowledged that (1) there were a number of different interpretations by economists of this principle in regard to electricity pricing in a regulated monopoly context, but (2) a general consensus that the cost of providing an additional increment of electricity varies considerably with time of usage.[6] As regulated monopolies, utilities are required to meet the demand for electricity at all times. Periods of very high demand require that special generating facilities (commonly referred to as peaking units) be available to meet this demand. These facilities are otherwise generally not used or are under-utilized. This contributes to a problem of excess generating capacity which must be built and maintained at excessive costs. Conversely, periods of normal demand also generally leave a significant portion of a utility's generating capacity underutilized. Thus there is the desire to spread out the demand or load as much as possible, sometimes using price and discount incentives as a strategy supported in some instances by special technologies. Within the context of rising fuel costs, a growing consciousness about environmental degradation attributable to building new energy facilities, and growing concerns for energy conservation, the issue of electric utility load management took on special significance.

Sant testified that the administration advocated time-of-day pricing (as a form of marginal costpricing) plus interruptible rates to get around the "needle-peak" problem which occurs after several days of high temperatures when residential consumers just ignore price incentives and consume more electricity, sometimes wiping out any benefits earned by off-peak consumption.[7] With interruptible rates, consumers agree to selectively drop portions of their electricity load (e.g., TVs, dishwashers, clothes dryers, etc.) upon signaling by the utility in exchange for a lower rate structure. Some interruptible rate agreements permit the utility to reduce electricity consumption by turning off major appliances, such as air conditioning systems, for brief periods each hour. In the case of some industrial users, energy consumption can be cut back significantly upon short notice from the utility. However, some peak demand cannot be curtailed significantly with ease, as in the case of commercial usage in keeping shopping centers open or in giving industry the option of running work shifts around the clock. Thus there is an aspect of intractability to the issue of peak demand and load management.

The chairman of the Federal Power Commission (FPC) presented testimony which largely echoed that of Zarb of the FEA. Richard Dunham spoke in opposition to the strong federal role set forth in the committee bill as a usurpation of state power and as not providing enough flexibility for states to experiment with various rate structures. He also objected to an Office of Public Counsel for representation of consumer interests within FPC proceedings arguing that the commission staff represented the public interest. Dunham argued that the new office would represent users whose interests were not necessarily the same as the public interest.[8] A similar argument against any new efforts to enhance consumer representation in state PUC proceedings, arguing that current mechanism were both adequate and effective, had been made by the FEA. The FEA position was that instead of more consumer representation, efforts should be made to assist the consumer to understand regulatory procedures.[9]

The idea of special lifeline rates also did not fare well with the administration. A detailed statement of the official administration position was given by Dennis Bakke, Deputy Assistant Administrator for Energy Conservation and Environment of the FEA. Bakke argued that the available evidence on lifeline was inconclusive and advised against its enactment into law, although the FEA intended to continue support of projects devoted to demonstrating lifeline policies. Bakke cited two studies, from California and Maryland, which utilized regression analysis and found that there was no statistically significant correlation between income and energy usage. According to these analyses, low-income households were not necessarily low users of electric energy and low users were not necessarily low-income households. (H.R. 12461 did not require a means/income test and simply provided for pricing an initial increment of electricity at a reduced rate. This had the effect of providing a discount for everyone regardless of need.) Bakke also cited a New York study which showed that many low-income citizens lived in multiunit rental housing, where energy costs were factored into their rent payments. Such low income households would not benefit at all from lifeline provisions and might indeed be hurt by such policies. Multiunit housing, particularly apartment buildings, were generally billed at commercial rates for electricity. If the costs of subsidizing lifeline rates were shifted onto the industrial and commercial classes of consumers, low-income consumers in the latter would be hurt by a remedy intended to help them. Furthermore, they were not necessarily low users of electric energy, nor could they readily and substantially control their usage because they were frequently dependent on electricity for their total energy needs.

There was another aspect of intractability associated with multiunit housing: the difficulty of ensuring or imposing effective energy conservation measures. Bakke cited an FEA study on master metering, or the billing for electricity usage based on one meter serving an entire building. The FEA study had found that in master-metered buildings, per-household residential usage was 30 percent greater than for individually metered households. A significant portion of this greater usage was generally attributed to the absence of direct price signals, which also meant the absence of incentives for conservation of energy. Any policy seeking to address the problems of master metering would have to take into account the costs of retrofitting existing buildings with individualized metering systems.

Bakke also raised the spectre of a more serious problem emerging from the implementation of lifeline policies. Bakke suggested that a shifting of the costs to subsidize lifeline onto commercial and industrial users might lead them to switch fuel and energy sources; and that if enough large industrial users switched away from electricity usage, utility load factors would decline, driving up electricity costs for everyone else, including the beneficiaries of lifeline. Moreover, Bakke argued, the goal of energy conservation would not be served by shifting energy costs from one class of consumers to another because those consumers who could switch fuels might help to reduce consumption of electricity but may in fact use more of other energy sources.[10]

In an interesting gesture of what one may characterize as political courtesy the committee invited the comments of several major executive branch agencies on H.R. 12461. As these agencies were under the leadership of the President, it was predictable that they would not express positions at variance with those contained or implicit in the administration's bill. Although some agency heads spoke critically of specific portions of H.R. 12461, all deferred to the official FEA position on the bill or otherwise argued against its enactment and in support of H.R. 2633/2650. Agencies submitting letters and statements for the record in response to the committee's invitation included the Environmental Protection Agency, the FPC, (which also sent officials to testify in person), the Department of Interior, the Interstate Commerce Commission, the Nuclear

Regulatory Commission, the Office of Management and Budget, and the TVA.

State Regulators

Although representatives of several state PUCs came to testify before the committee, PUCs as a group were represented by the National Association of Regulatory Utility Commisions (NARUC). Presenting the NARUC position was the organization's president, James McGirr Kelly, who had also been a member of the Pennsylvania PUC since early 1967. Kelly identified the NARUC as:

a quasi-governmental nonprofit organization founded in 1889. Within its membership are the governmental agencies of the 50 states and of the District of Columbia, Puerto Rico, and the Virgin Islands, engaged in the regulation of utilities and carriers. Our chief objective is to serve the public interest by seeking to improve the quality and effectiveness of public regulation.[11]

The NARUC position offered yet another definition of the problem. Although it concurred with the assessment of seriously high energy costs, the NARUC argued that H.R. 12461 ignored the two most pressing aspects of the problem: escalating plant and equipment costs and rising fuel costs. The committee bill was criticized for an undue emphasis on load management when, according to the NARUC, the problem of the future would not be one of excess generating capacity but one of improving technological processes to permit safe and environmentally acceptable uses of coal and uranium. Otherwise, much of the NARUC's opposition was directed toward what was perceived as federal preemption and usurpation of the state role in utility regulation. Thus the NARUC held that national or uniform federal standards for load management and rate structures were totally inappropriate, as was uniformity on fuel adjustment clauses and CWIP. NARUC saw no need for an Office of Electric Utility Assistance; it objected to compensation for the representation of consumer interests in ratemaking proceedings; and it opposed federal funds to improve PUC staff skills, arguing that states should pay to improve PUC staffs. After having referred to the section of H.R. 12461 which provided for lifeline rates as "particularly objectionable," Kelly indicated that the NARUC neither endorsed nor condemned lifeline but rather took the position that a uniform rule was not appropriate. NARUC also opposed the requirement of a State Energy Facility Management Plan as being a usurpation of state authority.[12]

At least one representative of a state PUC spoke in support of H.R. 12461. Edward Berlin of the New York PUC testified in support of the committee bill, specifically expressing support for national standards, marginal cost pricing, and efforts to ensure a reliable national power supply. Berlin argued that the legislation did not comprise an inhibition on effective state regulation.[13] Commissioner Berlin had been identified by Congressman Richard Ottinger as a noted consumer advocate. Thus, Berlin's position on lifeline was unlikely to be dismissed. He too expressed reservations about whether lifeline provision would indeed help its intended beneficiaries. Berlin's reservations paralleled those raised by other witnesses: that low-income users were not low energy users; and that many lived in poorly insulated homes or in multiunit dwellings and thus either could not easily practice energy conservation or could not make choices about sources of energy for specific uses. He recommended adoption of some form of income tax credit.

Investor-owned Utilities

As a group, the investor-owned utilities were represented by the Edison Electric Institute (EEI), with official testimony presented by the president of EEI, Donham Crawford. Perhaps not surprisingly, the EEI held that H.R. 12461 imposed severe adverse impacts on the ability of the utility industry to provide for the nation's electric power demands; and that whatever problems might have existed in the industry could be resolved by the industry and state and local regulators without federal intervention. Crawford challenged two major assumptions underlying the committee bill: (1) that the growth in demand for electricity was attributable to large industrial users; and (2) that large users were being subsidized by residential users. Crawford argued that most growth in demand was due to increases in the residential class of consumers and that, moreover, most industrial users were on interruptible service rates, which assured that much of their usage was offpeak. Crawford provided data for the record which showed average annual growth in residential and industrial electricity demand of 8.8 and 7.2 percent respectively for the period 1954-1964. However, at the time of the hearings these data were twelve years old.[14]

The EEI expressed strong reservations about the requirements for marginal cost pricing, arguing that there was no agreement within the industry or among regulators about the proper method for establishing marginal costs in a manner sufficiently precise for ratemaking. Thus the EEI and the Electric Power Research Institute (EPRI) had formed a joint task force to conduct an Electric Utility Rate Design study. The executive Director of the EEI/EPRI study reinforced the concerns about how to establish pricing structures to affect load management. The director also indicated that the study was being done at the invitation of NARUC and involved participants from all segments of the industry, including regulatory commissions, investor-owned utilities, publicly and cooperatively owned utilities, and representatives from state and federal governments.[15]   The EEI position was that more studying and testing was needed on the reliability of the technologies involved and on the ability and willingness of customers to accept the constraints imposed by load management techniques.[16]

The EEI presented data showing that the costs of constructing coal and nuclear powered electrical generating facilities had increased 27 and 17 percent, respectively, for the period 1969-1975. Thus the EEI argued that restricting FACs would only delay the recovery of financial burdens by utilities, causing damage to the industry. The EEI also presented the results of a 1974 NARUC survey on the provisions among the states for representation of consumer interests in formal PUC ratemaking proceedings.[17] The survey had found that consumer representation took one of four forms: commission staff, state consumer agencies, state attorney generals, and local government units. The notes to the survey revealed an array of nuances and exceptions to each of the categories of representation and generally left unanswered any questions about the condition and circumstances under which consumer representation occurred, the extent and effectiveness of representation, or how costs of representation were defrayed. The EEI opposed any new initiatives in consumer representation, characterizing the committee bill provision as having the potential for regulatory paralysis and as an open invitation for abuse by those with no interest in rate regulation. Lifeline rates were also opposed by the EEI as a drastic departure from cost-based ratemaking and as likely to be hurtful to many it would seek to help (i.e. the poor who lived in master-metered dwellings billed at commercial rates). The EEI argued that the rational approach to helping the poor with high energy costs was direct governmental assistance.[18]

The EEI found that it could support part of H.R. 12461 but did not express that support without taking the opportunity to make a major point, which was telling of the industry's overall attitude toward federal regulation. Malcolm Killop, appearing on behalf of the EEI, characterized section 502 of H.R. 12461 as a worthwhile provision with the worthy objective of expediting the construction of bulk power facilities requiring federal approval. However, he chastised the committee for failing to direct itself to the principal cause of regulatory delays in the construction of needed new electric power capacity. Killop argued that the critical sources of regulatory delay were the numerous special purpose federal statutes, each enacted with a single worthwhile objective but which together had become a Gordian knot of regulations and procedures required at both federal and state levels.

Killop proceeded to list examples of delay-causing laws and procedural requirements that affected the siting of power plants, including the Clean Air Act, the Coastal Zone Management Act, the Federal Water Pollution Control Act, the Atomic Energy Act, the Wild and Scenic Rivers Act, the National Trails System Act, the Wilderness Act, the Anadromous Fish Act, the National Historic Preservation Act, the National Forest Multiple Use Act, the Water Resource Act, the Bureau of Outdoor Recreation Organic Act, and the National Environmental Policy Act.[19]

Cooperatives and Rural Utilities

There was a great chasm of difference in terms of the condition of investor-owned utilities and rural cooperatives and the corresponding impacts likely to ensue from enactment of H.R. 12461. The National Rural Electrical Cooperative Association (NRECA) represented over 1000 non-profit, rural electric cooperatives, which served 25 million customers in forty-five states. Some 900 members were electricity distribution cooperatives, which provided power directly to endusers, and some fifty were organized as bulk power systems which generate and transmit at wholesale rates to the distribution systems. Rural cooperatives generated one third of the power they sold at retail rates; one third was purchased at wholesale from federal bulk power suppliers, and the remaining one third was purchased at wholesale from investor-owned utilities. Presenting testimony for NRECA was its executive vice president and general manager, Robert Patridge, who testified that rural cooperatives experienced problems in negotiating firm prices in long-term bulk purchase contracts with investor-owned utilities which were commensurate with requirements for obtaining long-term financing to support the contracts. He also testified about problems rural cooperatives had in obtaining the use of transmission lines of investor-owned bulk power suppliers, ranging from uncertain availability of transmission to restrictions on subsequent sale of purchased power. Thus the NRECA felt that Title III of H.R. 12461, with its provisions affecting joint use of bulk power supply facilities and unfair methods of competition, would be very helpful to its member utilities.[20]

There were other aspects of the committee bill which the NRECA saw as being detrimental to it because of the fundamental nature of the NRECA's administrative apparatus, its nonprofit status, and its rate base. Partridge testified that ·many rural cooperatives would have problems implementing load management techniques because they did not have daily demand meters, thus making the gathering of kilowatt-hour demand data very expensive. He argued that holding evidentiary hearings would also be expensive and recommended that an audit be substituted. He similarly argued that customers could save old bills as opposed to utility mailings of past consumption patterns. Perhaps one of the most compelling points raised by Partridge was the predicted dire consequences of attempts by rural cooperatives to implement the lifeline policy requirements in the Committee bill. Partridge stated that rural electric cooperatives get 65 to 75 percent of their revenue from residential consumers and less than one third from industrial and commercial customers in contrast to the typical urban utility, which usually gets one third of its revenue from residential consumers and the rest from commercial and industrial users. Thus for rural cooperatives, there was no customer class on which to shift the costs of subsidizing a lifeline rate. For rural cooperatives to shift costs onto commercial and industrial users would court the risk of driving out industry, resulting in a loss of jobs for rural economies.[21]

Environmental Groups

The Environmental Defense Fund (EDF) was a self-identified major player in efforts to reform the pricing policies of regulated electric corporations. The EDF was not so much a consumer interest group as what might be characterized as a special purpose public interest group, with a decided mission and set of objectives. The EDF was described to the committee as a "broad identity of interests between those concerned with protecting the environment, American consumers, workers, and investors with a total membership consisting of 38,000. As told to the committee, the purpose of EDF's energy program was to "minimize the total social costs of energy to society."

The EDF representative, Ernst Habicht, Jr., reminded the committee of the EDF's victories and interventions in a host of state regulatory proceedings dating back to 1974, asserting that "it is fair to say that we have virtually blanketed the nation with our ideas." Habicht attributed the EDF's success to its internal organizational structure wherein economists, scientists, and attorneys worked together to understand the need for rate reform and the economic and technical consequences of such reform. Thus the EDF endorsed marginal cost pricing as spelled out in H.R. 12461 as resting on solid analytical and economic grounds. Habicht charged that unfortunately the utility executives most inimical to change were those who dominated some of the industry-sponsored studies of rate reform and remained partly successful in placing the burden of proof on those who advocated change. The EDF also endorsed the provision for compensating public interest intervenors in utility rate proceedings and argued that the language of the bill be made clearly unambiguous to provide compensation to any organization which had at least one member who was an electric consumer.[22]

In regard to the lifeline provision of H.R. 12461, the EDF urged its deletion from the bill. The EDF criticized the lifeline provision for assuming that (1) electric corporations were a suitable instrument for the redistribution of wealth; (2) all residential customers should be treated equally with respect to their need; (3) that all residential customers could be treated as identical in regard to their physical living arrangements. Furthermore, the EDF criticized the lifeline provision for representing a departure from the fundamental principle that rates reflect marginal costs of supply. The EDF did not explicitly advocate direct financial assistance to the poor to offset high energy costs. Instead EDF argued that the poor made uneconomic consumption decisions in the purchase of electricity using devices. Thus the EDF proposed, as an alternative to lifeline rates, policies mandating energy efficiency labeling of even the smallest appliances. The EDF further urged that all institutional barriers to more intelligent consumer decisions be eliminated, including letting utilities reap profits in this effort.[23]

Positions similar to those taken by the EDF were expressed by a representative of the Sierra Club. The Sierra Club supported the implementation of marginal cost pricing in place of the practice of average cost pricing or declining block rates, consistent with the goals of energy conservation and environmental protection. However, the Sierra Club objected to lifeline provisions for anything above 150 kwh per month, the amount of electricity required for lighting and refrigeration. The reasoning for this position was the Sierra Club's objection to subsidizing a sector of the market in which demand was elastic and its opposition to subsidizing the uneconomic use of energy through poorly insulated housing, inefficient heating equipment, etc. The Sierra Club advocated assisting the poor in ways which affected energy conservation, but through a comprehensive plan carried out at the state or federal level, in addition to educating the poor in regard to the incremental costs of energy consumption.[24]

The strongest support for H.R. 12461 from an environmental group came from the Environmental Action Foundation (EAF), an independent research organization based in Washington, D.C. which served as a clearinghouse for environmental and consumer groups working on energy issues. The EAF expressed explicit support for almost all of the specific provisions of the committee bill but expressed opposition to the provision allowing for inclusion of CWIP by the FPC in setting rates for wholesale bulk power supplies. (H.R. 12461 prohibited the inclusion of CWIP by state PUCs in retail sales but permitted the FPC to allow it in wholesale rates.) The EDF also articulated the strongest and best formulated counterargument to the inclusion of CWIP in electrical rates:

In concept, CWIP is very simple. It would allow utilities to earn a profit on new power facilities while they are under construction. It means today's customers would be paying for tomorrow's power. The use of CWIP is similar to a landlord requiring his tenants to pay rent 5 years in advance. CWIP makes a mockery of the longstanding regulatory principle that utilities should earn a return only on equipment which is "used and useful" in the production of utility services. The use of CWIP would also allow the utilities to transfer most of their business risks to their customers.[25]

The EAF argued that the FPC had estimated that rates would rise as much as 11 percent due to the inclusion of CWIP, or a total cost to consumers of $5 billion per year in higher rates, whereas some others had estimated increases as high as 17.7 percent. Thus the EAF supported the prohibition of CWIP in retail and wholesale rates.[26]

Consumer Groups

The Consumer Federation of America (CFA) provided two witnesses for the hearings, who testified on different days and who presented slightly different positions. The president of the CFA, Lee Richardson, expressed support for uniform national standards of utility regulation, arguing that the states were unable to regulate the electric industry. Lee White, Chair of the Energy Task Force of the CFA, expressed reservations about national standards, arguing that the perspective of Washington did not always play in the states and urging the allowance of deviation from national standards on a showing by a state that compliance was wasteful. Otherwise the two representatives generally agreed in their support of most of the provisions of H.R. 12461. They both expressed support for lifeline but raised concerns about its effective implementation. The president of the CFA specifically spoke against the inclusion of the Office of Utility Ratemaking Assistance within the FEA, arguing that it would be in a position of conflict with the main body of the agency. He favored instead placement of the Office within another agency or its establishment as a separate, independent office.[27]

Industrial Users

An organized, select group of major industrial users of electrical power, the Electrical Consumers Resource Council (ELCON), presented testimony at the hearings. ELCON was identified as an unincorporated trade association of ten industrial electric consumers who manufactured chemicals, glass, steel, beer, plastics, machinery, etc., and which included Union Carbide, PPG, Olin, Anheuser-Busch, and others. Ronald Wishart, Executive Director of ELCON, testified that ELCON members had experienced increases in energy costs of up to 150 percent for the three-year period of 1972–1975. Wishart testified that ELCON opposed federal intervention in state PUC activities in setting rate standards. ELCON challenged H.R. 12461 as a bill embodying the philosophy that energy conservation and small consumer interests required rate structures that were antigrowth and anti-industry. ELCON further argued that rate designs should apportion costs in ways which were nondiscriminatory, rational, and efficient; that any policy should distinguish between peakload pricing and marginal cost pricing because the two were not Siamese twins; and that load management policies should await the results of the NARUC/EEI study. Lifeline rates were opposed by ELCON as being incompatible with any fair, cost-based rate structure and comprising a pure subsidy from some consumers to others. Wishart also testified that criticism of declining block rates was unfounded.[28]

SUMMARY

The issues in the 1976 legislative hearings shifted from a central focus on the need to alleviate the adverse impact of rising energy costs on the poor to a focus on the need to reform the regulation of electric utilities, with relief to the poor being one of several benefits of reform. Similarly, the role of Congress shifted from that of hosting generic hearings on rising energy costs to holding formal hearings in support of legislative proposals which incorporated varying definitions of the core problem and varying policy responses as well. Defining the problem and proposing solutions in formal legislation made the debate a far more serious one.

The legislative hearings illuminated three competing and conflicting definitions of the problem to be addressed. Two of these definitions were reflected in legislative proposals; the third was articulated by the main group representing utility regulators. One definition of the problem held that electric utilities were dominating the state regulators with the result that electricity was being priced in ways which encouraged wasteful consumption and made electricity cheaper to large users by way of a subsidy from small residential users. This, in turn, led to the need to build more generating facilities at greater economic costs, which again penalized residential consumers, especially the poor, and entailed the cost of continued degradation of the environment. Thus reform of electric utility regulation was needed to set into motion a series of developments, including rationalizing the pricing of electricity to ensure equity, to encourage energy conservation, to slow the pace of facility construction, and to lower economic costs overall, thereby benefiting the poor and yielding environmental benefits. This was the definition of the problem and the concomitant perspective on the appropriate solution as held by the dominant group on the Energy and Power Subcommittee and as reflected in the committee's bill, H.R. 12461.

A second definition of the problem held that electric utilities had been caught by enormous changes in economies of scale which were compounded by rapid escalation of energy fuel prices due to the oil embargo. Electric utilities had also been beseiged by angry residential consumers and hostile environmentalists, who had joined in successfully intimidating state regulators such that utilities were retreating from facing and accurately assessing the energy needs of the future. Thus what was needed was not more regulation, but an unfettering of utilities from the constraints of regulation so that they could rationally plan for the energy needs of the future. This definition of the problem and perspective of the appropriate solution was contained in the Ford administration bills, H.R. 2633 and H.R 2650, and underlay the testimony given by Ford administration officials.

The third major perspective was presented by the NARUC, the organization representing public utility regulators. The NARUC definition of the problem was that escalating plant and equipment costs and rising fuel costs would be compounded by an energy future based on a reliance on coal and nuclear fuels for the generation of electricity. Thus the challenge in crafting a policy response to this problem was how to meet the nation's future electric energy needs in safe and environmentally acceptable ways. Interestingly, this position was not reflected in any of the competing legislative proposals. The NARUC perspective was some years off in terms of acquiring a commanding role in policy discourse. The two major environmental groups took what might be characterized as an attempted pristine philosophical position, buoyed by considerable hubris. The poor got little support from these groups, who were at the time in a position to be particularly influential. Consumers as an organized interest suffered by not having a strong enough presence at these hearings.

In terms of the major legislative proposals, the Ford administration bill was simply not in the running in structuring the policy debate. This lent greater dominance to the committee bill. The considerable strength of the committee bill may be attributable to the then prevailing mobilization of bias engendered by the convergence of rising energy costs and a growing environmental movement; partisan dynamics given the tenuous status of the Ford administration; or simply the expectation that the committee's position, modified or not, would end up as law. Thus the major point of contention in response to the committee bill centered not so much around the question of whether electric utility regulation should be reformed, but rather the issue of federal intervention versus state autonomy. Thus much of the opposition expressed was primarily opposition to what was characterized as federal usurpation of a state government role. This was a debate as old as the federal relationship and one which almost inevitably pales in the face of policies which are advocated to bring about nationwide results in a manner which is seen as reflective of the public interest. Circumstances had converged such that the idea of electric utility regulatory reform had the popular saliency and political potency to prevail.

The idea of lifeline rates was a different story. Part of the problem had to do with the manner in which the argument supporting the idea was structured. Although the problem of income deficits induced by rising energy costs gave rise to what ultimately became a push to reform electric utility regulation, there was no comprehensive proposal which placed lifeline provisions first in priorities and thrust and which organized other issues around that idea. As it was, lifeline provisions stood out as a contradiction to the main thrust of the rate reform bills (i.e. the shift to cost-based pricing). The dedicated lifeline bills were not only duplicative of the provision in the committee bill, but within the context of competing legislative proposals, they were sidelines to the main discourse. There were also no major champions of lifeline rates. The two organizations representing the interests of the elderly had given only modest support to the idea when it emerged in the hearings before the Special Committee. They had not participated at all in the legislative hearings. Most other participants in the hearings opposed the establishment of lifeline rates. The FEA opposed lifeline rates as anathema to the principle of cost-based pricing. Industrial and commercial users opposed lifeline because the cost of subsidizing such rates would presumably be shifted onto the industrial and commercial rate structure. The more influential environmentalists opposed lifeline because such rates did not clearly contribute to their higher priority of energy conservation. At the end of the 1976 hearings, lifeline and the issue of income support which it represented had been significantly upstaged by other concerns and other ideas.

NOTES

1. U.S. Congress. House. Committee on Interstate and Foreign Commerce. Subcommittee on Energy and Power. *Electric Utility Rate Reform and Regulatory Improvement: Hearings on H.R. 12461 and Related Bills.* 94th Cong., 2nd sess., 1976, pt. 1, p. 1. Opening Statement of Congressman John Dingell.

2. Ibid., p. 588. Testimony of Honorable Frank Zarb, Administrator, Federal Energy Administration.

3. House. *Electric Utility Rate Reform*, pt. 2, pp. 1145–1156. Testimony and Prepared Statement of William Rosenberg, Assistant Administrator for Energy Resource Development, Federal Energy Administration.

4. House. *Electric Utility Rate Reform,* pt. 1, p. 594. Testimony of Honorable Frank Zarb.

5. Ibid., p. 594. Material submitted for the record by Honorable Frank Zarb.

6. House. *Electric Utility Rate Reform*, pt. 1, pp. 298–322. Testimony and supporting material submitted for the record by Robert W. Sant, Federal Energy Administration.

7. Ibid., p. 298.

8. House. *Electric Utility Rate Reform*, pt. 2, pp. 1417–1448. Testimony and prepared statement of Honorable Richard Dunham, Chairman, Federal Power Commission.

9. House. *Electric Utility Rate Reform*, pt. 1, p. 591. Testimony of Honorable Frank Zarb.

10. Ibid., pp. 706–713. Testimony and prepared statement of Dennis Bakke, Assistant Administrator for Energy Conservation and Environment, Federal Energy Administration.

11. House. *Electric Utility Rate Reform*, pt. 1, p. 195. Testimony of James McGirr Kelly, President of the National Association of Regulatory Utility Commissions.

12. Ibid., pp. 195–202.

13. House. *Electric Utility Rate Reform,* pt. 1, pp. 336–342. Testimony and prepared statement of Edward Berlin, New York Public Utility Commission.

14. House. *Electric Utility Rate Reform,* pt. 1, pp. 219–246. Testimony of Donham Crawford, President of Edison Electric Institute.

15. House. *Electric Utility Rate Reform,* pt. 1, pp. 382–386 Testimony and prepared statement of Robert Uhler, Edison Electric Institute and Electric Power Research Institute.

16. Ibid., pp. 219-246. Testimony of Donham Crawford.

17. House. *Electric Utility Rate Reform,* pt. 1, pp. 230–231. Materials submitted for the record by Edison Electric Institute.

18. House. *Electric Utility Rate Reform*, pt. 1, pp. 219–246. Testimony of Donham Crawford.

19. Ibid., pt. 2, pp. 1397-1398. Testimony of Malcolm Killop, Edison Electric Institute.

20. House. *Electric Utility Rate Reform,* pt. 1, pp. 1029–1035 Testimony and prepared statement of Robert Patridge, Executive Vice President, National Rural Electrical Cooperative Association.

21. Ibid.

22. House. *Electric Utility Rate Reform,* pt. 1, pp. 851–862. Testimony and prepared statement of Ernst R. Habicht, Jr., Environmental Defense Fund.

23. Ibid.

24. House. *Electric Utility Rate Reform*, pt. 2, pp. 1849–1855. Testimony and prepared statement of Lawrence I. Moss, Sierra Club.

25. House. *Electric Utility Rate Reform,* pt. 2, p. 1321. Testimony of Richard Morgan, Environmental Action Foundation.

26. Ibid., pp. 1320-1324.

27. House. *Electric Utility Rate Reform*, pt. 1, pp. 881–888. Joint testimonies and prepared statement by Lee S. White and Lee Richardson, Consumer Federation of America.

28. Ibid., pp. 246–250. Testimony of Ronald S. Wishart, Executive Director, Electricity Consumers Resource Council.

REFERENCES

Anderson. Douglas D. *Regulatory Politics and Electric Utilities*. Boston: Auburn House Publishing Co., 1981.

Gordon, Richard L. *Reforming the Regulation of Electric Utilities*. Lexington, Mass.: Lexington Books, 1982.

Chapter 4

Policy Responses by Congressional Action

A NEW CONTEXT FOR A CONTINUING DEBATE

In 1977, the entire discourse on energy-related issues was altered again by the initiatives of President Jimmy Carter's administration. The Carter administration sought to formally institutionalize a broad-based, comprehensive policy response to the nation's energy needs. Administration and congressional policymakers were pushed in the direction of examination and overhaul of the nation's entire energy policy apparatus. As a result, a national energy policy was developed and proposed in legislation which entailed a reorganization of all administrative, regulatory, and research and development efforts in the area of energy. The new administrative and regulatory thrust was designed to maximize economic efficiency and to encourage the use of energy sources in a more rational and efficient manner. As part of an integrated approach to energy planning, a vastly new and ambitious research and development effort was envisioned to expand the domestic energy production base through the development, testing, and deployment of an array of new and underutilized energy technologies, such as passive and active solar energy, geothermal energy, wind energy, biomass, and coal gasification and liquefaction. Energy conservation was to be practiced so aggressively that it would equal the energy contribution of a new source of fuel. With emphasis on more progressive regulation and end-use energy conservation, the issue of utility rate and regulatory reform came to be incorporated into the Carter administration's policy initiative.

The Carter National Energy Policy was introduced in the House as H.R. 6831 and in the Senate as S. 1469. Part E, Title I of the House bill addressed the issue of utility reform. However, the Carter proposal in this area was not an original effort. Instead, it built on the extensive work in this area which had been done by the Dingell Committee and its work, as discussed in Chapter 3. A key staffer, Robert Nordhaus (who had worked for the House Subcommittee on

Energy and Power) had joined the Carter White House staff in the Office of Energy Policy and Planning. Not surprisingly, the Carter proposal for utility rate and regulatory reform was very similar to the Dingell bill. Congressman Dingell had revised his original bill, H.R. 12461, in response to input from the 1976 hearings. Some changes in the Dingell bill were designed to incorporate new issues raised by the Carter administration and others. The revised bill, H.R. 6660 was titled The Electric Utility Act of 1977 and was introduced in 1977 with twenty-four cosponsors. The policy debate continued to address the array of issues raised in earlier hearings. Again, the new committee bill held sway.

In terms of national minimum standards for the retail sale of electricity, the abiding principle of cost-based pricing was retained. Thus, declining block rates were prohibited unless they could be justified by costs. Time-of-day rates (a variant of marginal cost pricing) were mandated for industrial and commercial users but were made voluntary for residential users. This exemption for residential consumers reflected concerns about the benefits to be derived from time-of-day rates versus the added costs of making add-ons to existing meters or installing new meters to measure usage by time-of-day as opposed to total consumption. There was also a concern about the willingness of residential consumers to make the necessary lifestyle adjustments, such as doing the laundry at 2 A.M., to reap the benefits of such rates. Utilities were still required to notify consumers of requests for rate increases as well as to provide periodic notification of all rates in effect for all classes of consumers. However, information on past consumption patterns was to be provided by utilities only upon request. A new requirement was imposed on utilities: that specific prior notice of intent to terminate service be provided to the consumer with a reasonable opportunity given to contest the termination. State PUCs were given the authority to prescribe specific procedures for this provision. Promotional and political advertising by utilities was prohibited, as in the earlier bill. Interestingly, this ban on utility advertising had not provoked protests from the industry during the hearings. There had been no defenses of utility advertising.

The revised committee bill did not mention the controversial CWIP provision, thereby eliminating the previous allowance of 66 2/3 percent (which, if enacted, would have been of great benefit to the utility industry). The provision establishing an Office of Utility Ratemaking Assistance within the FEA was eliminated, although the provision for grants to improve PUC staff, to support consumer representation, and to demonstrate load management techniques was retained. Also retained was the right of the FEA (specifically its administrator) to intervene in state-level ratemaking proceedings. In the absence of formal provisions for consumer representation in utility regulatory proceedings, utilities were still held liable for compensating prevailing intervenors. The FEA was given the authority to restrict or prohibit master metering of multiunit housing. This provision was included to encourage energy conservation and reflected acceptance of the FEA study (referred to in Chapter 3) which showed significantly greater per-household consumption patterns when master metering was used instead of individual metering.

In a major change from the committee's earlier position, the requirement for lifeline rates as a national standard was eliminated in the revised committee bill. Rather lifeline rates were permitted (i.e., explicitly not prohibited) as an exception to cost-based rates. Thus lifeline rates could be implemented on a voluntary basis. The Carter administration proposal contained the same voluntary provision for lifeline rates. This was effectively a legislative nod in the direction of the principle of equity in electric energy costs. However, the issue was not a moot one. Senator Gary Hart introduced S. 1364, which was apparently designed to stimulate support for lifeline by recasting the issue in its original context of assistance for the low-income elderly.

One of the faults of earlier lifeline provisions in both dedicated bills and in H.R. 12461 was the universality of its applicability. Earlier lifeline proposals simply provided for a discounted subsistence-level block of electricity, with the discount applying to the initial usage block and built into residential rates and made available to all consumers in that class, independent of need. Thus such universal provisions would have helped the low income while also needlessly providing a discount to those who were fully able to pay the real costs of electricity. However, each of the provisions made lifeline rates applicable only to primary places of residence, presumably eliminating second homes (which would likely have shown low usage but would likely not have met a needs test).

The purposes of the Hart proposal, S. 1364, included the following:

to provide an interim solution for the subsistence residential electrical needs of the elderly while Congress attempts to construct an equitable electric utility structure which adequately meets the needs of all classes of electrical consumers; to promote equity in electrical costing; to demonstrate the effects of lifeline costing on electric utility rate structures, consumption patterns and the operation of electric utilities; and to demonstrate the feasibility and desirability of action by Congress to extend lifeline costing to other segments of American society.

The specifics of Senator Hart's bill were somewhat similar to other lifeline provisions in that Hart's bill provided that lifeline rates could not exceed the lowest rates paid by any other electricity consumer. The appropriate regulatory authority was authorized to determine a subsistence quantity of electricity and the enduses which were to be considered in determining the subsistence quantity. However, the Hart bill differed from other lifeline provisions in two significant ways, which might have negated the objective of engendering broad-based support. First, the Hart bill explicitly mentioned "medical and other essential purposes" among the end uses to be considered in determining a subsistence level of electricity. In many instances, the inclusion of medical needs, which might have covered special medical equipment or the use of air filtration systems or constant air conditioning use for asthma sufferers, would have dictated a substantial level of electricity consumption as an essential subsistence level. This example reflected part of the difficulty of developing a lifeline policy. There was no easy way of establishing a generalized policy based on low-level subsistence needs which would be inclusive of all needy cases. Yet to opt for a more inclusive provision would, given conventional ways of approaching implementation of policies for the low income and needy, require a tangle of rules for certification of need and eligibility.

The second major difference in the Hart bill was its restriction of eligibility for lifeline rates to the low-income elderly. The specific age and eligibility criteria were sixty-two years of age. Although the impetus for consideration of lifeline rates emerged from concern about the adverse effects of rising energy costs on the low-income elderly, if the larger policy objective was to promote equity in energy costs, then discrimination among the low income was a basic contradiction to that objective.

Senator Hart's proposal did not appreciably advance the cause of lifeline electricity rates. Moreover, Hart was going against the legislative momentum in introducing lifeline rates on an interim basis under his proposal (they were to expire in three years) within the context of an assumption that other issues of electric regulatory reform were going to be postponed for further study. Not only had the issue of electric utility regulatory reform been under discussion and legislative consideration for some time, but the President's national energy policy initiatives gave an added sense of urgency to an already strong sense that Congress ought to enact legislation in this critical area of national policy. There was no better reflection of that sense of urgency than the statement made by Senator Henry M. Jackson at the opening of the hearings: "We will be engaged in an educational exercise of substantial proportions for our jurisdiction over these issues is new. Members of the Senate Committee on Energy and Natural Resources have not had extensive experience with this policy area. We are, however, a committee which knows how to move legislation."[1] There might well have been a lot of issues which warranted further study, but there was an overriding momentum for legislative action in the area of utility regulatory reform. For an issue which did not have strong support at the committee level or from the administration, as was the case with lifeline policy, the prevailing legislative environment was not a propitious one.

In 1976 the issue of lifeline policy had been diminished in the policy debate by an overriding emphasis on the need to rationalize electric utility rate structures and a prevailing conviction among key policymakers that cost-based pricing of electricity was the key to rationalizing rate structures. Lifeline policy stood out as a fundamental contradiction to that central policy thrust. Another major issue in the 1976 policy debate was that of enhanced citizen participation in utility ratemaking, which in turn supported the issue of rationalizing rates. However, within the context of energy conservation, which had emerged as an issue which undergirded the entire debate about all energy related-policies, the issue of lifeline policies was not presented in a way which depicted it as an issue which made a solid contribution to solutions which had a broader and ultimately higher value in the policy debate.

A NEW IDEA AND AN EXPANDING DEBATE

In 1977 a not so subtle and certainly not insignificant shift in emphasis had occurred in the debate about energy policy. The high-valence issue which the Carter officials were using to enshroud all aspects of energy-related matters was that of energy savings. Specific policies were preferred not because they contributed to or promoted energy conservation in an evident manner. Rather, energy savings which could be expressed in specific, quantifiable terms became the currency of the policy debate. Some specific policy ideas and proposals could readily conform to what was effectively a political requirement, whereas others could not. Lifeline was not a policy idea which conformed to this requirement. Again, lifeline was at a disadvantage because it did not contribute to an end goal which was given a higher value in the policy debate.

Before the 1977 hearings the argument for utility rate reform had not been presented within the context of specific quantities of energy savings. Perhaps the shift in the context of the debate was due to a shift in the institutional driving force behind the debate. In the 1976 hearings Congress was the driving force behind the debate, arguing that utility regulatory reform was necessary to rationalize the behavior of utilities and their regulators in terms of rationalizing rate structures, curbing wasteful consumption of electricity, and curbing what some saw as profligate ways of utilities in constructing more and more facilities which resulted in severe environmental degradation. In 1976, Congress was prodding a recalcitrant executive branch, resistant state regulators, and a resistant industry. Although Congress retained a significant role in 1977, the Carter administration emerged as the driving force behind utility regulatory reform. It did so by urging a heightened national concern about energy issues generally and by firmly taking hold of what had previously been nascent and disparate efforts to formalize an integrated and comprehensive approach to national energy planning and policy.

Although Congress had taken the approach of building the case for electric utility regulatory reform, the position held by the Carter administration was that major changes in the total approach to energy production and use were a forgone conclusion. Perhaps the more expansive approach taken by the Carter administration required an equally compelling undergirding context for successfully structuring the overall terms of the debate on energy policy. Thus utility regulatory reform was seen as a means of enhancing efficiency in energy production and use and as a means of directly contributing to producing net energy savings. The statement of David Bardin, Deputy Administrator of the FEA, in the Senate hearings on public utility rate proposals of the Carter energy program reflected the new thrust of the debate:

The proposals before you today will bring about savings of about 450,000 barrels of oil and gas per day by 1985. Two hundred and fifty thousand barrels of this savings comes mainly through a shift of electric utility load to more efficient generating plants that are fueled primarily by coal or nuclear [power]. The remaining 200,000 barrels of oil per day savings comes by stimulating the cogeneration of electricity and useful thermal energy. Moreover, the rate design proposals are conservatively estimated to lead to net savings in capital resources of almost $13 billion by 1985. These capital savings represent some 49,000 megawatts of new generating capacity that would otherwise be needed in 1985. That's about 9 percent of today's total installed capacity.[2]

Whether claims such as those of David Bardin were actually valid, within the context of the new debate they provided a compelling, "scientifically based" rationale for utility regulatory reform. They provided as well a critical political validation for the broader policy initiatives of the Carter administration. Moreover, the emphasis on net energy savings provided the basis for expanding the scope of utility regulatory reform beyond its initial formulation. The Carter administration expanded the scope of utility regulatory reform to include a major emphasis on encouraging and facilitating cogeneration and to include as well some initial steps in reforming the regulation of natural gas utilities.

Cogeneration was defined (in a statement prepared by a staff analyst for the Congressional Research Service) as the deliberate coupling of the production of electricity with the production of low-grade steam (or vice versa) and the recovery and use of the by-product energy. In the normal course of the production of electricity, low-termperature steam (400 to 500° F) is also generated as a byproduct, classified as waste heat when the low-grade steam is not used. On the other hand, low-grade steam is produced as a major energy source to support industrial processes and manufacturing. Analysts held that these two situations amounted to deliberately producing steam in one place and throwing it away in another. Within the context of a major concern for maximizing net energy savings, the challenge was to capture the waste energy for productive use. For the future, policies could encourage the proximate siting of central power plants and major industrial users of low-grade steam because the transmission of such steam over long distances was expensive and inefficient, and low-grade steam (like electricity) is not easily stored.

The claim made by some analysts was that the energy efficiencies of cogenerating process steam and electricity could double the efficiency of separate generation. The thrust of the Carter initiative was to eliminate the legal and regulatory barriers to cogeneration. Thus under the Carter proposal, ownership of cogeneration facilities would not be restricted to electric utilities but could include industrial consumers of electricity and independent investors. Cogeneration facilities would be exempt from certain provisions of the Federal Power Act, the Public Utility Holding Company Act, and certain restrictions imposed by state electric utility regulators. Cogeneration would not be limited in terms of the types of fuel but could consider all fuel types, including oil and natural gas. Tax credits were to be given to owners of cogeneration facilities, and utilities would be required to offer transmission, interconnection, and wheeling to cogeneration facilities as well as providing back-up electricity supply as required.[3]

There was some opposition from electric utilites to the manner in which cogeneration was to be imposed by federal fiat, as well as some concern about the prospect of utilities losing customers to cogenerators. However, the industry offered no counterclaims to some of the impressive energy savings claims made in support of cogeneration. Senator Gary Hart had introduced a dedicated cogeneration bill, S. 1363, as an alternative to the administration's proposal for cogeneration. In testimony before the Senate Committee, he made the following energy savings claim about his bill: "The Library of Congress states that within 10 years, the bill that I have introduced will stimulate enough cogeneration to: first, substitute for the capacity of 10 to 14 large nuclear powerplants, cutting projected plants by 13 to 20 percent; second, reduce the country's total fuel consumption by 5 to 10 percent; third, cut oil imports by 18 to 37 percent; and, fourth, reduce electric utility bills by about 10 percent."[4] As stated earlier, the effect of making such impressive claims of net energy savings made an issue such as cogeneration a compelling one in the ongoing discourse on energy policy. Moreover, cogeneration was a popular issue with environmentalists, who were prominent participants in the energy debate. The availability of a legislative proposal on electric utility reform which had been debated and made ready for enactment into law provided an ideal vehicle for advancing a policy plank on cogeneration.

The President's proposal for public utility regulatory reform was brought full circle by including provisions for reforming the regulation of natural gas utilities in addition to electric utilities. Although there were significant differences between cost incurrences and distribution among electricity and natural gas utilities, the administration proposal extended the central rationale for reforming electricity pricing to gas utilities: that rate designs should, to the maximum extent possible, reflect the costs of providing service to different classes of customers. Because natural gas can be stored (unlike electiricity), gas utilities are not affected by greater costs for peak demand in the same way as electric utilities. Therefore, there were no requirements for time-of-day rates or major concerns about load management. However, in keeping with the emphasis on energy conservation, declining block rates were prohibited in gas rate structures, and gas utilities were required to collect cost of service data. The FEA was authorized to study alternative gas utility rate designs for possible further changes in the future. The stage was set for enacting a new public policy.

PURPA: THE MAJOR LEGISLATIVE POLICY RESPONSE

Electric utility reform had grown out of concerns about the impact of rising energy costs on the elderly poor. The idea of reform had not emerged so much as the solution to the energy affordability problems of the elderly poor and others similarly affected but as a way of fixing electric utility regulation. The momentum provided by the national energy crisis provided an opportunity for federal policymakers to propose reform of an area of regulatory policy which was conventionally the domain of state regulators. The idea of reform also became an ideal mechanism for advancing President Carter's goals of institutionalizing a national energy policy based on maximizing efficiency in the use of energy resources. Electric utility reform was greatly propelled by a policy debate on national energy policy which was structured around quantifiable measures, or claims, of energy savings. The result was a policy response, the Public Utility Regulatory Policy Act of 1978 (PURPA, P. L. 95-617), which embraced the main issues of a transformed debate, but which gave only a polite nod in the direction of lifeline policy.

PURPA covered some ancillary issues which went beyond the reform of electric utilities, such as retail policies for natural gas utilities, financial incentives for establishing small hydroelectric power projects on dams not being used to generate electricity, and provisions for pipeline systems for transporting crude oil. The major thrust of the Act was Title I, which addressed "retail regulatory policies for electric utilities." The objectives of Title I were (1) conservation of energy supplied by electric utilities; (2) optimization of the efficiency of use of facilities and resources by electric utilities; and (3) equitable rates to electric consumers. Title I was cleverly crafted in a way which encompassed the original intent and thrust and many of the specifics of regulatory reform as set forth in the earlier legislative proposals, but in a manner which lessened the coercive force of the federal role. As opposed to dictating the adoption of federally mandated standards, PURPA instead required the formal consideration of eleven specific federal standards within the context of furthering the objectives of Title I.

After engaging in a formal consideration of each of the eleven standards, states were required to make a determination concerning whether it was appropriate to implement such standards to carry out the purposes of the title. The issues raised in the policy debate were covered in the eleven standards and/or the procedural requirements set forth in the Act. The standards included six ratemaking standards and five regulatory standards set forth as follows:

Ratemaking Standards

1. *Cost of Service Standard:* Rates to each class of consumer shall be designed to the maximum extent practicable to reflect the costs of providing service to that class, including the cost consequences of both additional kilowatt-hour usage and peak kilowatt demand;
2. *Declining Block Rates Standard:* Declining block energy charges that are not cost-based shall be eliminated;
3. *Time-of-Day Rates Standard:* Declining block energy charges that are not cost-based shall be established, if cost-effective, where costs vary by time of day;
4. *Seasonal Rates Standard:* Seasonal rates shall be established where costs vary by season;
5. *Interruptible Rates Standard:* Interruptible rates based on the costs of providing interruptible service shall be offered to commercial and industrial customers;
6. *Load Management Techniques Standard:* Load management techniques shall be

offered to consumers where practicable, cost-effective, reliable, and useful to the utility for energy or capacity management.

Regulatory Standards

1. *Master Metering Standard:* Master metering shall be prohibited or restricted for new buildings to the extent necessary to carry out the purposes of Title I of PURPA;
2. *Automatic Adjustment Clauses Standard:* Automatic adjustment clauses shall not be allowed unless they provide efficiency incentive and are reviewed in a timely manner;
3. *Information to Consumers Standard:* All consumers shall receive a clear and concise explanation of applicable and proposed rate schedules and annual consumption, upon request;
4. *Procedures for Termination of Service Standard:* Service shall not be terminated except pursuant to certain enumerated procedures; and
5. *Advertising Standard:* Political or promotional advertising shall not be charged to ratepayers. [5]

The standards were set forth in varying detail to structure what was to be considered formally in regulatory proceedings. For example, states were to formally consider a cost-of-service standard in which "rates charged by an electric utility for providing electric service to each class of electric consumer shall be designed, to the maximum extent practicable, to reflect the cost of providing electric service to such class." Title I further specified that state PUCs could prescribe the methods for determining cost of service. However, special rules for standards were set forth which required that the methods used by state PUCs permit identification of specific variables, cost factors, and cost relationships. Similar special rules were specified for each of the remaining ten standards. Title I set forth certain procedural requirements to undergird the consideration and determination processes.

The consideration process was to take place after prior public notification and in a public hearing. The determination was (1) to be presented in writing; (2) to be based on findings included in the determination and on evidence presented at the hearing, and (3) to be made available to the public. States were given the option of implementing any standard determined to be appropriate to carry out the purposes of Title I, or of declining to implement any such standard pursuant to its authority under otherwise applicable state law. If a state PUC found that implementation of a standard would further the objectives of Title I but yet chose not to implement the standard, the PUC was required to state its reasons in writing and to make such statement of reasons available to the public.

The procedural requirements were integral to defining the nature of reforms the Act sought to induce. The procedural requirements were collectively designed to open up the PUC ratemaking process to lay, residential consumers by increasing public awareness of PUC activities and procedures; to enhance consumer participation by providing for paid consumer intervenors; and to rationalize the PUC decisionmaking process by requiring the presentation of specific and pertinent data and evidence in ratemaking cases. Thus the analytical requirements in the consideration and determination processes and the requirements for a broadly participatory process became the main points of leverage in ensuring compliance with the Act.

Lifeline was not established as a standard under PURPA. However, an exclusion was made to the cost-of-service standard to permit state adoption of a rate for essential needs of residential electric consumers which was lower than rates otherwise established under the standard. If states had not adopted lifeline policies by November 1980, PURPA required state regulators to determine, after an evidentiary hearing, whether such a lifeline rate should be implemented. An evidentiary hearing required the presentation of pertinent data and analysis and, coupled with other procedural requirements of the Act, strengthened the possibility of adoption of lifeline policies.

Did PURPA make a difference in changing the way in which PUCs set electric rates and the kind of rates set? PURPA required that consideration of regulatory standards be carried out within two years of the date of enactment of the law and that consideration of the ratemaking standards be started by the end of the second year and completed by the end of the third year. Tracking of compliance with the Act was facilitated by a review of the second annual report to Congress of the Economic Regulatory Administration of the Department of Energy (DOE). The DOE was the successor agency to the FEA as a result of the reorganization of federal energy functions included in the Carter national energy plan.

At the time of preparation of the second annual report (covering the period from November 9, 1978 to June 30, 1980), consideration of standards had begun in three quarters of the minimum number of required situations (state regulators could choose to consider some standards as a group, thereby reducing the required consideration). Final decisions had been made in one third of the required cases. The DOE reported "significantly greater" progress in considering the five regulatory policy standards than for the six ratemaking standards. However, greater progress had been made in considering the other ratemaking standards, with consideration begun in 73 percent of the required cases. Significant compliance with the procedural requirements of PURPA were found. State and local regulatory authorities were found to have (1) provided public notice of hearings prior to conducting them, (2) held hearings open to the public, (3) provided opportunity for public intervenor participation and compensation, and (4) made available to the public relevant data about decisions made and the underlying written determinations. Finally, the standards adopted at the state level were found in most cases to be consistent with congressional intent in regard to prescriptions for identifying demand-related costs and energy-related costs, prior notice before termination of service, and consideration of possible dangers to health of consumers in termination.

In sum, significant progress was being made by the states in complying with the requirements of PURPA. During FY 1980, the DOE had distributed $15.9

million to state regulatory authorities and nonregulated utilities to support technical assistance in a range of areas, including basic PURPA grants, consumer office grants, innovative rates grants, and support of analytical techniques and approaches through the national Regulatory Research Institute established by PURPA.[6] The requirements of the PURPA standards were being met. Significantly less progress was being made in regard to consideration of lifeline rates which were not part of a standard under PURPA. The second annual DOE report revealed that only 18 of the 328 electric utilities and 200 gas utilities covered by Title I of PURPA had adopted some type of lifeline policy. These 18 utilities served a total of 7.6 million residential customers, or about 11 percent of this class of customers nationwide. However, only a small percentage of these customers would have been eligible for lifeline rates based on need. In a telling gesture, the DOE report did not provide any substantive discussion about the nature of lifeline rate programs or their adoption. However, the Senate Special Committee on Aging commissioned a fifty-state study, which showed that many states had implemented lifeline rates on a restricted, demonstration basis, and a few had adopted lifeline rates as a permanent part of the rate structures for some utilities.[7]

No one claimed that the PURPA-mandated changes in electric price structures would result in significant cost reductions for electricity consumers. Indeed, it was expected that energy prices would continue to rise due to increasing costs of constructing generating and transmission facilities and the increasing costs of energy fuels. However, there was an expectation that long-term price increases would be lessened by the reforms. The mechanism chosen for providing relief for low-income energy consumers—special lifeline rates—had been vigorously opposed by various parties at various points in the policy formulation process. In the final policy decision to emanate from the original policy debate, lifeline had been effectively vitiated. The initial policymaking effort had run its course and there had been no federal initiative which guaranteed relief for low-income residential energy users.

FROM ENERGY LIFELINE TO ENERGY SECURITY: A SECOND WINDOW OF OPPORTUNITY

The problem of providing relief to low-income consumers from rising energy prices was not solved by enactment of the PURPA. After a hiatus during 1977, in 1978 both House and Senate Select Committees on Aging resumed hearings on the impact of rising energy costs on the low-income elderly. During the period of 1978–1980, hearings were held in a dozen cities nationwide. These hearings ensured that the issue remained on the policy agenda. A window of opportunity was opened for enacting legislation to provide for the low income and for funding such a relief effort by the continuing push by President Carter to institutionalize a comprehensive national energy policy. In an April 5, 1979 address to the nation, President Carter further outlined the contours of his comprehensive energy policy. His latest proposal was to decontrol domestic crude oil prices as a means of spurring the production of oil, boost energy conservation through the pricing mechanism, and reduce U.S. reliance on foreign oil. The new policy idea was that of energy security for the nation.[8]

The immediate impact of price decontrol on domestic crude oil would be additional price increases for all crude oil derivatives. Residential energy prices would particularly be affected by increases in electric rates and prices for home heating oil. All talk about energy conservation and energy independence aside, price decontrols would result in massive income transfers—billion of dollars—from energy producers to energy consumers. Energy consumers could already see that they could not control their energy costs by sharply reducing their energy consumption. This was the kind of straightforward, direct impact which consumers could see and feel, and the simplicity of its poignancy made the issue of relief for the low income more compelling. Thus, at the same time that President Carter announced price decontrols, he announced a proposal to place a tax on the windfall profits which would accrue to oil companies as a result of domestic price decontrols. President Carter further proposed that revenues from the windfall profits tax be used to establish an energy security fund to support a broad range of energy research and development activities, as well as to fund an assistance program to provide economic relief to low-income consumers.

THE RATIONALE FOR PRICE DECONTROL AND A WINDFALL PROFITS TAX

In hearings before the House Ways and Means Committee, Michael Blumenthal, Secretary of the Treasury under President Carter, explained the origins of domestic crude oil price controls and tried to set the tone for congressional action on the windfall profits tax:

The system originated with the comprehensive wage and price controls instituted by the Nixon administration in 1971 and has operated in its present form since 1973. The system has grown steadily more complicated. At present, no single expert can pretend to understand how all the regulations work or whom they benefit...What is clear about the system is that it intensifies our energy problems. It does so by disguising from the American people—consumers, investors, and industry alike—what we are really paying for oil. The system is, quite literally, an exercise in economic self-deception. Because of it, we use and import more oil than we should; we produce less domestic oil than we should; and we neglect to make economically sensible and necessary investments in alternative energy sources and technologies. Could there be any greater condemnation than this?[9]

The President was committed to decontrol of domestic crude oil prices, especially as a means of reducing reliance on foreign oil and as a means of inducing a greater measure of energy conservation. Partially in response to political instability in Iran and reduced exports, the President had agreed with U.S. allies and the International Energy Agency to reduce U.S. imports by up to

1 million barrels a day below the level prior to the 1979 OPEC price increases.[10] Increases in domestic production were necessary to partially offset this reduction although the President was pushing a range of energy conservation measures, including adjusting thermostats in public facilities and private homes. The President could on his own authority decontrol domestic oil prices and had indicated his intention to initiate phased decontrols starting on June 1, 1979. The President's objective was to bring domestic crude oil prices up to world oil prices by October 1, 1981.

However, congressional action was essential for facilitating the remainder of the President's program. In addition to providing assistance to low-income households, the Carter administration outlined a range of uses for monies from the energy security fund which fell within the objectives of energy conservation and the development of alternative energy sources. These included added support of mass transit (including increased grants for bus purchases and rail rehabilitation for cities with existing rail transit services) and increased support for energy investments (including loan guarantees for construction of nonnuclear demonstration projects, development of a synthetic liquid fuels program, coal research and development, tax credits for shale oil production, development of renewable energy resources such as solar energy and solar industrial process heat).[11] The specific uses of the Energy Trust Fund reflected the continuing emphasis on energy savings and a determination to pursue exploitation of the full range of domestic sources of energy.

The Windfall Profits Tax would be a complex one, differentially applied to old oil and new oil, a distinction based on the date of extraction, with as well a different tax applied to oil extracted by tertiary recovery programs.[12] The President sought a middle ground of giving oil companies some of the windfall profits to encourage them to increase production while using part of the windfall profits to develop alternative sources of energy and to support low-income assistance programs. The White House projected revenues from the new tax to total between $1.8 and $2.5 billion for FY 1981 and $3 and $4.7 billion for FY 1982 depending on OPEC prices.[13]

Under the President's larger proposal, the President's objective of alleviating the energy-related burdens of the low income was contingent on the outcome of three distinct policymaking decisions: (1) passage of the windfall profits tax as a prerequisite for generating the necessary revenue base; (2) the establishment of an energy security fund with a specific authorization for low-income assistance; and (3) decisions about how to structure the specifics of the assistance program. Although passage of a windfall profits tax was by no means a forgone conclusion, the idea of taxing the perceived bloated profits of big oil companies that never paid their fair share of taxes was one which garnered considerable public support. As might be expected, the oil companies supported decontrol but opposed any new taxes. However, no doubt recognizing the inevitability of a new tax, they directed their greater energy to structuring the tax, and the plans to enact a windfall profits tax moved forward. However, the plans for low-income assistance were vulnerable on the question of the means used to provide the assistance.

THE DEBATE ON LOW-INCOME ENERGY ASSISTANCE

Given the overall sense of urgency which accompanied all of the Carter energy initiatives, consideration of Phase III, the Windfall Profits Tax and related items, was being pushed on several tracks simultaneously. Thus part of the debate on low-income energy assistance—issues relating to the more general questions of establishing the Energy Trust Fund—took place within the context of hearings on the Windfall Profits Tax. This was a critical phase of the debate because assistance to the low-income was largely contingent on establishing the Energy Trust Fund and authoring its specific use for low-income energy assistance.

The set of groups which participated in this phase of the debate on assistance for the low income was an eclectic one, dominated by environmental groups. The low income were not represented as a distinct constituency by any of the groups which could be defined loosely as consumer groups, and few of the consumer groups provided what could be characterized as solid, committed support for low-income energy assistance. The strongest support was given by the League of Women Voters, which held that the only use of the proceeds from the windfall tax should be to reduce the burden on the poor. However, the League objected to the establishment of a special trust fund deeming it unnecessary, favoring instead a progressive system of rebates based on economic need.[14]

Environmental groups—including the Natural Resources Defense Council, Environmental Policy Center, the Sierra Club, and Friends of the Earth—differed strongly with the administration on the size of the tax. They supported a tax of 85 to 90 percent compared to what they argued was the effective 20 percent level of the administration's proposal. They also opposed the establishment of a trust fund, favoring instead a general system of rebates. The Sierra Club and Friends of the Earth held that decontrol would lead to environmental degradation and support of inefficient energy technologies with undetermined environmental impacts.[15] The Consumer Federation of America took the opportunity provided by the hearings to direct a harsh attack against the President and his energy policies:

It is little wonder that in the eyes of consumers the credibility of the government is shrinking. Decontrol is a regressive and economically unsound policy that will not work, and the windfall profits tax is nothing more than an attempt to distract the public from the basic bankruptcy of a policy based on senselessly high energy prices. . . . It is no consolation at all to consumers facing skyrocketing energy prices if a windfall profits tax is passed since such a tax will not reduce energy prices by 1 cent and the hypothetical uses of the energy trust fund for low-income consumer protection, mass transit, and solar [energy] should be funded regardless of whether a tax is passed.[16]

The House passed a version of the Windfall Profits Tax on June 28, 1979, including a provision for the establishment of an Energy Security Trust Fund, and sent it to the Senate for consideration. Before the issue of the windfall tax was settled, attention shifted to the second phase of the debate and questions of how to structure the assistance program for low-income energy consumers. Hearings on legislative proposals for low-income home energy assistance opened before the Senate Labor and Human Resources Committee in late September 1979 at the full committee level. These hearings overlapped with similar hearings before the Subcommittee on Public Assistance and Unemployment Compensation of the House Ways and Means Committee. A host of bills were considered, with the majority initially being taken by the Senate. There was a great deal of disagreement on issues such as whether assistance should be provided directly to eligible participants or whether payments should be made to energy suppliers on behalf of eligible recipients; whether energy stamps should be provided instead of cash payments (an idea denounced years earlier as unacceptable to elderly consumers); and whether to restrict eligibility to elderly consumers or to include the total low-income population. There were also questions of how to define the low-income population: as those eligible for food stamps only; those eligible for benefits under Titles XVI (SSI) and IV (Aid to Families with Dependent Children or AFDC); or those with incomes up to 125 percent of the Bureau of Labor Statistics (BLS) lower living standard. Each criterion defined a different population. The latter criterion would define a larger population of eligible beneficiaries and would cost more money.

As usual, most of the discussion about how to structure the program for low-income energy assistance was not anchored in any data, definitive or otherwise, which defined the scope and dimensions of the problem or the population to be served. However, a report submitted to the Department of Energy by its Fuel Oil Marketing Advisory Committee (FOMAC) offered a reasonable database. The FOMAC was composed of consumers, refiners, wholesalers, retailers, and representatives of state government. The committee advised the DOE on a range of consumer issues emanating from the effects of the national energy crisis and provided an updated assessment of the dimensions of the problem and the size of the needy population to be served by an energy assistance program. The FOMAC report was introduced into the record of hearings held by the House Ways and Means Committee. The point of this presentation by FOMAC was to show that (1) low-income households spent a disproportionately higher percentage of income on household energy costs, and (2) cost-of-living adjustments in income maintenance programs (such as social security, SSI, AFDC, etc.) based on the CPI significantly understated the impact of rising energy costs.

FOMAC recommended that the population for a low-income energy assistance program be defined as follows:

The Committee determined that households at or below 125 percent of poverty should be eligible for energy assistance. At 1978 levels, the income of a family of four (4) at 125 percent of poverty was $7,750 per year. . . .

The only exception to the 125 percent eligibility criterion recommended by the

Committee was the inclusion of elderly households with incomes up to 150 percent of poverty. Given the special needs of the elderly poor, the fixed nature of their income and their usually small household size, the Committee recommended that income eligibility levels be set at 150 percent of poverty.

Using the above income eligibility criteria, there would be approximately 16.2 million households initially eligible for assistance. Of these 16.2 million, almost 7.2 million households (44 percent) are headed by persons 60 or older.[17]

Actual assistance to income-eligible beneficiaries would be based on a formula which factored in the percentage of income spent on household energy, the number of degree days for heating or cooling, and regional variations in energy costs. Unlike the case of lifeline rates, the proposal for providing direct assistance to low-income energy users (from what would actually be general revenue funds) garnered the strong support of the end-use household energy supply industry. Although the various components of this industry would clearly benefit from a larger population of consumers who were able to afford the costs of energy, there were useful insights to be gained from viewing the problems of low-income energy consumers from the perspective of energy suppliers. Moreover, in a deliberative process which did not benefit from strong advocacy groups representing the poor, in an interesting way energy suppliers gave some voice to the plight of the poor.

The American Gas Association (AGA) expressed strong support for a permanent program of assistance for low-income energy users. The AGA was identified as comprised of 300 natural gas transmission, distribution, and integrated companies serving 150 million customers or 85 percent of utility sales. The AGA saw benefits of an assistance program deriving from an improvement in timely payments to utilities, reduction in billing disruptions and administrative costs, and a reduction in uncollectible accounts. The AGA reported that gas utilities had experienced a rise in uncollectibles from $109 million in 1976 to $163 million in 1978. The AGA urged dropping the requirement used in emergency assistance programs that beneficiaries have a termination notice in hand before they are granted assistance. This requirement was seen as encouraging nonpayment by some consumers and as effectively penalizing those individuals who made the difficult choice to pay utility bills over other pressing needs. The AGA also supported provisions that beneficiaries pay a portion of their utility bills as an incentive for energy conservation; that states with a moratorium on service cutoffs be ineligible for grants under the program; that payments be made directly to utilities; and that states, not utilities, certify eligible participants.[18]

The Edison Electric Institute voiced "four square" support for a low-income energy assistance program including the setting aside of an emergency assistance fund. However, the representative for EEI made a point of disagreeing with any underlying assumption that the energy crisis was a long-term one and expressed the opinion that a home energy assistance program was only a temporary necessity.[19] Perhaps the most poignant insights about problems of affordability at the residential end-use level were offered by the representative of the National Oil Jobbers Council. The Oil Jobbers were described as a federation of forty-four state and regional groups representing small, independent petroleum product marketers (including 8000 heating oil dealers distributing 80 percent of residential heating oil). The Oil Jobbers were very supportive of a solution to the affordability problem which went beyond crisis intervention, because they asserted that even in a mild winter, many low-income consumers could not pay heating costs. Home heating oil companies were described as more directly and adversely affected by the inability of consumers to pay heating costs. They are small companies, operate on a limited cash flow, cannot provide credit as needed, cannot afford to have uncollectible accounts, and know their customers well—frequently on an individual basis—so that ceasing delivery for nonpayment is painful to the supplier.[20]

A host of congressmen and governors testified in the hearings before the House Ways and Means Committee in support of various relief measures, with all expressing the need for immediate action. Governor Julian Carroll of Kentucky represented the National Governors Association (NGA). He expressed the NGA's support for a windfall profits tax but urged that low-income energy assistance not be tied to such a tax. The NGA argued for a permanent, comprehensive program which included a crisis assistance component to aid families with emergencies who would otherwise not need assistance. The NGA further held that although income criteria should be set, preferably above 100 percent of the BLS lower living standard, an assets test should not be used, particularly for the elderly. A major NGA position was that the states should be given flexibility to choose between providing assistance via an energy stamp program or a direct cash assistance program.[21] Although conspicuously absent from the debate on PURPA, the National Retired Teachers Association and the American Association of Retired Persons (NRTA and AARP) reemerged to participate in the debate on low-income energy assistance. NRTA and AARP urged that more aid be given to single-person households and to households headed by elderly persons. They were consistent in their sentiment expressed in the early days of Special Committee hearings on energy prices and the elderly—that a fuel stamp program was not acceptable (largely due to the welfare stigma associated with such a program). NRTA and AARP favored a program of direct cash assistance using existing income maintenance programs.[22]

Part of the difficulty in defining the population of low-income lay in the fact that they had never been defined definitively. There existed no single program which identified and served the poor as a discrete or comprehensive population. Rather federal and state assistance programs were a hodge-podge of programs which each defined and served a specific segment of the poor. Both AFDC and SSI were means-tested, income maintenance programs directed toward special and different segments of the poor. AFDC was part of the original Social Security Act. It pays a monthly benefit to dependent children and their caretaker, usually their mother. The program is jointly funded by the national and state governments and is administered at the state level, and benefit levels are based on a standard of need established by each state. State need standards are not based on the federal poverty index, and less than one half of the states pay 100 percent of the standard of need set for their AFDC program.

The SSI program was created in 1972 under Title XVI of the Social Security Act by consolidating the original programs of aid for the indigent aged (the old Title I), and for the blind (old Title X), and aid to the disabled (created in 1950 as Title XIV). With the establishment of SSI, the federal government assumed responsibility for administration and set national eligibility criteria to guarantee a minimum amount of support. About one third of the states supplement the federal SSI payment. Because SSI is a designedly income support program rather than a retirement insurance program, some social security recipients who receive benefits at the lowest levels are eligible for SSI benefits. The food stamp program is the most cross-cutting of the income support programs. It is an in-kind program, wholly federally funded, with eligibility criteria set in relationship to the federal poverty level. The food stamp program served the young, old, unemployed, and so on, depending on need as established by eligibility criteria for a range of individual or family circumstances. In the end, the eligibility criteria for all of the income support programs were largely arbitrarily set. The size of the population served by each of these programs could be altered by simply changing the eligibility criteria, making them more generous or more restrictive.[23] By adopting an eligibility criterion which used the federal poverty index or the BLS lower living standard as a ceiling, the energy assistance program would be directed toward a more inclusive population of the poor.

POLITICAL URGENCY AND AN INTERIM BUREAUCRATIC RESPONSE

The already urgent legislative process for consideration of a windfall profits tax and a low-income energy assistance program was upstaged by an even more urgent desire of the Carter administration to get assistance in the hands of low-income citizens for the winter of 1979–1980. Deliberations on new legislation in late September would not permit that. The administration estimated that under the most hurried preparations, getting the administrative apparatus in place to disburse funds to eligible beneficiaries and the actual disbursement of funds would take sixty to eighty days after enactment of all formal legislation. Any legislation requiring certification of vendors would require even more time. Although these assertions showed the cumbersome nature of governmental processes and the inability of government to respond effectively to crises, the administration's alternative plan demonstrated just the opposite. The administration's plan also embodied the essence of take-charge politics; a determination to use the power and resources of the executive branch to initiate immediate and direct action to address a problem in a manner which co-opted Congress and limited the range of congressional actions.

The essence of the administration's plan was presented by the Honorable Patricia Roberts Harris, Secretary of HEW, to the Senate Labor and Human

Resources Committee as follows:

One, we will transmit to the Congress a supplemental request for $1.2 billion, under the Community Services Administration Authority, and contingent upon passage of a windfall profits tax.

Two, we propose to use the existing Community Services Administration energy crisis assistance program to make block grants available to states this winter. All low-income people with incomes below 125 percent of the CSA poverty line and assets no higher than those permitted for food stamps would be eligible.

Three, energy assistance payments will be made early in January to those elderly and disabled poor people who participate in the supplemental security income program. Specifications for those payments must be determined by early October in order to make an early January payment.

Four, energy assistance payments will also be made in early February to those poor families participating in the aid to families with dependent children program. Specifications for those payments will also be needed no later than early October.[24]

And so it was. Many congressional members in both houses argued for inclusion of assistance for needy lower-middle-class citizens, but the administration was unwilling to accept such an expansion of its aid package. The administration's proposal anticipated making cash payments averaging $200 annually for multiperson households with a high of $300, and about $100 for low-income elderly and other individuals. The size of payments to individuals would vary from state to state, with half of the payment based on a uniform amount and the other half varying due to climatic variations.[25] The proposed $1.4 billion in aid was the amount of money to be used from the first year's proceeds from the windfall profits tax, not the total expected revenue. The idea was that the administration would be reimbursed for its supplemental appropriation from the new tax revenues.

The administration made it clear that its plan for a relief package for the oncoming winter required that the windfall profits tax be passed. Although there was some indication that a windfall profits tax would eventually pass the Senate, there was concern expressed by some senators that the debate on the tax would be prolonged given the intense lobbying against the measure by the oil companies. The administration proposal was characterized by some members of congress as "using the distress of the poor as a club over the Congress." Not to be denied the opportunity to debate the Windfall Profits Tax and not wanting to be blamed for blocking emergency energy assistance to the poor, Congress adopted an Interior Department appropriations bill amendment to make appropriations for the administration proposal. On November 27, 1979, President Carter signed into law a supplemental appropriations bill allocating an additional $1,350,000,000 to the existing CSA energy assistance, for a total of $1.6 billion for the winter of 1979–1980. The money was to be transferred to HEW for distribution to the poor.[26]

A POLICY FOR LOW-INCOME ENERGY ASSISTANCE

In April of 1980, Congress passed the Crude Oil Windfall Profit Tax Act of 1980, Public Law 96-223, exactly three years after President Carter had initially submitted the tax proposal to Congress. Although an Energy Security Trust Fund was not specifically established, the Act did specify the uses of the tax revenues which the President had sought. Basic net revenues from the tax were to be divided as follows: income tax reductions for individuals and businesses, 60 percent; low-income energy assistance, 25 percent; and energy and transportation programs, 15 percent. Title III of the Act provided for low-income energy assistance and was titled the Home Energy Assistance Act of 1980. The Home Energy Assistance Act provided that the Social Security Administration of HEW award grants to states that would provide eligible low-income households assistance to offset the rising costs of home energy. Eligible households were those with incomes at or below the BLS lower living standard, and households with members eligible for AFDC, SSI, food stamps, and certain income tested Veterans Administration benefits. Assistance was to be in the form of direct payments or vouchers to eligible beneficiaries, or on behalf of such beneficiaries to an energy supplier or an operator of certain publicly subsidized buildings for energy costs.

The Act provided for an outreach program for elderly beneficiaries to inform them of the program and included a crisis intervention component to provide emergency assistance to households otherwise not eligible for assistance. State plans detailing guidelines for implementation of and compliance with program provisions were required for the receipt of grants under the Act In 1982 the Home Energy Assistance Act was repealed and replaced by the Low-Income Home Energy Assistance Act of 1981, as Title XXVI of the Omnibus Budget Reconciliation Act of 1981 (P.L. 97-35). The provisions of the original program were substantially retained in the new legislation and remained in effect in late 1992.

SUMMARY

The larger issue which originally framed the debate on low-income energy assistance was transformed as the issue of electric utility reform was incorporated into President Carter's national energy plan. The currency of the debate changed to that of energy savings, making the idea of lifeline rates a policy misfit.

Congress responded to the problem of adverse effects of rising energy costs on the poor and elderly, albeit by no means in a timely fashion. The issue of severe impacts on the low-income elderly due to rising energy costs was initially raised in 1973. A series of interim assistance programs via existing bureaucratic apparatus were implemented. Congress facilitated these bureaucratic responses by appropriating necessary funding, but it did not enact a definitive assistance measure until 1981. Congress did not provide assistance in a manner consistent with the problem solution embodied in the concept of lifeline rates. The concept of lifeline rates was an intriguing policy idea, but it offered a rather narrow definition of and solution to the problem: that the problem was the structure of electric rates and that the solution lay in changing electric rate structures and providing a subsistence amount of electricity to the poor and/or all residential consumers at a discounted rate. Within this context, the major failing of the concept of lifeline rates was that it conflicted with the fundamental premise of electric rate reform. In making the case for electric rate reform (i.e., in arguing that electric rates should be based on actual costs of generation and service) the argument for a special subsidized rate was undermined.

Although lifeline rates as a policy idea failed, they did advance a line of argument or reasoning—that of tying assistance to the poor to the immediate stimulus of increased costs. In this sense, the spirit of lifeline was retained and an important divide was crossed in regard to social welfare policy formulation and legitimation. There was the implicit recognition of the social costs of major societal developments or the adoption of specific public policies, such as energy conservation or energy independence, although there had been no explicit argument made for addressing social costs. During the hearings, there had been the routine assertions of the need to provide relief to the poor from rising energy costs, but that assertion or plea had not been set within any broader philosophical context.

The linking of the problem solution to its immediate origins in terms of assignment of increased energy costs was, in effect, temporary and somewhat less than definitive. Linkage of assistance for the poor to the Windfall Profits Tax was ephemeral. Although this was a kind of earmarking of taxes—the setting aside of specific tax revenues for specific uses—because it was a temporary tax measure destined for demise when domestic oil prices reached world market levels, this earmarking of tax revenues amounted to a grander symbolic gesture than to a major substantive policy change. In the end, energy assistance to the poor became a program funded like all social welfare programs, out of general revenues. What was of lasting significance was the establishment of another dedicated assistance program. The continuation of the home energy assistance program acknowledged and addressed a special area of need by the poor, that of relief from high energy costs.

NOTES

1. U. S. Congress. Senate. Committee on Energy and Natural Resources. Subcommittee on Energy Conservation and Natural Resources. *Public Utility Rate Proposals of President Carter's Energy Program: Hearings on Part E of S.1469 and Related Bills.* 95th Cong., 1st sess., 1977, pt. 1, p. 125. Opening statement of Senator Henry M. Jackson.

2. Ibid., p. 167. Testimony of David J. Bardin, Deputy Administrator, Federal Energy Administration.

3. Senate. *Public Utility Rate Proposal,* pt. 1, pp. 195–252. Materials submitted for the record by David J. Bardin, Federal Energy Administration.

4. Ibid., pp. 125–133. Testimony of Senator Gary Hart.

5. U.S. Department of Energy. Economic Regulatory Administration. *Public Utility Regulatory Policies Act of 1978: Annual Report to Congress.* Vol. 1. Washington, D.C.: GPO, May 1981, pp. 3–4.

6. Ibid.

7. For the most comprehensive survey and discussion of state lifeline programs, see U.S. Congress. Senate. Special Committee on Aging. *Energy Assistance Programs and Pricing Policies in the 50 States to Benefit Elderly, Disabled, or Low-Income Households.* 96th Cong., 1st sess., 1979. Committee print.

8. President Jimmy Carter, Address to the Nation, April 5, 1979, *Public Papers of the President,* Office of the Federal Register, National Archives and Record Service, General Services Administration, p. 609.

9. U.S. Congress. House. Committee on Ways and Means. *Windfall Profits Tax and Energy Trust Fund:* Hearings. 96th Cong., 1st sess., 1979, p. 8. Testimony of Honorable Michael Blumenthal, Secretary, Department of Treasury

10. Ibid., p. 9.

11. House. Windfall Profits Tax and Energy Trust Fund, pp. 4-17, and 17–24. Testimonies and prepared statements of Honorable John F. O'Leary, Deputy Secretary, Department of Energy and James T. McIntyre, Jr., Director, Office of Management and Budget.

12. In addition to the hearings cited earlier, for a detailed discussion of the pros and cons of decontrol and legislation to structure the Windfall Profits Tax, see U.S. Congress. House. Committee on Interstate and Foreign Commerce. Subcommittee on Energy and Power. *Domestic Crude Oil Decontrol, 1979: Hearings.* 96th Cong., 1st sess., 1979; and U.S. Congress. Senate. Committee on Finance. *Crude Oil Tax: Hearings.* 96th Cong., 1st sess., 1979.

13. U.S. Congress. House. Committee on Interstate and Foreign Commerce. Subcommittee on Energy and Power. *The President's April 5, 1979, Energy Address: Hearings.* Materials submitted for the record by Honorable John F. O'Leary, Department of Energy, pp. 72–73.

14. House. *Windfall Profits Tax and Energy Trust Fund.* pp. 364–368. Testimony of Dorothy K. Powers, League of Women Voters.

15. Ibid., pp. 385–386, Testimony and statement of Jonathan Lash, Resources Defense Council, pp. 400–409, Testimony and prepared statement of Jonathan Gibson, the Sierra Club; pp. 391–400. Testimony and prepared statement of Gary Delors, Environmental Policy Center; pp. 409–417. Testimony and prepared statement of David C. Masselli, Friends of the Earth.

16. House. *Windfall Profits Tax and Energy Trust Fund,* pp. 369–376. Testimony of Michael Podhorzer, Consumer Federation of America.

17. U.S. Congress. House. Committee on Ways and Means. Subcommittee on Public Assistance and Unemployment Compensation. *Administration's Low-Income Energy Assistance Program: Hearing.* 96th Cong., 1st sess., 1979, p. 101. Material submitted for the record by the National Oil Jobbers Council.

18. U.S. Congress. Senate. Committee on Labor and Human Resources. *Home Energy Assistance Act: Hearings on S. 1724 and Related Bills* 96th Cong., 1st sess., pt. 2, pp. 203–218. Testimony and prepared statement of Stephen Schachmano, American Gas Association.

19. Ibid., pp. 219–226. Testimony and prepared statement of Frederick Webber, Edison Electric Institute.

20. Senate. *Home Energy Assistance Act,* pt. 2, pp. 227–228. Testimony of

Robert Sullivan, National Oil Jobbers Council.

21. House. *Administration's Low-Income Energy Assistance Program*, pp. 47–53. Testimony and prepared statement of Governor Julian Carroll of Kentucky, representing the National Governors Association.

22. Ibid., pp. 62–70. Testimony and prepared statement of James Hacking, National Retired Teachers Association and American Association of Retired Persons.

23. This discussion of income support programs draws on Andrew S. Dobelstein, *Social Welfare Policy and Analysis*. Chicago: Nelson-Hall, 1990, Chap. 6.

24. Senate. *Home Energy Assistance Act,* pt. 2, p. 349. Testimony of Honorable Patricia Roberts Harris, Secretary, Health, Education, and Welfare.

25. Ibid., p. 350.

26. *Public Papers of the Presidents of the United States: Jimmy Carter 1979,* p. 2154. Washington, D.C.: GPO.

Part III

THE POLICY DEBATE ON LIFELINE RATES AND TELECOMMUNICATIONS POLICY

Chapter 5

Defining the Public Interest in Telecommunications

THE BELL SYSTEM MONOPOLY AND THE STRUCTURE OF THE TELECOMMUNICATIONS INDUSTRY

In the mid-1970s, at the behest of AT&T, Congress began to explore the implications of a series of decisions rendered by the Federal Communications Commission (FCC) which promoted competition in an industry which had long been characterized by monopoly control and governmental regulation. Telecommunications had been regulated as a monopoly since passage of the Communication Act of 1934 in an industry overwhelmingly dominated by the Bell system. Historically the Bell system had operated with competitors upon the expiration of the original Bell system patents in 1893. Access to the Bell patents and legal prohibitions in most states against the granting of exclusive franchises enabled Bell competitors to build and operate competing telephone companies. However, Bell was successful in purchasing many of its early competitors. Otherwise, competition succumbed to the economic hazards of building duplicative facilities. In the early days, some cities were briefly served by as many as four competing telephone companies whose lines were not interconnected. This rendered the telephone service of any one company severely restricted in its benefits. This situation led to public demands for an integrated system, with a single provider if need be. The demise of Bell competitors was also hastened by state PUCs' adoption of the economic theory of the efficiency of natural monopolies based on the observed tendency of direct, duplicative competition to produce inferior results, leading to the failure of numerous businesses in a given industry. Due to economies of scale, the ability of one firm to supply the entire market at decreasing per-unit costs leads to a natural monopoly. In the case of services vital to the public wellbeing (which, due to their nature, cannot readily be obtained except from a sole provider), government intervenes with active regulation. This premise became part of the rationale or legal standard for federal regulation of telecommunications.

Telephone companies were required to assume certain responsibilities to the public and to accept certain constraints on their activities in return for what amounted to a protected monopoly status. They were made to operate as common carriers and required to render adequate service at fair rates. The rates charged for services were regulated, as was the allowable rate of return on investment. Prior to federal regulation, state laws supported PUC requirements that a telephone company extend service to an unserved locality, improve its service in a certain area, and obtain PUC approval prior to discontinuing of facilities or services in a given area. These obligations were carried over into the 1934 Act.

The enactment of the Communications Act of 1934 and the establishment of the FCC resulted in the consolidation of administrative and regulatory control, which had been dispersed among several agencies. Originally, the Interstate Commerce Commission (ICC) had jurisdiction over wire and radio common carriers, the Federal Radio Commission oversaw operations of radio companies, and the Postmaster General regulated telegraph companies and telegraph lines. The 1934 Act set a public interest standard for the regulation of telecommunications and other industries under its statutory authority. The public interest standard was embodied in the requirement that the FCC evaluate and establish "the public interest, convenience, and necessity" in approving or disapproving the entry of new firms into the telecommunications industry and in approving or disapproving all of the activities of existing dominant firms in the industry. That was one major premise of the public interest standard for federal regulation. The other major premise was embodied in the stated purpose of the 1934 Act "to make available, so far as possible, to all the people of the U.S. a rapid, efficient, nationwide and worldwide wire and radio communication service with adequate facilities at reasonable charges." These two regulatory standards placed the FCC in the position of being responsible for defining the public interest over time in relationship to emergent conditions and developments and made it responsible for realizing and preserving the goal of "universal service." Universal service thus became institutionalized as a pivotal public policy and regulatory standard in telecommunications.[1]

Since passage of the 1934 Act, regulation of the telecommunications industry has traditionally been divided between the FCC and state public utility commissions. The FCC regulated the interstate market through regulation of entry and rates for long-distance telephone service, and state PUCs regulated rates of companies providing local exchange service. From the early 1900s up to the mid-1960s, the domestic telecommunications industry had been dominated by the Bell system with some sharing of territory with a host of small, independent (non-Bell) companies. The Bell system was extensive. Prior to divestiture, AT&T was the largest company in the world with one million employees and assets of $155 billion. AT&T Long Lines, which was the giant of long-distance telecommunications service, handled all Bell System calls made between states and the twenty-two Bell operating companies (BOCs). The BOC's provided local and regional telephone service and frequently carried the Bell ownership in their names (Southern Bell, Southwestern Bell, etc.). The BOCs were the local telephone companies with the most direct dealings with local consumers. In addition to providing local telephone service, they operated regional, intrastate long-distance networks; handled telephone installation and repair; and published the local directories and yellow pages. AT&T Long Lines and the BOCs were the major purveyors of voice communications.

These core components of the Bell operations were supported by Bell Laboratories, a world-class scientific and engineering, research and development operation. Bell labs enjoyed the fame of having developed the transistor and were supported by revenue contributions from the BOCs and Western Electric. Western Electric was the manufacturer of all equipment used throughout the Bell system including telephones and switching and transmission equipment.

A host of non-Bell telephone companies operated locally and regionally providing basic local exchange service. Numbering around 1450, they were collectively known as the independents. From the earliest days, Bell had taken for itself the densely populated and more lucrative urban markets, leaving unserved the rural and more sparsely populated areas of the country. Enterprising entrepreneurs had been assisted in providing telephone service to these rural areas by a generous loan program administered by the federal Rural Electrification Administration (REA). Thus, although the independents accounted for only 20 percent of local telephone service, they covered about 44 percent of the country geographically. To avoid duplication of services and facilities, the BOCs and the independents did not hold overlapping franchises for local exchange service (i.e., neither operated in an area served by the other). However, the independents' networks were interconnected with the Bell system's intrastate and interstate networks. Prior to the changes which came to maturation in the mid-1970s to early 1980's, there was little question of the dominance of AT&T. AT&T held 90 percent of the long-distance transmission market, 80 percent of the local transmission market, 100 percent of the local geographic markets it served, vertical integration into and dominance of the manufacture of communications equipment, and dominance in communications research and development.

THE EROSION OF MONOPOLY BY ADMINISTRATIVE RULINGS

As the regulator of the telecommunications industry, the FCC had rendered a number of decisions which undermined the AT&T monopoly.[2] However, the pivotal forces which threatened the Bell monopoly were new technological developments and associated competitive pressures. Advances in technology brought pressures for competition in the private line service industry (as distinct from the public switched telephone system network). Private line services were point-to-point, interstate, dedicated communication lines reserved for specific customers on a 24-hour-a-day, seven-day-a-week basis. AT&T and Western

Union initially engaged in some limited competition for hig- volume business clients who made up the bulk of the private line service market. The private line market was composed of four basic submarkets:

1. Telegraph grade private lines were principally used by the newspaper wire services.
2. Telephone grade private lines were principally used by large businesses for voice communications.
3. Audio-radio private lines were used by broadcasters.
4. Audio and video private lines were used by the television networks.

This was a rather homogeneous market, with each class of users having essentially the same communications requirements, and it was assumed that AT&T and Western Union would continue to satisfy all of the private line communications markets.

The emergence of digital computer technology greatly expanded and altered the potential usage of the telecommunications network, first by creating a demand for specialized terminal equipment and second by creating a demand for specialized private line data transmission capabilities. The demand for terminal equipment was rapidly being defined beyond the functional capabilities of the traditional black telephone "main station," PBXs (private branch extensions), or customer premises-based local switching systems which permitted routing of communications channels among a host of customer telephone stations. Terminal equipment quickly came to mean data terminals utilizing MODEMs to translate voice and electrical signals into signals compatible with digital computers, facsimile machines, and a host of other specialized terminal devices. Because the telephone network was based on analog technology refined for high-quality voice transmission, it was inherently incompatible with the on-off digital signals of computers. Although special interface devices (MODEMs) and other special conditioning of telephone private lines could be utilized to facilitate nonvoice communications, such modifications did not overcome the obstacles of high error rates and a low speed transmission rate. These limitations drove the demand for specialized networks for data transmission. Thus there were two major demand areas: for diverse, specialized terminal equipment; and for specialized data transmission services, which aroused the interest of entrepreneurs outside the monopolized telecommunications world. From a public policy perspective, the issues for federal regulators were whether it was in the public interest to rely on a single terminal equipment supplier, AT&T, and just two providers of specialized data transmission services, AT&T and Western Union.

The cumulative effect of a series of FCC decisions rendered over two decades was to support new entrants and competition in the equipment and special services components of the telecommunications industry. In the *Hush-A-Phone Case* of 1956 (*Hush-A-Phone v. U.S.*, 238 F. 2d 266), the U.S. Court of Appeals laid the groundwork for the use of non-Bell terminal equipment in ruling that the customer had a right to use the public telephone network in a manner which was privately beneficial but not publicly detrimental. The principle of the *Hush-A-Phone Case* was expanded and made a general policy in the 1968 *Carterfone Case* (Carterfone 13 FCC 2d 420, 1968) in which the FCC ruled that it was the customer's right to interconnect a device to the telephone system which improved the utility of the system for his use and did not otherwise adversely affect the telephone network operation and utility for others. AT&T had vigorously resisted the connection of non-Bell equipment to its network, arguing that such interconnections impaired the technical functioning of its network facilities. In what became an interim resolution of this conflict, the FCC adopted a set of technical standards and a registration program for the use of non-Bell terminal equipment.

With regard to competition in private line services, the initial pivotal regulatory decision was rendered in the *Above 890 Decision,* 27 FCC 359 (1959). Although the FCC had been liscensing private microwave systems to large businesses (such as pipeline companies, railroads, and mining o perations)with communications needs which could not readily be met by the established telecommunications companies, temporary frequency assignments had initially been made. In the *Above 890 Decision,* permanent frequency assignments were made upon a finding that an adequate number of frequencies in the microwave range were available to serve the foreseeable needs of the common carrier and private point-to-point microwave systems. The FCC found that despite the arguments of AT&T and Western Union, there was no evidence produced in its inquiry that the established common carriers would suffer any loss of revenues or other adverse economic effects from the liscensing of private, point-to-point communications systems. In 1969 the FCC granted a liscense to Microwave Communications, Inc. (MCI) to provide specialized common carrier services between Chicago and St. Louis via a terrestrial (land based) microwave system. In this action, the FCC issued a finding that competition in specialized private line services was reasonably feasible and beneficial to the public, although at the time the ruling was applicable to the activities of a single company on a restricted basis.

In 1971 the FCC made a broad-based, more definitive ruling in favor of new entry into the specialized private line services in the *Specialized Common Carrier Decision,* 29 FCC 2d 870 (1971). The commission found that the market for specialized data communications services was likely to expand rapidly and that new entrants would be developing and providing new services not met by the established carriers. Again, AT&T claimed that such multiple new entries would result in substantial loss of revenue, thus impairing its ability to continue to provide basic telephone services at reasonable costs. However, the Commission found that only a small percentage of AT&T's existing total market was vulnerable to the type of competition which would be provided by specialized carriers; that the growth rate of AT&T's basic services was substantial; and that AT&T would enter and obtain a substantial share of the new data transmission markets. The FCC found that these factors made it unlikely that AT&T would incur any substantial adverse economic impact due to new entry in the specialized common carrier market. In a 1972 decision, the FCC extended the policy of multiple entry to domestic satellite communications services. In the *Domsat Decision*, the commission determined that multiple entry was the policy most likely to test fully the economic benefits to the public of satellite technology. At the same time, the FCC made what was to become an important precedent in regard to incubating and encouraging competition in telecommunications. Despite a determination that AT&T should be granted use of satellite technology to test its utility in carrying the heavy measured (MTS) and wide area telephone service (WATS) traffic, the commission determined that AT&T could too easily control the costs of satellite-borne specialized services and could too easily subsidize such services from its monopoly service base. Thus the commission prohibited AT&T from utilizing its satellite facilities for private line services for three years.

Another decision by the FCC also served to further a policy of competition. In 1973 the FCC issued a ruling, *Packet Communications, Inc.,* 43 FCC 2d 922 (1973) which approved a packet switching communications network that utilized digital technology to package, store, and transmit bits of data at high speeds and low error rates. This added-value service in the transmission process would permit computers of disparate speed, codes, etc. to communicate with each other. The providers of these services were termed value-added carriers. The commission determined that the types of services proposed by the value-added carriers were not likely to be provided immediately by either the established common carriers or the specialized carriers.

By 1976 the cumulative effect of the several FCC decisions was to create a competitive private line communications industry described by the FCC as follows:

First, the established telephone industry provides a variety of private line services through voice grade services and up to video transmission services. These services are provided on a partnership basis by AT&T Long Lines, Bell System Companies and the Independent Telephone Companies. Western Union Company offers private line service as well as public message telegraph services and switched teletype service. Western Union provides private line services over both terrestrial facilities and its domestic satellite system. Specialized common carriers also provide private line service via terrestrial microwave facilites. They princiaplly offer voice and data services, but are not limited to those offerings. Another group of carriers, the miscellaneous carriers, use the microwave transmission method to supply video transmission service to television broadcast stations and CATV systems. Additionally, domestic satellite carriers offer a wide range of services via domestic satellites and another group, the value-added carriers, typically lease channels from Bell, the specialized carriers, or the satellite carriers and add terminal equipment, switching equipment and/or concentration equipment to enhance the basic communications service. [3]

Although the FCC had effectively adopted a policy favoring competition in a previously wholly monopolized industry, it had been careful to restrict competition to a portion of the industry and only to that portion which could validly be characterized as new in its origins. Thus only private line service was opened to competition, and essc..tially that portion of private line service which was driven by new technology and the service opportunities and demands created by new technology. Basic public telephone service (MTS and WATS) as well as basic long- distance toll service were still offered under monopoly conditions. The Bell system was required to make available to new carriers its local network distribution facilities on a reasonable and nondiscriminatory basis. The commission ordered such interconnections in the interest of full and fair competition. However, the commission also pursued a range of actions to ensure that competition in customer-premises terminal equipment and the interconnections of new entrants to the specialized common carrier market did not render technical harm to the Bell System or otherwise impair the quality of service to the public. Indeed, many of those actions required that new terminal equipment and transmission services be provided in accord with engineering standards prescribed by AT&T and sanctioned by the FCC.

THE 1976 EXPLORATORY HEARINGS: QUESTIONS OF COMPETITION AND INSTITUTIONAL AUTHORITY

When the House Committee on Interstate and Foreign Commerce, Subcommittee on Communications, convened what it termed exploratory hearings on competition in the telecommunications industry in the fall of 1976, AT&T's dominance of the industry was being eroded by the consequences of the aforementioned series of FCC decisions. The nature and structure of the telecommunications industry were being altered by the forces of new technology and concomitant innovative uses of that technology by new entrants to the industry. Although AT&T would warn against the spectre of huge increases in the costs of basic telephone services and many congressmen were clearly concerned about the prospect of such rate increases, the dominant concerns were not yet those of rising costs for basic telecommunications services. The dominant concern for AT&T was that a new telecommunications policy was necessary, one which restored and protected AT&T's dominance of the industry. Many others shared the view that a new policy was necessary, although not all agreed with AT&T's reasons. Some members of Congress in particular believed that a new national communications policy was needed to replace the Communications Act of 1934, which was considered woefully outdated and outmoded because the new technologies of communications were not envisioned by the 1934 Act. Perhaps in part a as prelude to considering a new communications policy, and no doubt in response to a major lobbying effort by AT&T, Congress apparently felt compelled to consider at least informally a proposal for revamping telecommunications policy which originated with the telephone industry.

Although the House hearings were not officially called to consider a specific piece of legislation, a bill pertinent to the focus of the hearings, H.R. 12323, had been introduced. Officially titled the Consumer Communications Reform Act of 1976, the bill was unofficially and openly referred to as "the Bell bill." The hearing record did not carry a printing of the bill even though the bill had combined cosponsorship of 175 in the House and sixteen in the Senate. Thus, the specifics of H.R. 12323 had to be discerned from the statements and testimonies of those appearing before the committee. Although some specifics of the bill were addressed in the hearings, much of the testimony was directed toward justifying the activities of new entrants to the telecommunications industry as fulfilling new and unmet needs not detrimental to the provision of basic telephone service. Thus, as the first phase of what was to be prolonged congressional consideration and debate, the 1976 hearings centered around the issue of institutional authority in restructuring telecommunications policy. The specific question was whether the FCC could effectively restructure the most profound aspects of regulatory policy through a series of disparate rulings, or whether Congress was the appropriate body for exercising such broad authority. Indeed, the preferences of AT&T and many others was for Congress to rewrite the 1934 Communications Act in a manner which remedied the consequences of the FCC decisions and in a manner which reined in the authority of federal regulators in the area of telecommunications policy.

The hearings opened with the traditional rhetorical flourishes but with a clear signaling of an intended and desired shift to Congress as the institutional locus for setting telecommunications policy. There was also an interestingly explicit statement of a necessity for Congress to direct its efforts toward a determination of the public interest in telecommunications policy. Two statements illustrate these observations. Subcommittee chairman Lionel Van Deerlin opened the hearings, stating that "we come to the third act of a continuing drama, the first [two] of which have been performed before the Federal Communications Commission and the courts."[4] In reflecting on the opposing views of the FCC and the telephone industry regarding the propriety of permitting competition in some aspects of telecommunications, Congressman Louis Frey attempted to frame the overall issue context:

Rather than cast this issue in academic economic schools of thought—monopoly versus competition—I believe that we have to drive it down to the basic issue. That is: What course of action is in the best interest of the public?

Certainly it is not the job of this committee to tinker with the detailed rates of the telephone industry. However, the broad impact of telephone rates is more than an industry question. It concerns the affordability of a basic service to all the people. It concerns the broad social question of who should bear the cost of a nationwide telecommunications policy and whose interests should be protected. It also concerns whether the telephone industry should be responsible for a subsidization of local phone service or whether such an activity could be more effectively administered by a Government agency.

. . . [T]hese exploratory hearings should be held, and I hope that they will pave the way for full hearings on the issues, in which *all arguments can be examined, data sifted, and the public interest discerned.*[5] (emphasis added)

As the lead sponsor of the Bell bill, Congressman Teno Roncalio offered opening remarks broadly consistent with AT&T's main arguments. However, Congressman Roncalio indicated that he had introduced H.R. 12323 at the request of the owners and operators of three independent telephone companies in the state of Wyoming. He alluded to the interconnection between these independents and Bell, which resulted in capabilities of calling to or receiving calls from anywhere in the world. Congressman Roncalio argued that such a phone system should be "maintained and not jeopardized by actions of our regulatory authorities." In apparent anticipation of a major thrust of AT&T's argument about huge increases in rates for basic telephone service, Congressman Roncalio made another interesting assertion, which much later would become a central part of the debate over telecommunications policy. That assertion also further expanded Congressman Frey's framing of the issues:

I believe the time has come in the American public utility law that there must be a new element fused into law, a "life-line base rate," and that life-line base rate, whether telephone company, light and power company, natural gas or propane distribution firm, will be a base rate for the average family. Commercial users will pay proportionately more.

I think this case might be a benchmark in establishing a new basis to govern ratemaking and the base rate, itself, in determining that "life-line" concept.[6]

However prescient Congressmen Frey and Roncalio were, the issue of lifeline rates would not become a part of the central debate for some time.

THE STATUS QUO POSITION: AT&T AND THE INDEPENDENTS

In keeping with the implicit sentiment conveyed in the title of H.R. 12323, the AT&T posture in these hearings was that of protector of the interests of residential telephone subscribers. Chairman of the Board and Chief Executive Officer John D. de Butts argued that he was not at the hearings to protect the profits of AT&T or to circumvent a pending Justice Department antitrust suit but simply and only to protect the interest of AT&T customers. He left little doubt that by "customers" he meant residential subscribers because he characterized the FCC actions as designed to help big business and as resulting in significantly higher charges for everyone else. The FCC came in for harsh criticism because de Butts charged it with undermining congressional intent of the 1934 Communications Act and the policy goals of an efficient nationwide telecommunications system at reasonable charges. Furthermore, de Butts charged the FCC with choosing to legislate rather than regulate.[7]

The de Butts testimony offered some interesting historical insights into AT&T's role in defining the regulatory and pricing policies of the telecommunications industry. De Butts explained how it had been Theodore Vail, the first president of AT&T, who had defined the industry's goal as that of "universal service." Indeed, the phrase had preceeded the adoption of the 1934 Act and was not contained therein, although over time it would come to be seen as an implicit standard in regulatory policy and a concept highly valued by Congress and consumer advocates. De Butts further alluded to the contents of the first advertisement for the telephone, which appeared in May 1877: "The terms for leasing two telephones for social purposes connecting a dwelling house with any other building will be $20 per year; for business purposes $40 a year." That was the beginning of what AT&T defined as value-of-service pricing. This rate structure favored the residential telephone user and, according to AT&T, was aimed at making telephone service as widely affordable as possible. De Butts argued that the alternative to value-of-service pricing was to relate rates to cost of service. A shift to cost-of-service pricing was the predicted effect of FCC policies, and AT&T argued that the result would be a major burden on individuals on fixed incomes, retired persons, and the urban and rural poor. De Butts cited a statistic of 11 million families with incomes less that $5000 per year for whom basic telephone charges would be beyond their means to pay, whereas the cost of telecommunications was being decreased for large business users.

The other major thrust of AT&T's position was that the FCC had selectively authorized competition without first examining the implication of such action for the existing pricing system and had permitted competition in ways which disadvantaged AT&T vis- à-vis its new competitors. AT&T complained that the new entrants were free to choose to serve only lucrative markets whereas it had to serve every customer in its territory regardless of costs; and that the FCC had raised a protective regulatory umbrella over the new entrants. This argument was coupled with AT&T's argument that nationwide quality of service depended on an integrated telecommunications system which was centrally planned and designed and which operated according to common standards. This was part of AT&T's argument against connecting non-Bell equipment to the Bell system: that the system should be technically integrated and economically integrated as well through the paced investment in new capacity. De Butts argued that there was no serious quarrel with this position from any responsible quarters. He asserted that the Office of Telecommunications Policy, the National Academy of Sciences, the 1988 President's Task Force on Communications Policy, and even the FCC agreed, although the FCC had not decided that way.[8]

The central thrust of AT&T's position was supported by testimony from both the for-profit independent telephone companies (telcos) as well as the cooperatively owned independent telcos. The descriptions given of the service areas of these two groups privide more specific insight into the distribution of telephone service between them. Paul H. Henson, Chairman of the Board of United Telecommunications, Inc., the second largest non-Bell telco, charged that decisions by the FCC had placed the industry in chaos in its shift from the traditional public utility concept of regulation to one of regulated competition. Henson argued that the vast majority of users did not benefit from the FCC's selective competition. Like Bell, United Technologies was actually a holding company engaged in manufacturing switching equipment and providing a range of computer services, in addition to providing basic telephone service. Henson charged the FCC with stressing competition wherever possible in the industry without a concomitant evaluation of the social and economic impact of competition. He called on Congress to adopt a national telecommunications policy giving definition and direction with respect to those areas of telecommunications to be provided under public utility regulation and those areas, if any, to be provided under competitive conditions.[9]

Also testifying in support of the Bell position was Theodore F. Brophy, Chairman of the Board of General Telephone and Electronics Corporation (GTE). GTE owned and operated independent telcos in 7500 communities, with 12.6 million telephones, in parts of thirty-three states. Brophy charged the FCC with pursuing a policy, unsanctioned by Congress, which lowered rates for certain big-business customers but which abandoned the philosophy of universal service. He further argued that FCC policies had been piecemeal and revisionist resulting in the absence of any coherent national telecommunications policy.[10] The collective position of the independent telcos was represented by Frank Barnes, President of the U.S. Independent Telephone Association. The 1600 independent telcos were credited with providing 27 million telephones in parts of forty-eight states and directly employing 158,000 workers. Barnes leveled harsh criticism against the FCC, charging it with being an interested party incapable of an impartial judgment. He further expressed doubt that the benefits of pursuing FCC policies in support of competition could outweigh the potential for a deterioration in quality of service and significantly higher rates for most telephone subscribers. Barnes acknowledged that, in essence, the subcommittee was being asked to define the public interest. He asserted that only Congress could be the source of the far-reaching national policy necessary for setting the future course of U.S. telecommunications.[11]

The nonprofit telephone cooperatives were represented by Leroy Schecher, General Manager of West River Cooperative Telephone Company in Bison, South Dakota. Telephone cooperatives were said to number 240, with fourteen in the state of South Dakota. The cooperatives frequently provided basic telephone service in the most remote rural areas and owed their existence to support from the Rural Electrification Administration. The cooperatives strongly supported what Schecher described as the Bell system toll rates based on social or public interest pricing policies which made them uniform nationwide or statewide despite substantial differences in the cost of service in various locations. The cooperatives greatly benefited from such a pricing arrangement. With an average subscriber density of 4.86 per mile of route line for REA-supported rural cooperatives compared to an average of 81.95 subscribers per route mile of line for the Bell companies, the cooperatives would have to impose extraordinary rate increases under a cost-based pricing scheme which, it was assumed, would be a main consequence of competition in the telecommunications industry.

Subscribers of rural cooperatives were expected to be hit with higher toll rates for service over the higher-cost routes to which they were connected, plus a steep rise in rates for local service. The toll usage of rural subscribers was predicted to drop with increases in toll rates, leading in turn to a decrease in toll settlement or division of revenue payments from the Bell system. Under the then existing Bell system division of revenue, a rural cooperative earned revenue from every toll call placed to or from any rural cooperative subscriber. The result was that for some cooperatives, toll revenue settlements accounted for up to 58 percent of total system revenue. This revenue, in turn, contributed to keeping local service rates low.[12] Schecher concluded his testimony by charging the FCC with studying the economic impact of its actions only after they were *a fait accompli* and irreversible, and he called on Congress as the appropriate body to act in setting national telecommunications policy.

THE OTHER SIDE OF THE STORY: THE NEW ENTRANTS

The testimony presented by the opposition, the new entrants into the telecommunications industry, provide useful insights into the structure of the competitive areas of the telecommunications industry. It also shows how the new entrants benefited from specific FCC decisions and how they, in turn, provided innovative telecommunications services. Generally, the Bell competitors were concerned about convincing Congress that their services did not pose a threat to the quality or cost of basic telephone service. They also had to make a specific and compelling case against the adoption of H.R. 12323. There was one section of the Bell bill, section 8, which was most threatening to the Bell competitors. It specified the findings to be included in FCC authorization of specialized carriers:

The commission shall not grant or authorize any construction permit, station license, or certificate, for the construction, acquisition, or operation of any communication or transmission line facility, or extension thereof, or any modification or renewal thereof, that otherwise might be granted or authorized pursuant to any provision of this Act, to any specialized carrier that furnishes or proposes to furnish interstate communication service unless the Commission shall find, after full opportunity for evidentiary hearing on the record, that such permit, license, or certificate will not result in increased charges for telephone exchange service or in wasteful or unnecessary duplication of communication lines, facilities, equipment, and instrumentalities of any telephone or telegraph common carrier, and will not significantly impair the technical integrity or capacity for unified and coordinated planning, management, design, and operation of the nationwide telephone network...The commission shall determine, among other things, that the proposed service or services of specialized carriers, which are the subject of the proposed grant or authorization, (i) are not like or similar to any service or services provided by a telephone or telegraph common carrier, and (ii) cannot be provided by available communications lines, facilities, equipment, or instrumentalities of a telephone or telegraph common carrier. At any hearing involving a matter under this subsection, the burden of proof to support the requisite findings by the Commission shall be on the applicant for such permit, license, or certificate.

The chairman of the FCC testified that the Bell bill would impose an almost impossible burden on specialized and domestic satellite carriers because any applicant would not only have to show that its services were not duplicative of those of a telephone or telegraph carrier but demonstrate that existing carriers could not then or in the future provide the proposed services. In addition, sections 6 and 7 of H.R. 12323 would transfer from federal (FCC) authority to the authority of the fifty states regulatory jurisdiction over any and all terminal equipment, terminating facilities, exchange, and other like instrumentalities and apparatus used for, or in connection with, telephone exchange service or interexchange service regardless of the use of such equipment in interstate or foreign communications service. The FCC held that sections 6 and 7 would deprive the FCC of jurisdiction over interstate communications services; dispense regulatory authority over matters affecting the nationwide communications network to fifty state regulatory bodies; and permit individual states to veto FCC decisions in the terminal equipment and private line fields which had already received judicial affirmation.[13]

The three nonmonopoly telecommunications companies providing interstate business and data communications services had joined together to form an industry trade and lobbying group, the Ad Hoc Committee for Competitive Telecommunications (ACCT). The group consisted of MCI Telecommunications Corporation, Southern Pacific Telecommunications Company, and U.S. Transmission Systems, an ITT subsidiary. ACCT was represented at the hearings by Herbert Jasper, Executive Vice President of ACCT. Jasper opened by stating that a fourth member of the group, DATRAN, had recently filed for bankruptcy and had filed a $285 million lawsuit against AT&T alleging anticompetitive business practices. Jasper traced the origins of ACCT's member firms to several pivotal FCC decisions: the 1959 *Above 890 MHz* proceeding which allowed for construction and operation of private microwave relay systems; the 1959 *Microwave Decision* which allowed construction and operation of specialized common carrier (SCC) microwave facilities; *the 1970 Domestic Satellite (DOMSAT) Decision*; and the *1971 Specialized Common Carrier Decision* which allowed microwave relay communications carriers to begin constructing and operating business and data communications systems. Jasper argued that the emergent SCC industry posed no threat to AT&T's monopoly in message telephone service because the new entrants sought to satisfy new and diverse data communications needs of businesses which could not be provided by AT&T.

In addition to providing flexibility and choices to business users, the SCCs were depicted as helping to disperse the risks and burdens of supplying the rapidly growing markets for new and specialized services. To counter AT&T charges of impending financial threat, Jasper quoted FCC statistics which showed AT&T's net income for the second quarter of 1976 at $1.012 billion, in contrast to total 1975 combined earnings for all interconnect equipment suppliers and SCCs of $186 million. Jasper likened AT&T's sole control of the entire communication network in the information age to having a single company in the industrial age controlling all of the transportation arteries of industrial commerce—all railroads, trucks, ships, pipelines, aircraft, and canals.[14]

Interestingly, MCI Corporation provided two representatives, the president and the senior vice president, to give testimony in succession on the same day. The MCI representatives spoke directly to the implications of the Bell bill, section 8 in particular. Their position was that the Bell bill would eliminate companies like MCI because they could not design a system which AT&T could not duplicate. Thus, section 8 was described as comprising a series of roadblocks which no specialized carrier could ever surmount. Moreover, the MCI representatives contended that the Bell bill represented an abuse of AT&T's right to petition Congress as the effect of the bill pending before Congress would be to support a claim that competition might be legislated out of existence and which would scare off investors and potential competitors. MCI urged the committee to cease further consideration of the Bell bill. MCI submitted a 58-page formal statement for the record and the committee's review. In it MCI attempted a point-by-point rebuttal of the major sections of the Bell bill. The MCI statement also listed twenty-seven "difficult" concepts which the committee was reminded it "must learn to understand" before it could "possibly try to second guess the FCC and the Office of Technology Policy (OTP), which are the expert agencies which you and the President have created to deal with communications—and which have been dealing with or studying these matters for a long time." The committee was also reminded that it would need to familiarize itself with a long list of FCC proceedings and court decisions because it was being asked to overrule those decisions.[15] The MCI statement attempted to explain these concepts and proceedings within the context of sections of H.R. 12323. Apparently, MCI was hoping that an informed Congress would be its best supporter.

The argument for continuation of competition in the area of satellite transmission was made by Emanuel Fthenakis, President of American Satellite Corporation (ASC). Fthenakis expressed particular pride in putting America in the satellite communications business after the Soviets and Canadians had launched satellite systems, (the latter used American-built equipment). This lag on the part of U.S. industry to deploy satellite technology was attributed to obstacles erected by AT&T. ASC had been formed in 1972,and after it initiated transmission in 1974, two other firms joined the industry within a matter of months. To avoid any possible confusion, ASC's operations were carefully described as involving no wiring of telephone sets in buildings, no selling of telephone equipment, and no placing of cable in streets, but only the provision of satellite transmission from one unique location in a city, government, or commercial installation to another similar point in a distant location. Some, ASC operations made use of the local telephone network in various places, a service for which, Fthenakis asserted, ASC paid handsomely. ASC operations were defined as high-speed data transmission with an extremely low error rate. For clients such as the U.S. Meteorological Service, ASC transmitted weather data, including actual pictures in digital form for receipt at remote U.S. bases. Its services for the *Wall Street Journal* permitted the paper to be set in Massachusetts, broadcast via satellite in the form of virtually error free high-speed data, and received and reproduced at remote locations. These were examples of the innovative services provided by ASC and not provided by AT&T. Despite ASC's innovative services, Fthenakis acknowledged that with a $10 billion annual construction budget, AT&T could provide any and all communications services required by the public. Thus the question for Congress, Fthenakis argued, was whether it wished to sustain the competition permitted by the FCC as being in the public interest.[16]

Representatives from the new packet-switching industry and the emergent interconnect equipment industry also testified against H .R. 12323. The packet-switching industry was represented by Philip M. Walker of Telenet Communications. Packet switching had grown out of Department of Defense (DOD) research programs devoted to developing a technology to meet the communications requirements of computer users. It permitted the high-speed and error-free transmission of data among remote access data processing computers and computer terminals. Specifically, Telenet made use of high-speed data communication lines, both analog and digital (leased from AT&T and others) which interconnected Telenet's switching offices from coast to coast. Telenet's services permitted error correction in transmission (because each switching device was actually a small computer) and provided code and speed conversions to enable otherwise incompatible computers to communicate. Thus, Telenet considered itself a value-added carrier, utilizing the same transmisison lines as the telephone but adding innovative services and greater efficiency in its use of existing transmission lines. Telenet's position was that because AT&T was itself seeking to offer new competitive services, traditional rate regulation was no longer workable for a company such as AT&T. The alternative, Walker argued, was for AT&T's competitive services to be offered by a totally separate corporate entity.[17]

Richard B. Long testified on behalf of the North American Telephone Association, which represented a majority of the 400 interconnect firms engaged in the manufacture and installation of telephones and switchboards. The interconnect industry was credited with having created employment for 37,000 in thirty-eight states and having handled the $1 billion investment (in value, not sales) customers had made in owning their own communications systems. The interconnect industry traced its origin to the 1968 FCC *Carterfone Decision* which provided a wedge into the communications industry. The interconnect industry was taking advantage of available technology to offer a blend of computer and telephone equipment that would provide a host of programmable telephone features for clients such as hospitals, brokerage houses, banks, and transit systems. These services enabled clients to design communications systems to suit the needs of their operations. Again, the issue was not that

AT&T could not provide these services but whether it should be the only provider of these services.[18]

THE REGULATORS DISAGREE

The FCC had been accused by representatives of the established telephone industry of not being an objective party and, moreover, not the appropriate body to continue to decide the issue of permitting competition in the telecommunications industry. Thus, whether it had objectively fulfilled its responsibilities or not, the FCC was placed in a position of defending its actions. FCC chairman Richard E. Wiley offered six pages of oral testimony, a section-by-section commentary on H.R. 12323 numbering eighteen pages, and a 156-page report entitled an "Overview of the Domestic Telecommunications Industry and the Commission's Policies Concerning Terminal Equipment and Private Line Services." The latter report was extensive and detailed in its coverage, entailing a chronological review of the development of the telephone industry; the specifics of developments in computer and electronic technologies as catalysts for change; major FCC decisions permitting use of new technologies; new service offerings by new entrants; specifics of common carrier regulations; and details of ratemaking and revenue policies. This information package was designed to give Congress a basis for a critical review of the Bell bill. Perhaps the FCC also hoped that an informed congress would be its best supporters.

In his testimony, chairman Wiley essentially took on AT&T and the established telephone industry. He opened by charging that the Consumer Communications Reform Act of 1976 (the Bell bill) was not consumer legislation but was special interest legislation. Chairman Wiley reiterated the FCC's commitment to universal service as evidenced by its past refusal and intended future refusal to authorize the establishment of competitive communications systems which offer services essentially identical to basic message telephone service or which adversely affect the technical integrity or economic viability of the public telephone network. He insisted that no FCC actions were likely to require changes in the pricing of basic telephone service and stated that there was considerable evidence to contradict the assertion by Bell that it practiced value-of-service pricing such that business users subsidized residentials. Wiley informed the committee of two investigations of AT&T tariffs (pricing schemes) conducted by the FCC. In one, completed prior to the *Specialized Common Carrier Decision*, the FCC had concluded that AT&T priced interstate private lines below full costs. In the second investigation, Dockett 20003 *Economic Inquiry*, the FCC had found no credible evidence that terminal equipment covered its full costs. In both cases, basic telephone charges were said to provide a cross-subsidy for other competitive services. Chairman Wiley testified that overall, the FCC had concluded that the public interest was served by the open marketplace, especially given the proliferation of communication needs and the emergence of computer and electronic companies outside the traditional voice telecommunications industry.[19]

The FCC recommended that Congress reject H.R. 12323. However, the commission had a lone dissenter on this position, Commissioner Benjamin Hooks. Hooks did not testify before the committee, but submitted twenty-one pages of dissenting commentary written in regard to several FCC decisions. Hooks took pains to assert his support of competition in a number of areas of communications common carriage and his many votes on the commission in support of competition. However, Hooks claimed that the commission had not always followed a course of permitting "full and fair" competition but rather had implemented policies with a "curious neutrality" in favor of competitive entrants. Commissioner Hooks took issue with the commission report of its *Economic Inquiry* (Docket 20003), which it had submitted as a retort to the question of whether some competitive services would lead to a loss of revenue by the major providers of basic telephone services and lead to sharp increases in the cost of telephone service for the ordinary consumer. Hooks's recounting of the thrust of this report differed from that given by chairman Wiley. Hooks pointed out that although *Economic Inquiry* did not tell the whole story, the report did concede, for the first time, that some FCC policies could prove dangerous to the independent telephone companies and that local household rates would have to be subsidized by a separations charge to offset revenue loss from competitive offerings. He raised questions about the feasibility of higher separations but reserved his opinion on the matter. Commissioner Hooks also indicated that *Economic Inquiry* seriously underestimated the magnitude of revenue diversion if stronger competitors ,such as IBM or ITT chose to enter some service areas long held to be the province of telephone companies. The commissioner expressed special concern about the prospects of a court review of the commission's *Execunet* case, which might permit competition in some areas of message telephone service.

Moreover, Commissioner Hooks pointed out that although competition in the terminal equipment market had had only a minimum impact on telcos' revenues up to 1976, that situation was likely to change significantly with the entry of larger competitors with greater financial and marketing clout. In an interesting observation on the impact of the emergent interconnect industry, Hooks cited a report submitted to the FCC by the Stanford Research Institute (SRI). The SRI report stated that since the *Carterfone* decision, Japanese and European companies had captured more than 75 percent of the U.S. interconnect market for PBX and key equipment; that business users had been the major beneficiaries due to tax depreciation advantages of ownership over leasing; and that there had been surplus revenues from the business interconnect equipment area which the telcos insisted had been used to support basic residential rates. Hooks framed his dissent within the context of his concern for the ordinary consumer, who lacked the lobbying clout or financial resources to fight competing industry interests. Hooks had been the lone dissenter in this regard on the FCC.[20]

The association representing state regulators of telecommunications, (National Association of Regulatory Utility Commissioners (NARUC), unquestionably took the FCC to task on its pro-competition policies. The NARUC was represented by Edward P. Larkin, who testified that NARUC's principal concern was with the cost of basic telephone service and that NARUC's members were closer to their constituency than were the FCC and were thus likely to be more emotional in their concerns. Larkin summed up the NARUC position:

Now again we are not defendants of AT&T as we have been accused. Nor are we in essence monopolists. But, gentlemen, if it will bring to the individual user of telephone service the best possible telephone service at the lowest possible cost, then, gentlemen, I and my colleagues are for monopoly and the Congress of the United States in the Communications Act of 1934 so ordained. . .
I am a believer in the integrated telephone network as it presently exists.   I think the telephone service starts off with the local household owner and he is the one with whom my concern rests basically. It is an integrated thing. It is not something that you can pick apart.It is a whole. It is an entity. What you do in any part of this system is going to affect every other part.[21]

Larkin sought to focus the committee's attention on what NARUC considered the already great disparity in the rate burden borne by local users and that borne by users of interstate telephone service. The NARUC position was that this growing disparity was the result of the FCC having structured federal and state ratemaking procedures in such a way that Bell system long-distance interstate telephone rates had remained much the same since 1953. Larkin pointed out that between January 1, 1969 and April 15, 1974, the FCC granted a net increase of $163 million to the Bell system whereas during that same period, state commissions were forced to grant Bell system companies intrastate rate increases of approximately $2.9 billion. Reductions in interstate rates were attributed to technological advances such as coaxial cable, microwave transmission, and satellites. There were no comparable advantageous uses of these technologies to offset local rate costs. Moreover, with growing competition, common carriers were said to oppose vigorously increases in interstate rates, with the burden of lost revenues being shifted to residential subscribers who had no place to go. Larkin indicated that NARUC had conducted an evidentiary inquiry into the impact of competition in terminal equipment and in specialized common carrier services. The inquiry concluded that the new FCC policies encouraging competition would result in a substantial adverse economic impact on local exchange telephone subscribers. Specifically ,NARUC estimated that by 1980 the cost of new competition in terms of higher local rates would be minimally $600 million to $1.0 billion annually; reaching $1.5 to $1.7 billion annually by 1984; and reaching a cumulative total of $6.7 billion to $9.6 billion by 1984. These increases were projected in addition to otherwise normal cost increases.

Larkin also referred to a bill which NARUC had proposed in 1975, the Home Telephone Act of 1975, H.R. 8189. The NARUC bill would have had Congress make it a goal of national communications policy to establish and maintain rates for local exchange service which were, to the extent practicable, within the economic reach of every home in the United States. A second goal was to provide for the joint federal-state board to set procedures for crediting revenues from interstate and foreign services against the costs of residential service. These new procedures would supplement the traditional separations procedures and would result in a sharing throughout the system of cost efficiencies due to technological innovations. The NARUC thus proposed that Congress adopt both the Home Telephone Act of 1975 and the Consumer Communications Reform Act.[22]

THE FORD ADMINISTRATION POSITION

FCC policies were supported by the Director of the White House Office of Telecommunications. The Director, Thomas J. Houser, was new to his post and not familiar with the issues. Houser expressed general support for competition but urged that special consideration be given to the unique problems of small independents serving rural subscribers.[23] Given that the Justice Department at the time had an antitrust suit pending against AT&T, it is somewhat surprising that the Assistant Attorney General for the Antitrust Division appeared to present testimony before the committee. However, one of the provisions of H.R. 12323 was to extend to AT&T an exemption to antitrust laws if it sought to acquire any of the specialized common carriers. The Assistant Attorney General submitted a 37-page formal statement for the record, in which he cited the advantages already accruing from competition; questioned the premise of cross-subsidies from business to residential services, and supported governmental policymakers as the appropriate source of any policy of cross-subsidization in telecommunications. Not surprisingly, the Justice Department expressed strong criticism of AT&T's anticompetitive behavior and strong support for the FCC's policies in support of competition.[24] At least at this stage, the administration of President Gerald Ford was clearly one which supported competition in telecommunications.

THE CONSUMER SPEAKS?

When chairman de Butts of AT&T had given testimony earlier in these hearings, he had been asked how many national consumer groups backed the Bell bill. De Butts responded that he was unaware of any who had come out in favor of the bill and aware of only one that had come out against the bill; that AT&T was working closely with national consumer groups; and that their position at the time was neutral.[25] AT&T had not been successful in persuading any national consumer groups to support H.R. 12323 in testimony before the committee. Representatives of two consumer groups, Public Citizen Congress Watch and Public Interest Research Group appeared before the group and offered joint testimony. They testified that H.R. 12323 was not in the consumers' interest but was special interest legislation. These consumer representatives objected to AT&T's insistence that business services revenues were being used to subsidize residential rates, arguing that the reverse appeared to be the case. Moreover, they argued that it was not for AT&T to establish a policy of income distribution but this was a decision to be made by government. They offered a strong argument for a presumption for competition in the American economy but also pressed for legislation to create a nonprofit Residential Utility Consumer Action Group (RUCAG) comprised of lawyers, accountants, economists, and organizers and supported by voluntary contributions through utility payments. RUCAG would represent the consumer on all utility matters before regulatory commissions, the courts, and legislatures.[26] At this point, consumer interests were not well articulated or represented by distinctively consumer organizations. Rather, many others who arguably had vested interests were dubiously the strongest proponents of consumer interests.

SUMMARY

In three days of exploratory hearings, the Subcommittee on Communications had obtained 1331 pages of testimony and supporting materials submitted for the record. The basic contours of the debate had been set in place. At this point, the question around which the debate pivoted was whether emergent competition in the telecommunications industry should be quashed. The FCC had already decided in the affirmative the prior question of whether competition should be allowed in a traditionally regulated monopoly. The presence of numerous new and growing industries had given reality to this FCC policy shift. In a societal context which values a competitive free market, new entrants to the telecommunications industry had only to downplay any harm their presence might cause residential consumers and tout the benefits of their services to American businesses and larger society. AT&T and others who expressed deep concerns about the adverse impacts of competition on residential consumers were in a difficult position of appearing to be protectionist of their own interests and reactionary in the face of progress. They were swimming against the tide—a tide propelled by the forces of technology and competition. Although the issue of lifeline telephone rates had been raised as an implied remedy for the threat to universal service posed by competition in telecommunications services, this issue had not yet become an integral part of the emerging debate.

At the end of the third day of hearings, Congressman Timothy Wirth introduced into the record the text of a speech he had given to the North American Telephone Association entitled "Telecommunications Policy and the Bell Bill." Congressman Wirth delivered the speech eleven days prior to the start of the exploratory hearings of 1977. That speech is excerpted here for the wealth of insights it provides into the context within which public policy issues are debated:

Telecommunications policy is not something my colleagues in Congress have spent a lot of time thinking about since the Communications Act was written 40 years ago. In fact, it is a subject—I would say—that fewer than a half dozen Members of

Congress can speak about with authority today. And I do not include myself in that group.

However, this period of Congressional neglect of telecommunications is about to come to an end. The House Subcommittee on Communications, on which I serve, is presently laying plans to conduct a total review of the Communications Act in the next Congress.

The question that is certain to be uppermost in the minds of my colleagues is, "What are the advantages and disadvantages of allowing competition in the telephone industry?" On the surface this may seem like a very easy question to answer; but I can assure you that for every advantage you can cite, Ma Bell will have a disadvantage to point to. She will be raising the question in the following form: "Won't competition harm the world's best telephone system? And won't it cost the consumer more?"

As far as I am concerned, the burden is on the Telephone Company to prove that competition in the interconnect and specialized common carrier areas is not in the public interest. However, many of my colleagues who extoll free enterprise and competition do not share my approach to these questions. There are a number of reasons for this—lack of information: pressure; the pervasiveness and comfort of our telephone system; and lots of misunderstanding of what competition in the interconnect industry really means.

If you expect your Congressman or Congresswoman to be well-informed about the problems your industry faces then it's up to you to inform him or her.

You must learn, if you don't already know it, that Exxon, George Meany, Ralph Nader, and others concerned with the currently squeaking wheels are experts in getting their views across to harrassed, overworked and confused members of Congress who are expected to know everything about everything from the Alaskan pipeline to the Angolan civil war—maybe more to the point, these advocates know that public policy decisions are no longer made in genteel, bucolic atmosphere. What may once have been a gentleman's game is, in 1976, a fierce contest for scarce resources of time, energy and, on the bottom line, votes.[27]

In March of 1977, the Senate held four days of exploratory hearings to parallel the House hearings held the previous fall. The Senate hearings served largely to provide a forum for parties offering a rebuttal to points scored against their positions during the House hearings. However, there were some new participants in the Senate hearings, most notably a new national consumer organization, the Consumer Federation of America (CFA). The two consumer organizations which provided testimony for the 1976 House hearings did not participate in the 1977 Senate hearings. The CFA was represented by Andrew Horowitz, who also identified himself as a founding member of the Public Interest Satellite Association (PISA). PISA had been founded to promote the establishment of a low-cost satellite communications system tailored to serve the needs of the nonprofit sector. Thus, Horowitz took the opportunity to advance a somewhat dual agenda. The CFA position was to support competition as a spur to providing the public with a variety of high-quality communications services on a just and equitable basis. It opposed the Consumers Communications Reform Act.

The CFA called for a national telecommunications policy which would specifically provide for (1) a basic telecommunications service package made universally available at a reasonable cost to all income levels; (2) uniform average intrastate and interstate rates, with the disparity between the two eliminated; (3) special reduced-rate concessions for nonprofit groups, especially voluntary, consumer, public interest, and educational organizations; (4) healthy competition in the sale of communications equipment to all telephone companies, equipment vendors, and consumers; (5) consumer choice concerning the purchase or rental of terminal equipment from either equipment vendors or telephone companies; (6) elimination of "protective umbrellas" or artificially pegged rates to protect individual companies from competition; (7) equal application among all telecommunications carriers of service limitations, cost allocations, price structures, and an accounting system; and (8) preservation of the quality and integrity of the telephone network through the establishment of itnerconnection regulations while furthering competitive services and equipment in all monopoly communications sectors.[28]

The CFA's rationale for its argument regarding special reduced rates for satellite telecommunications was that this technology was produced by public subsidies via governmental appropriations in the form of research and development expenditures. It was not enough, CFA argued, to turn these technologies over to private vendors and declare them available to the public. The CFA also made a poignant point about the participation of consumer groups in the hearings in relationship to their stake in the making of telecommunications policy. The CFA Congress to consider making available funds to consumer and public interest organizations to cover their travel and other essential costs incurred in participating in policy proceedings. The point of this argument was that consumer groups generally did not have available to them the arsenal of legal and other expert resources which industry groups could call on in pressing their positions.[29] Perhaps the significance of the CFA's participation in these exploratory hearings, in which the major debate was being structured, was that consumer interests had been articulated in a more expansive manner by an organization with an impressive identity and profile and a relatively strong presence in national policymaking arenas. The CFA proposal was as much pro-competition as it was pro-consumer. The CFA had not made an explicit call or argument in support of lifeline rates as a means of protecting the interests of low-income consumers.

NOTES

1. U.S. Congress.   House.   Committee on Interstate and Foreign Commerce. Subcommittee on Communications.   *Communications Act of 1934, Section 214: Legislative Background.*   96th Cong., 1st sess., April 1979.   Committee Print 96-IFC18.

2. This background section on changes in the telecommunications industry due to technology and administrative rulings draws on several sources. See U.S. Congress. House.   Committee on Interstate and Foreign Commerce.   Subcommittee on Communications.   *Competition in the Telecommunications Industry: Hearings:*

Exploring the Subject of Competition in the Domestic Communications Common Carrier Industry. 94th Cong., 2nd sess., 1976, pp. 781–934. Report submitted for the record by the Federal Communications Commission. See also Harry M. Shooshan III, ed. *Disconnecting Bell: The Impact of the AT&T Divestiture.* New York: Pergamon Press, 1984.

3. Ibid., pp. 868–869. Competition in the Telecommunications Industry.

4. House. *Competition in the Telecommunications Industry*, p. 1. Opening Statement of Congressman Lionel Van Deerlin.

5. Ibid., pp. 4–5. Opening Statement of Congressman Louis Frey.

6. House. *Competition in the Telecommunications Industry*, p. 7. Opening Statement of Congressman Teno Roncalio.

7. House. Competition in the Telecommunications Industry, pp. 10–27 Testimony and Prepared statement of John D. de Butts, Chairman of the Board and Chief Executive Officer, AT&T.

8. Ibid.

9. House. *Competition in the Telecommunications Industry,* pp. 57–62. Testimony and prepared statement of Paul H. Henson, Chairman of the Board, United Telecommunications, Inc.

10. Ibid., pp. 128–133. Testimony of Theodore F. Brophy, Chairman of the Board, General Telephone and Electronics Corp.

11. House. *Competition in the Telecommunications Industry*, p. 1 Testimony and prepared statement of Frank Barnes, President, U.S. Independent Telephone Association.

12. Ibid., pp. 238–244. Testimony and prepared statement of Leroy Schecher, West River Cooperative Telephone Company, Bison, South Dakota.

13. House. *Competition in the Telecommunications Industry*, pp. 733–739, Testimony of Honorable Richard E. Wiley, Chairman, Federal Communications Commission and pp. 774–775, materials submitted for the record by the Federal Communications Commission.

14. Ibid., pp. 257–287. Testimony and prepared statement of Herbert Jasper, Ad Hoc Committee for Competitive Telecommunications.

15. House. *Competition in the Telecommunications Industry*, pp. 325–398. Testimonies of Kenneth A. Cox and William McGowan, MCI, and report submitted for the record by MCI.

16. Ibid., pp. 463–492. Testimony and prepared statement of Emanuel Ethenatis, American Satellite Corporation.

17. House. *Competition in the Telecommunications Industry*, pp. 493–531. Testimony and prepared statement of Philip M. Walker, Telenet Communications.

18. Ibid., pp. 545–578.Testimony and prepared statement of Richard B. Long, North American Telephone Association.

19. House. *Competition in the Telecommunications Industry*, pp. 733 739. Testimony of Honorable Richard E. Wiley.

20. Ibid., pp. 740–761. Dissenting commentary of Commissioner Benjamin Hooks, submitted for the record by the Federal Communications Commission.

21. House. *Competition in the Telecommunications Industry*, p. 953. Testimony of Edward P. Larkin, National Association of Regulatory Utility Commissioners.

22. Ibid., pp. 955–969. Prepared statement of Edward P. Larkin.

23. House. *Competition in the Telecommunications Industry*, pp. 1027–1034. Testimony and prepared statement of Thomas J. Houser, Director, White House Office

of Telecommunications.

24. Ibid., pp. 1072–1113. Testimony and prepared statement of Donald I. Baker, Assistant Attorney General, Antitrust Division, Department of Justice.

25. House. *Competition in the Telecommunications Industry,* p. 30, Testimony of John D. de Butts.

26. Ibid., pp. 1214–1223. Joint testimony and prepared statement of Andrew Feinstein, Public Citizen Congress Watch, and Mantin H. Rogol, Public Interest Research Group.

27. House. *Competition in the Telecommunications Industry,* pp. 1225–1227. Speech submitted for the record by Congressman Timothy Wirth.

28. U.S. Congress. Senate. Committee on Commerce, Science, and Transportation. Subcommittee on Communications. *Domestic Telecommunications Common Carrier Policies: Hearings.* 95th Cong., 1st sess., pt. 2, pp. 1036–1044. Testimony and prepared statement of Andrew Horowitz, Consumer Federation of America.

29. Ibid.

Chapter 6

Challenges and Competition in Policy Formulation

THE INITIAL REWRITE EFFORT

After two sessions of exploratory hearings in 1976 and 1977, in 1978 Congress began the ambitious task of rewriting the Communications Act of 1934. The task was ambitious because the rewrite effort sought to set new national policies which would take into account the consequences of technological developments as they had affected telephony, radio broadcasting, conventional television broadcasting, and cable television broadcasting. An effective new policy would have to incorporate the cumulative set of relevant administrative and judicial rulings rendered in each of these areas over the years. The new national policies would also seek to provide a basis for resolving future conflicts in areas of U.S. domestic and international communications in a changed environment of expanded competition and limited regulation. The discussion presented in this chapter focuses only on domestic telecommunications issues pertinent to redefining the role and status of the telecommunications common carriers as related to the shift from monopoly to competition. Other issues which also relate to competitive pressures, such as those pertaining to the debate over the entry of telcos into the cable television industry, are generally not included in this discussion. Although these issues were important ones, they were essentially at the periphery of the telecommunications policy debate of the 1970s and early 1980s.

Unlike the situation in 1976, when Congress had held what it called exploratory hearings on the controversial question of competition in the telecommunications industry, in 1978 Congress faced a different and somewhat more daunting challenge. Congress was faced with the tasks of defining a specific policy course, legitimating an already emergent policy of competition, and establishing its position as the premier formulator of telecommunications policy.

It was clear that through a series of decisions the FCC had not only regulated according to policy mandates of the 1934 Act, but it had made new policy, and in the latter case, it had laid the foundation for a redefinition of the public interest in telecommunications. This is not to say that the FCC had acted irresponsibly. However, the FCC had certainly helped to create a major policy dilemma. The FCC actions were not only controversial but were also sweeping in their implications for (1) changing the nature of the telecommunications industry (2) affecting the functions and profits of the world's largest telecommunications companies and other would-be commmunications giants, and (3) affecting the costs of telecommunications services for the average consumer. Thus, given the scope of these changes, the policy dilemma entailed a question of legitimacy. There was the question of whether the initiatives taken by the FCC reflected the proper and legitimate responsibility of a regulatory agency. Although it is in accord with conventional regulatory practices that regulatory agencies can and do make policy, they are expected to do so within a relatively narrow scope, directly derived from a broader legislative mandate. Many participants in the telecommunications policy debate argued that actions such as those taken by the FCC with regard to initiating competition in the telecommunications industry were the exclusive prerogative of Congress. The legitimacy of the FCC's actions was called into question. Thus, an attempt to rewrite the 1934 Act was an attempt by Congress to reassume the role of chief policymaker in telecommunications (and other areas of communications policy as well). The rewrite bill was H.R. 13015, the Communications Act of 1978. It was the first of what would be numerous attempts over the next seven years in which Congress sought to make a major policy statement regarding the impact of new technologies and the provision of new services in telecommunications.

The major issue driving the debate in 1978 had shifted from that of 1976. In 1976 the major issue was one of whether competition should be permitted and sanctioned in the telecommunications industry. By 1978 that question had been answered in the affirmative (and not just by the FCC). In 1978 the debate pivoted around the issue of how competition in telecommunications would be accommodated. The issue was not a simple one for it too embodied a major policy dilemma. Indeed, the dilemma had been recognized by the telephone industry. The chairman of the Telecommunications Policy Task Force testified in regard to a report submitted on request to the subcommittee, entitled "The Dilemma of Telecommunications Policy," in which the crux of the policy dilemma had been identified. J. Stephen Vanderwoude testified that the dilemma dealt with two conflicting national policy goals. The first was the desire to maintain and expand the universal network with low residential rates generally low rates for rural service (which was in reality high-cost service) and nationwide averaged long-distance rates. The second goal was the desire to broaden the availability of largely business customer choice in telecommunications services. These two goals were seen as inherently in conflict but subject to balancing in a carefully conceived policy.[1] The challenge was one of how to craft a specific policy which achieved this balance.

There was little doubt that the House Communications Subcommittee had been persuaded of the viability, if indeed not the imperative, of competition in telecommunications. When it was introduced, the main finding of the rewrite bill (H.R. 13015) was that

regulation of interstate and foreign telecommunications is necessary, to the extent marketplace forces are deficient in order to make available to the people of the United States nationwide and worldwide telecommunications services which are diverse, reliable, and efficient, and which are available at affordable rates.

This prescription of a regulatory function limited to supporting deficiencies in market forces in effect became the new regulatory standard, supplanting the "public necessity and convenience of the 1934 Act." The proposed legislation also left little doubt about the desire for change in regard to the roles and functions of the FCC. The agency's name was changed to the Communications Regulatory Commission (CRC), and its membership was reduced from seven to five members to reflect a reduced workload under what would be the new conditions of competition. Members would be limited to a single ten-year term as opposed to being eliglble for unlimited reappointments. Appointees were to reflect a balance of professional backgrounds pertinent to communications, and their confirmation would be subject to a vote by both houses of Congress. That the last provision would require a constitutional amendment apparently did not trouble the bill's sponsors.

The main provisions of H.R. 13015 with regard to telecommunications, found mainly in Title III, were

1. To place maximum feasible reliance on marketplace forces to achieve the purposes of the Act
2. To permit the CRC to classify common carriers and interstate telecommunications services as competitive or noncompetitive, and to reclassify carriers and services accordingly
3. To require every common carrier to establish connection with any other carrier, except where the CRC found that such connection would result in substantial technical or economic harm
4. To prohibit the provision of noncompetitive telecommunications services by companies also engaged in the manufacture of equipment and in furnishing domestic common carrier services
5. To permit any common carrier to hold or acquire shares of any separate company which engaged in activities related to telecommunications notwithstanding any other law or judicial decree
6. To require any intercity carrier which connected with local exchange switching facilities to pay access charges to a universal service compensation fund
7. To require the CRC to establish and administer a universal service compensation fund to maintain toll telephone service and local exchange telephone service rates at affordable levels and to ensure nationwide availability of basic voice telephone service.

The rewrite bill proposed what amounted to a sea change in telecommunications, from a system dominated by a regulated monopoly to an openly competitive, deregulated industry with regulation only when competition was somehow defective. The bill attempted to pull together and respond to the disparate streams of demand for change in the telecommunications industry. The traditional regulatory standards of "public interest" and "public necessity and convenience" of the 1934 Act were replaced by "maximum feasible reliance on competition" to sustain the objectives of the new Act. The new CRC would be the arbiter in deciding which services were competitive or noncompetitive and thus subject to limited or no regulation. However, the bill did not specify any criteria for such a distinction. Interconnections were required between the Bell system network and its non-Bell competitors thus overriding AT&T's reluctance to grant competitors access to the local and intercity network.

Under the rewrite bill, AT&T would also have been required to divest Western Electric, its equipment manufacturing arm, and thus further loosen AT&T's lock on the terminal equipment industry. However, as if to offer AT&T a trade-off, the bill would have lifted the restrictions of the 1956 Consent Decree, which prohibited AT&T's participation in activities incidental to telecommunications (such as cable television and data processing services). Thus AT&T would have lost shares in some markets but would have been able to be a competitor in some new markets. By giving AT&T unfettered entry into ancillary activities, by forcing the divestiture of AT&T's manufacturing arm, by deregulating rates in all competitive services, and by authorizing full and open entry into specialized private line and long distance services, the bill was effectively restructuring the telecommunications industry. As a substitute for the Bell system separations and settlements procedures for cost allocation and sharing, the bill required all intercity carriers to pay an access charge for connecting to local exchange switching facilities. The implication of the bill was that the CRC would declare or classify interstate, long distance telephone service to be a competitive service with open entry and thus the traditional separations and settlement process would not be sufficient or necessarily operative. Under the proposed bill, rates for competitive services were not to be regulated and were to be presumed to be equitably determined by market forces. Obviously, in such a competitive environment, AT&T would not be able to singularly burden its long-distance rates with the special subsidies which were allegedly incorporated into the separations and settlement procedures.

Thus the traditional provisions made by the Bell System for national rate averaging and subsidization of high-cost service areas would no longer pertain under the new competitive arrangements. The bill's provision for a universal service compensation fund (USCF) was an acknowledgment that absent the separations and settlement arrangement, intrastate toll service and local service rates would rise. In short, the USCF was the proposed answer to the problem of ensuring universal service under conditions of competition. However, the bill offered no specifics on how the fund would be operated or what companies or individuals would be its beneficiaries.

The bill was similarly vague with regard to other major provisions. In an apparent determination to establish competition unequivocally as the governing principle of telecommunications practices and regulation, the bill imposed competition as the criterion for both triggering an otherwise dormant or secondary regulatory function and for evaluating all issues in areas requiring regulatory attention. However, neither the primary elements on which competition was established, nor the principles of promoting and relying on competition were deemed sufficient by some experts for realizing the goals of the Act or for enabling the new CRC to carry out its expected function. These points were made bluntly in testimony by FCC chairman Charles Ferris. Ferris's comments highlight not only the great difficulty of establishing competition as the new regulatory standard but also the difficulty of establishing any new regulatory standard in a mature industry:

I see four main areas where further discussion or clarification is needed. They are: the definition of markets; the meaning of market deficiencies, or, the other side of the coin, workable competition; the meaning of equitable and affordable as used in rate-related proceedings; and lastly, the division of Federal and non-Federal jurisdiction.

The threshold economic issue raised by the proposed act is: Which markets or submarkets should the Commission regulate? The legislation would give the Commission authority to set up separate regulatory schemes for competitive and noncompetitive services, and would allow the Commission to make the basic determination that a particular market is one requiring regulation because "market forces are deficient." Because of this we must take a hard look at the criteria for defining competitive and noncompetitive markets.

Regulation under the bill is preceded by a two-step process: (1) Defining the market, and (2) determining whether it is noncompetitive. The history of enforcement of antitrust laws establishes the difficulties of defining markets for public policy purposes. Whether or not a market is noncompetitive often turns on the activities or services defined as constituting that market as well as on the market shares of particular competitors. The problems of making a competitive determination are central to achieving the purpose of the bill, since the Commission's authority to use any regulatory tools ultimately depends on a finding that market forces are deficient in a given market. . . .

In establishing ratemaking standards, the bill uses language which is different from that in the 1934 act. The public interest touchstone of the 1934 act is deleted. No other broad standard is substituted. The traditional just and reasonable rate standard and the prohibition of unjust or unreasonable discrimination in rates or practices are eliminated. A regulatory standard of affordable and equitable rates is used in their place. Affordable and equitable are not yet defined. They have no clear and established meanings in the telecommunications field.[2]

Here we see what appears to be a paradox in which intended specificity in a piece of legislation is judged to be not only insufficient, but effectively meaningless, wherein a vague and supposedly outdated standard is preferable to attempted specificity in establishing a new standard. Although these new criteria could be defined eventually by the CRC and the courts, there was no anchoring standard within the proposed law on which the commission could base its actions until these new criteria could be given settled meaning in telecommunications policy and regulation.

The intentions of the bill sponsors regarding the traditional role played by state PUCs in regulating local service and intrastate toll rates were not clear. There was no mention of a state role regarding matters of rates or an explicit assertion that all rates would be determined at the federal level. The apparent intention, and certainly the implication, was that rates for competitive services would be determined by market forces. However, in the crucial areas of essentially noncompetitive local rates, the bill was silent. The NARUC, the organization of state regulators, naturally expressed alarm over this omission, charging that the bill effectively granted federal authorities power over all intrastate rates and emasculated the rights of states to oversee intrastate rates. Richard A. Elkin, President of the NARUC, argued that the authority to oversee intrastate rates was the most potent weapon for defending the preservation of universal service. The failure of the bill to mention any role for federal-state Joint Board procedures was taken as further proof of the elimination of the states' role in telecommunications regulation. The Joint Board, comprised of three FCC commissioners and four state commissioners nominated by NARUC, was created by a special act in 1971. This act provided for the mandatory convocation of a joint board in matters pertaining to the jurisdictional separation of common carrier property and expenses between interstate and intrastate operations or any other matters relating to common carrier communications of joint federal and state concern. The NARUC complaint predicted that the elimination of a state regulatory role in telecommunications would lead to significantly higher rates for basic residential service and the loss of such service by many Americans.[3]

Judging by the testimony given by the chairman of the FCC and the president of NARUC, one can conclude that neither federal nor state regulators believed that the rewrite bill was an adequate or satisfactory replacement for the 1934 Act. The FCC agreed with the principle of establishing competition as a clear policy goal but deemed the proposed act ineffective in providing a standard for implementing the principle. The NARUC complaint was that state regulators had been left out of the regulatory scheme. These two deficits in the proposed bill effectively rendered it a moot issue barring a major rewrite of the rewrite bill.

Interestingly, the position of AT&T with regard to competition in the telecommunications industry had changed considerably since 1976, when it supported legislation designed to prohibit competition. In a written statement submitted for the record and given at the time of his oral testimony on the rewrite bill, Vice Chairman of the Board, William M. Ellinghaus, stated that

the question today is not whether there should or should not be competition in telecommunications. That has been settled. Competition is a fact of life in the industry in terminal equipment, in intercity private line services, and in manufacturing and supply.

The question is one of balance. I am convinced that there are areas in telecommunications where the benefits of competition lag the benefits, to society as a whole, of regulated monopoly.[4]

With regard to the continuing need for some components of the industry to be maintained as a unified, regulated monopoly, Ellinghaus referred to the public switched network on which universally available basic telephone service was dependent, on which much of the Bell system was based:

What is crucial for further progress, in my view, is that there continue to be, at the core of the information infrastructure in this nation, a basic telecommunications network designed and managed as one entity. Such a core network, a nationwide public network, can serve to link an infinite variety of specialized services offered by a wide range of suppliers, I might add, and yet the indiscriminate interspersion of specialized carriers in the public switched network as contemplated by the bill can serve only to fragment, not enhance responsibility for the efficient, reliable functioning of that network.[5]

Ellinghaus also decried the absence of a public interest standard in the rewrite bill as well as the absence of a state regulatory role, both of which he deemed crucial to maintaining universal service. He offered a prescient and expansive statement about the concept of universal service in the emerging new world of communications services: "Looking at the future, however, the concept of universality takes on a much broader meaning. We look forward to the prospect of extending throughout our society a wide diversity of communications services matched to the individual needs of the American people and the institutions that serve them."[6] This was a very interesting statement in a debate that would soon shift to an explicit definition of universal service as the availability of basic, totally unenhanced voice telephone service.

Although AT&T's apparent acceptance of competition in telecommunications might have been genuine, its competitors were not persuaded. The position of Telenet, for example, was that the bill seemed to assume that with Congress having decreed a policy of competition, it would then be sufficient for the commission simply to step back and let it happen. Telenet argued that given the dominance of the established common carriers in monoploy markets and their freedom to participate in new markets, competition would not just happen, but would have to be implemented. There was particular concern that AT&T would cross-subsidize its competitive services from its monopoly service revenue base; that it would structure its tariffs (fees and charges) selectively to damage or drive out the competition; or that it would discriminate against one class of customers or one set of geographic locations over another within the same tariff.[7] The position of the Ad Hoc Committee for Competition in Telecommunications (ACCT) was even more pointed. ACCT requested a three to five-year transitional period to arrive at a truly free, fair, and competitive environment. During this period, the CRC would retain some of the old regulatory powers of the FCC which would permit the commission to suspend, reject, and prescribe rates for various telecommunications services.[8] Thus the new entrants to the telecommunications industry sought to add a broader dimension to the policymaking task. They desired not just a policy which legally permitted competition, but one which structured the path to competition and ensured its implementation while retaining regulatory constraints on the established common carriers.

PRESCRIBING POLICY FOR AN UNKNOWN CIRCUMSTANCE

Although there was general consensus on the desirability of retaining universal service, there were mixed opinions on the desirability and necessity of the proposed access charges and the universal service compensation fund, which the access charges were designed to support. There was some concern that the bill was silent about how access charges were to be calculated and that it was silent as well with regard to guidelines concerning how the fund would be administered. However, the greater source of concern about the access charges and the fund was the lack of confidence in the assertion that the Bell system separations and settlement procedures actually existed, or that they functioned to maintain nationwide averaged toll rates and affordable local service rates. (The separations and settlement arrangement was credited with transferring revenues from the interstate long distance market to the intrastate market and to rural, high-cost areas, thereby offsetting the cost of local service and ensuring universal service.) AT&T and the independents consistently made assertions about the objectives and significance of the separations and settlement procedures, but their assertions were just as consistently disparaged. Past and current members of the FCC made statements in testimony that either disparaged the claims of the separations and settlement procedures or further confused the issue.

In testimony on the rewrite bill, former chairman of the FCC, Dean Burch, chided the subcommittee for tacitly accepting the proposition that rate averaging existed and that it was beneficial to the public. He further chided them for accepting the proposition that interstate facilities subsidized local exchange facilities. Burch declared both of these arguments unproven. He thus characterized the provision for the USCF as amounting to "telecare," to be perceived as a basis for compensating every telephone company for every dollar lost for whatever reason.[9] The Chairman of MCI, William McGowan, asserted that the Department of Justice had found the separations process to be "a shell game."[10] The numerous disparagements of the separations and settlement procedures were challenged in a statement by Paul Henson, Chairman of United Telecommunications, Inc. Henson's remarks carried a strong ring of plausibility:

It is not a welfare fund for the independent telephone industry. It is simply a sharing of costs and revenues, recognizing the investment and costs of each participating element of an integrated network. It is nothing more than an accounting procedure.

Some now claim that this is the telephone industry's way of distributing welfare payments to those who need welfare. This is a gross misrepresentation. These separation procedures were approved by both the federal communication commission and the NARUC. State regulators and federal legislators, not the telephone industry, designed and adopted these practices and principles.

The fact that we allocate a considerable amount of local exchange plant to the interstate jurisdiction is simply the recognition by federal and state regulators of the economics of scale and technology in the provision of interstate services. They have decided, therefore, that interstate services should help support the costs of the local exchange network.[11]

Were Henson's claims accurate? In the 1976 exploratory hearings, FCC chairman Wiley had testified that the commission expected that a competitive market for terminal equipment and private line services would result in economic effects which would alter the division of revenues between interstate and intrastate operations and which might require regulatory intervention in the interest of the general ratepayer. He indicated that the commission had proposed changes in the separations procedures for consideration by the Joint Board so that the distribution of interstate revenues to local exchange services would remain unaffected by competition. Chairman Wiley had made these remarks almost as an aside despite the cruciality of this issue to the major policy determinations Congress was seeking to make. Buried deep within the final eight pages of a 148-page report on the development of FCC policies regarding telecommunications (which was entered into the official record by chairman Wiley) was a section that explained the jurisdictional separations and settlements procedures. This FCC report indicated that the separations procedures were initially and formally set forth in a *1947 Separations Manual*, with an update and revision of the procedures as late as 1971. The responsibility for creation, codification, and modification of the separations procedures was attributed jointly to the NARUC and the FCC.[12]

That the separations procedures would continue to be disparaged and even denied by some as late as 1978 during a crucial period of policy formulation was testimony to the ideological tone of much of the debate over the prospect of competition in the telecommunications industry. Supporters of competition simply announced it as an imperative driven by the twin forces of technology and the tradition of the American free enterprise system. Opponents of competion depicted themselves as the protectors of the public interest and defenders of the residential ratepayers against the special interests of big business. At the beginning of the debates, AT&T and some of the independents had attacked the FCC and had "told on them to Congress." This was done in a manner which contributed to the FCC being more of an active and partisan participant in the policy struggle than an official arbiter responsible for defining and protecting the public interest. Consequently, there was an obscuring of some issues due to the offensive and defensive postures assumed by the key parties. The question of the impact of competition on residential ratepayers was one which some parties simply preferred to avoid. However, the validity of the assertions regarding the functions and significance of the separations procedures was directly linked to the question of whether special provisions would have to be made to preserve universal service in the postmonopoly, newly competitive world of telecommunications. That question eventually would emerge as the pivotal policy question confronting Congress, and numerous legislative proposals would be introduced to address this issue. That phase of the policy debate is addressed in Chapter 7.

THE INEFFICACY OF CONSUMER INPUT

Despite the clear cruciality of the debate on the rewrite bill to the interests of residential ratepayers, such consumer interests were not well represented at these hearings. Thus, there were no strong consumer interest responses to such critical issues as the proposed elimination of state-level regulation of telephone services and the establishment of the USCF. Consumer groups testifying at the hearings included the National Rural Center, the Communications Institute of Boulder, Colorado, and the National Citizens Communications Lobby.

The National Rural Center was identified as "an independent, nonprofit corporation established to develop policy alternatives and provide information which can help rural people improve the quality of life for themselves and their communities." The National Rural Center was concerned about a number of issues in the rewrite bill, including provisions affecting cable TV, broadcast radio, etc. The primary concern expressed in regard to telecommunications issues involved questions about the adminstration of a proposed rural telecommunications loan program, which was to be established within the national telecommunications agency. The concern was the relationship between the proposed loan program and the existing loan program operated under the Rural Electrification Administration (REA). The rewrite bill did not include provisions for terminating the REA loan program (which had provided very low-interest loans to build the telecommunications facilities of most of the independent telcos serving rural areas) or a repeal of the enabling legislation establishing the REA program. The bill did not link the proposed loan program to the issue of preserving universal service in rural areas.[13] The testimony given by the representative of the National Citizens Communications Lobby was restricted to issues of radio and TV broadcasting.[14]

The Communications Institute of Boulder was identified as "a nonprofit corporation devoted to the research and development of humanistic approaches to telecommunications technology, and the promotion of the expanded role of citizens in communications and telecommunications policymaking." The Institute representative expressed general support for the goal of competition in telecommunications but otherwise focused his testimony on an elaborate plan to enhance citizen participation in telecommunications policymaking. The Institute's argument was that only those few citizens groups with substantial funds and paid lobbyists had been successful in participating in policymaking activities. Thus the Institute plan was to have the CRC members appointed on the basis of geographic areas, with each of ten commissioners representing geographic districts of equal population. Each district commissioner would have full authority in all policy matters affecting his or her district. The district commissioners would chair regional advisory committees comprised of representatives from each state within each region. Citizen committees would be established as needed to advise the regional advisory committees. The Institute's representative went on to outline a dozen potentially desirable effects of utilizing citizen committees.[15]

Except for the testimony provided by the representative of the National Citizens Communications Lobby, the testimony from the other two citizens/consumer groups on the rewrite bill was not likely to have much effect on the debate. In the aforementioned instances, the representatives "testified amiss." Neither presented solid positions on specific issues being addressed by the legislation under consideration. Although the issue of citizen participation was a significant one, the proposal presented by the Communications Institute represented such a stark departure from conventional governmental arrangements that it was dismissed by the subcommittee. H.R. 13015 did contain a provision for greater citizen participation in telecommunications policymaking via an Office of Consumer Assistance within the CRC. The proposed Office of Consumer Asistance was charged with assuring that consumer interests were considered by the commission in the formulation of policies, rulemaking, and other administrative proceedings; publishing materials to inform consumers of matters of import to their interests; and assessing the impact of commission actions on consumers.

HOW H.R. 13015 SHAPED THE POLICY DEBATE

With the question of whether to have competition in telecommunications decided if not settled, the debate on H.R. 13015 had shifted to a question of how to accommodate competition via official policy. At this point, the prevailing consensus was that it was necessary for Congress to take actions to legitimate a new telecommunications policy based on competition. Although the FCC had initiated a policy of competition, its ability to initiate a more expansive policy was constrained by compelling questions of the legitimacy of its role in this regard,as well as by its limited statutory authority as a regulatory agency. For example, it was not clear that the FCC could singularly deregulate the telecommunications industry,or that could it singularly force the divestiture of AT&T. The FCC's actions had served to open the door to competition in a way which greatly empowered the principle of competition as a formative policy idea in telecommunications. Thus Congress was now being pressed to implement the policy idea of competition via statutory provisions.

There were three main contrasting and contending views of the prospect of a telecommunications policy based on competition. One view was held by AT&T, which was uniquely, though clearly not objectively, able to see the whole universe of telecommunications—the local Bell telcos, the independents, and the specialized common carriers—and could see its position atop this universe being diminished. AT&T was now arguing for maintenance of a unified, national public switching network as the core of a superior national telecommunications system which would be centrally managed and planned. AT&T argued that such an arrangement was truly in the best interest of the entire nation. State regulators and some independent telcos argued that a shift to competition carried the certainty of major rate increases for basic residential telephone service and therefore posed a sure threat to universal service. They saw protection of the residential ratepayer and preservation of the universal availability of basic telephone service as defining elements in any policy which would lay claim to being implemented in the public interest. The specialized common carriers and other new entrants based their demands on new technologies and the capability of that new technology to provide a host of new services to businesses and institutions. Their demands were buttressed by linking them to the venerable American traditions of free enterprise and the unfettered use of technology in the service of enhancing social and economic development.

Although it would not be enacted into law, the rewrite bill was a starting point in formulating a new telecommunications policy. Congress had attempted to formulate a policy which not only gave primacy to competition but which established it as a new regulatory standard. There are two main sources of difficulty in this line of policymaking. A major source of difficulty was inherent in the necessary attempt to legislate competition. Competition as a policy idea was on target in terms of the demands and sentiments which gave momentum to the debate, and it was an idea which captured congressional interest. However, there were major obstacles to endowing this policy idea with the substantive meaning and legal rigor which was necessary to pursue a purposive course of action. For example, not only was competition likely to be slow in coming to an industry long dominated by a monopoly, but the presence of two or three providers of a particular service would not automatically make for a competitive market for that service. Ironically, what was needed was a policy that permitted and ensured competition without the necessity of defining it.

A second obstacle to establishing a policy based on a new standard of competition was inherent in the difficulties of legislating in a mature policy area, especially when the attempt was to enact and implement a wholly new "basement to attic" policy. The congressional subcommittee failed to appreciate that public policy comes not just from a piece of legislation passed by Congress, but is rather a cumulative process that results in a cumulative mass. Particularly in the area of regulation, policy accumulates from years of enforcement under a piece of legislation; from promulgation of numerous administrative rules, inquiries, and specific rulings; from judicial decisions; and from compromises and adjustments by key players in a given policy arena. Any effort to rewrite policy in a mature policy area thus faces a serious challenge in which nullification of all existing policy could create chaos, and attempts to substitute definitive new provisions to fill all of the functions of existing policy deemed worthy of retention and to establish new policy initiatives as well become a task of enormous magnitude.

A third obstacle that was apparent from a first-hand reading of the record of the congressional hearings was that the House Communications Subcommittee was attempting to assert policy leadership over an unfamiliar terrain. The subcommittee was not expert in telecommunications issues as they had developed over time. It was not knowledgeable about the intricacies of the structure and operations of the telecommunications industry. Most important, it was not knowledgeable about how a whole landscape of foundational ground had been laid over the years by the FCC and court rulings that gave interpretations and meanings to varied elements of the 1934 Act. In short, Congress might have possessed the official constitutional and statutory policymaking prerogative, but Congress was an interloper of sorts, and an uninformed one.

FOCUSING POLICYMAKING INITIATIVES: PROGRESS AND REDUNDANCY

Judging from the explicit and implicit sentiments expressed in the hearings regarding H.R. 13015, nobody (other than the bill's sponsors perhaps) expected that this legislation would become law. Rather, the bill was seen as a starting point in structuring the debate. However, given that the subcommittee, and especially its chairman, Van Deerlin, had committed to a "basement to attic" rewrite of the 1934 Communications Act, it was not surprising that the effort to legislate new policy would continue. In early 1979, Van Deerlin cosponsored a second bill, H.R. 3333, the Communications Act of 1979.

Using as a backdrop the preceding discussion of the initial efforts to rewrite telecommunications policy, we are now in a unique position to observe the committee's efforts to refocus its policy formulation in response to feedback and insights obtained from the first round of hearings. Utilizing this perspective also enables us to assess the emergence and evolution of policy ideas and to witness the ongoing development of the policy debate.

The 1979 bill continued with an emphasis on competition as the prevailing policy, with regulation being utilized only to the extent that market forces were deficient. The attempt to define competition was dropped. However, the bill breached the murky mire again with a requirement that the CRC classify carriers engaged in interexchange (or interstate) telecommunications service and regulate the activities of dominant carriers. (The relevant market for determining dominance included all interexchange telecommunications services, not just a submarket such as MTS, private line services, etc.). If a carrier was found to be a dominant carrier, CRC regulation would extend to all services provided by that carrier. The bill anticipated that only AT&T would be classified as a dominant carrier. Elimination of the term *common carrier* was characterized as an attempt to displace the various common-law attributes of common carriage. Only interexchange services of the dominant carrier were to be regulated. All other interexchange services by other carriers were to be deregulated. The bill looked to the long-term total deregulation of all interexchange services, because after ten years there would be no dominant carriers for the purposes of the act.[16] The sponsors of the bill obviously assumed that they were laying the groundwork for the flourishing of competition and envisioned a world in which the need for all regulation of interstate services would end.

The significant thing about H.R. 3333 was that by confining regulation to the dominant carrier, it sought to deregulate the activities of the new entrants to the telecommunications industry as a means of spurring competition. H.R. 3333 also proposed access charges and extended such charges to local subscribers as well as interexchange carriers seeking to utilize the exchange or local networks. As a reflection of the continuing ambivalence about the impact of competition on local service rates, the universal service compensation fund were dropped. Pooling of revenues from the access fees were to be done at the state level as a replacement for the old system of separations and settlements procedures and to offset any undue rise in local rates. In contrast to the first rewrite bill, H.R. 3333 did not require the divestiture of Western Electric; it only required that AT&T deal with Western Electric on an arms-length basis and permit it to provide equipment to other telcos as well. The bill also permitted independent local telcos to enter new markets under state regulation without having to establish separate subsidiaries. The expressed need for management of the core public switching network was to be carried out by meetings and/or an association between telecommunications carriers.[17]

It is not clear that the 1979 legislation was an improvement over the initial rewrite effort of 1978. Both bills contributed to structuring the broad contours of a policy for a shift to full-fledged competition in interstate services. However, the debate had not yet yielded clarity nor a generalized consensus on a set of critical issues such as how best to facilitate competion, how best to facilitate the maintenance of universal service, and how to ensure against cross-subsidization by AT&T. However, H.R. 3333 did not become law, thus ensuring the continuation of the telecommunications policy debate.

In an apparent effort to sustain momentum and the initiative in rewriting telecommunications policy, representatives Van Deerlin and James Broyhill of the Communications Subcommittee of the House Committee on Interstate and Foreign Commerce introduced a third policy iteration, H.R. 6121. This bill was introduced on December 10, 1979 and became known as the Telecommunications Act of 1980. H.R. 6121 represented a significant departure from previous subcommittee proposals in that subcommittee chairman Van Deerlin had abandoned his "basement-to-attic" approach in rewriting telecommunications policy and had decided instead to focus on amending the 1934 Communications Act to deal exclusively with matters of domestic telecommunmications policy. Two other legislative proposals introduced in the Senate in March 1979, S. 611 and S. 622, had been put forward as amendments to the 1934 Act; this suggested something of a consensus on the need to refocus congressional efforts on more urgent policy issues and to pursue a more focused and manageable legislative task. H.R. 6121 also abandoned efforts to change the name of the FCC and the internal structure of the organization. The FCC would remain as it had been authorized under the 1934 Act.

H.R. 6121 carried a heavy emphasis on deregulation and continued the focus on efforts to redirect the regulatory function as a means of spurring competition and as a means of reshaping the telecommunications industry. The bill set aside part of the 1956 Consent Decree, which had barred AT&T from participating in unregulated markets. Under H.R. 6121, any dominant carrier could offer any services, facilities, and products incidental to telecommunications on a deregulated or unregulated basis if done through a separate subsidiary with a cost accounting system which ensured against cross-subsidization. The legislation anticipated that only AT&T would be classified as a dominant carrier. Thus, under this legislation AT&T could enter new, unregulated markets. However, the dominant carrier was prohibited from offering any electronic alarm services, cable TV, mass media, or mass media product. The prohibition was designed to keep major telecommunications carriers out of the basic activities of newspapers and cable TV providers. The dominant carrier could provide facilities to others on a nondiscriminatory basis for the provision of such services. Other carriers without significant market power were to be deregulated completely with regard to all of their activities, thus ending FCC regulation of the entire telecommunications industry.

The FCC was specifically prohibited from regulating data processing services. The research activities of Bell Laboratories were to be conducted under contract only and on an auditable basis. Contract charges were to be charged to the various Bell entities to avoid cross-subsidization of any unregulated activities. AT&T was required to file with the FCC information on the physical and electric characteristics of the regulated network at points of interconnection with the Bell system for provision of services. The bill supported full competition in long-distance services, but to preserve universal service at affordable rates, the proposed legislation required telcos to continue offering basic local and long-distance service on a fully regulated basis.

Although the separation and settlement procedures figured prominently in the debate over telecommunications policy and resulting policy solutions, there was continuing ambivalence about the contribution of this process to the preservation of universal service. In offering a rationale for the uses of access fees, the following quote from the subcommittee report accompanying H.R. 6121 not only reflects this ambivalence but also suggests something of a general discounting of the separations process in rate equalization:

Following the Supreme Court's decision striking down board-to-board cost separation (Smith v. Illinois Bell Telephone Co., 282 U.S. 133 [1930]), long distance traffic has been required to bear a portion of local distribution costs. The system which has developed since that time is known as Separations and Settlements (or "division of revenues" among Bell System entities). The System is controlled by established carriers, primarily AT&T, with minimal regulatory supervision. It is characterized by a tenuous relation to actual cost causation, result orientation, a mixing of economics and social policy subsidies, and incentives for inefficient capital investment. Moreover, it was designed to serve the needs of carriers, which for the most part did not compete with each other. Through this system flow billions of dollars each year.

The Committee has determined that no one knows precisely what the costs of various classes of service are, or the size or direction of subsidies. This view was confirmed by a report from the Commission's Office of Plans and Policy early this year. The Committee believes, however, that it is critical that these facts be determined for competition and deregulation to succeed, and for the continuance of local service at reasonable and affordable rates.[18]

Nonetheless, H.R. 6121 provided for a system of access fees which would take the place of the separations and settlements procedures. Access fees would compensate intraexchange carriers for the direct, traffic-sensitive costs of interconnecting interexchange carriers and would contribute to the fixed costs of jointly used plant. Access fees would also provide revenues to subsidize local service rates where they exceeded the national average. The bill incorporated a return to the idea of a special fund supported by access fees to provide subsidies to needy telcos. A National Telecommunications Pool (NTP) was proposed to ensure that local and long-distance rates did not go up "substantially or unduly." The NTP was to consist of three accounts: (1) an account to compensate small telcos serving 50,000 or fewer main stations for any costs of service above 110 percent of the national average; (2) an account to compensate any telco for which the costs of interconnecting with the long-distance networks exceeded 110 percent of the national average (companies serving Alaska and Hawaii were expected to fall into this category); and (3) a transitional account to compensate any local telco in making up the difference between what it received under the separation procedures and revenues received from the access charges. The bill further provided for the deregulation of terminal equipment and the removal of its cost from the rate base as a way of protecting the ratepayer from the costs of competition in the sale of equipment. However, in something of an offsetting provision, the bill also provided for the phasing out of revenues earned from yellow pages advertising from the local rate base. This would mean the possible loss of a revenue stream which would have to be made up by the ratepayers.

H R. 6121 anticipated the need for new and flexible regulatory arrangements to shepherd the domestic telecommunications industry into a new era of substantial competition, substantial deregulation, and substantial restructuring envisioned by the bill sponsors. A special Transitional Joint Board consisting of three members of the FCC and two state regulators was given interim regulatory authority to

1. Oversee the establishment of local or interexchange boundaries
2. Establish rules to implement deregulation of terminal equipment
3. Change the separations and settlement procedure as necessary to facilitate the transition to access fees
4. Determine the percentage of non-traffic sensitive costs to be recovered from interexchange services
5. Oversee the phasing out of revenues from printed directory advertising (the Yellow Pages) from rate bases.[19]

The Transitional Joint Board represented a significant heightening of participation of state-level regulators in national level regulation. Traditionally, the Joint Board had served in an advisory capacity to the FCC on a generally sporadic basis.

Overall, H.R. 6121 represented the restoration of the policymaking initiatives of the House Communications Subcommittee. The bill clearly built on earlier legislative efforts and the feedback obtained in hearings on earlier bills. Judging from the choices and directions taken in this bill, the overlap with proposals set forth by the FCC, and the absence of discussions in the hearings records of many specifics incorporated in this bill in the hearings record, one is left to conclude that the subcommittee and its staff apparently engaged in behind-the-scenes efforts to develop a broadly acceptable legislative proposal. This is just one example of the virtual impossibility of capturing the totality of interactions and dynamics which comprise the policy debate and the policymaking process.

MULTIPLE CHECKS ON POLICYMAKING INITIATIVES

H.R. 6121 was not to become law and at least part of the specific causes which contributed to the failure of this bill is discernible from the record. H.R. 6121 converged with the ripening of the Department of Justice (DOJ) antitrust lawsuit which had been pending against AT&T since 1974. The bill also converged with some issues of turf with regard to the legislative jurisdiction and concerns of the House Judiciary Committee.

Representative Peter Rodino, chairman of the House Judiciary Committee, had written to Harley Staggers, chairman of the full House Interstate and Foreign Commerce Committee, expressing concern about the antitrust issues in H.R. 6121, particularly the lifting of critical portions of the 1956 Consent Decree. Rodino had sent a second letter to Representative Van Deerlin, who chaired the Communications Subcommittee, in which he detailed substantial concerns and offered suggestions to lessen the negative impact of the bill on the ongoing antitrust litigation. Rodino's urgings and suggestions were generally not accepted at either committee level. However, upon its favorable report out of the full Commerce Committee, instead of scheduling the bill for floor debate, the Speaker of the House referred H. R. 6121 to the Judiciary Committee.

The subcommittee on Monopolies and Commercial Law of the House Judiciary Committee held hearings on September 9 and September 16, 1980 during which seventeen individuals testified in person and fifteen others submitted written testimony. Testifying in support of H.R. 6121 were its original sponsors, Van Deerlin and Broyhill, the Assistant Secretary of Commerce for Communication, and AT&T. A written statement of support was submitted by the International Communications Workers union. Testifying against the bill were the chair of the FCC, a former Attorney General, two former chiefs of the FCC Common Carrier Bureau, the Director of the Federal Trade Commission's Bureau of Competition, Consumers Union, two members of the House Commerce Committee, and several of AT&T's competitors.

On September 25, 1980, the Subcommittee on Monopolies and Commercial Law adversely reported H.R. 6121 to the full Judiciary Committee, which in turn adversely reported the bill to the full House on September 30. The thrust of the Judiciary Committee's report was that the bill was so defective that it would have emerged as an entirely new bill to overcome the concerns of that committee. Reflecting support for major portions of the bill, the Judiciary Committee reported the bill without prejudice, meaning that the committee left open the door to consideration of a similar bill in the next session of Congress.[20] However, the long-running legislative initiatives of the House Communciations Subcommittee had been checked. Any successful legislation on the House side would have to be a joint effort involving the House Judiciary Committee, and any successful legislation would have to await introduction in a new session of Congress.

COMPETING INSTITUTIONAL THRUSTS

The issues raised and solutions set forth in H.R. 6121 did not see a demise with the death of this legislative proposal. In May 1980, between the December 1979 introduction of H.R. 6121 and its September 1980 demise, the FCC issued its *Computer Inquiry II Ruling.* In the *Computer II Decision,* the FCC abandoned the practice of requiring the traditional common carriers to submit tariffs (rates) for customer premise equipment (CPE) for FCC approval. This had the effect of totally deregulating the CPE market. The new interconnect companies were already able to offer CPE without seeking FCC approval of charges for such equipment. The ruling required that AT&T establish a wholly separate subsidiary for the provision of CPE. AT&T complied by establishing a separate subsidiary, named AT&T Information Systems, Inc. The other common carriers were required to establish strict accounting practices which separated regulated from unregulated activities in a manner which was readily auditable. In both cases, the FCC was acting to ensure against cross-subsidization of unregulated, competitive activities from regulated activities, the latter having a guaranteed rate of return. The *Computer II Decision* also applied to the provision of enhanced interstate communications services or those incorporating some aspects of computer or data processing. A sizeable cadre of new entrants referred to as value-added networks (VANs) or value-added carriers had emerged in this service area, leasing private line circuits from common carriers, adding new components in the preparation and transmission of data, and reselling these new services to the public. In authorizing these new entrants in 1973 the FCC had spurred competion in the telecommunications industry but had later determined that they were common carriers subject to regulation under the 1934 Act. The *Computer II Decision* lifted regulation of providers of enhanced services.

The significance of the *Computer II Decision* should not be overlooked. First, with this decision the FCC had assumed a major expansion of its traditionally defined role. It had shifted from the role of regulator to the role of active deregulator. To many observers, the FCC did not have the authority to deregulate under its existing statutory mandate, the 1934 Communications Act. This action by the FCC added to ongoing questions of the legitimacy of its policies. Over thirty court petitions were eventually filed against the *Computer II Decision* challenging FCC authority to deregulate and/or lift the 1956 Consent Decree. The *Computer II Decision* was later upheld in federal court.[21] Although Congress was viewed by many as the sole institution with the authority to deregulate even portions of the telecommunications industry, the FCC had seized the initiative (which had been proposed in H.R. 6121). Moreover, the *Computer II Decision* effectively lifted the constraints which had been imposed on AT&T by the *1956 Consent Decree*, which had restricted AT&T to offering only regulated common carrier activities. Within the terms of this agreement, AT&T had been able to continue to offer CPE as a part of its common carrier services packages, thus retaining its near monopoly on CPE. The third important aspect of the *Computer II Decision* was the severing or unbundling of the cost of transmission services from the cost of equipment with regard to deregulation of CPE. This meant that the rate base for basic telephone service would be affected and that consumers would be able to purchase telephone sets and other equipment from a host of vendors. This was the first step in what would later become a major policy of unbundling and repricing telecommunications services and equipment.

DEREGULATION AS A NEW POLICY THEME

In June 1981, the Senate Committee on Commerce, Science, and Transportation opened hearings on S. 898, the Telecommunications Competition and Deregulation Act of 1981. The congressional policy initiative had at least temporarily shifted to the U.S. Senate. In March 1979, members of the Senate committee had introduced two bills, S. 611 and S. 622 to amend the Communications Act of 1934 to provide for increased competition, deregulation of terminal equipment, etc. The committee had held combined hearings on both bills, receiving testimony from 171 witnesses. It had then utilized input from these extensive hearings to craft a third bill, S. 2827, which was introduced in June 1980. There were no hearings held on S. 2827. When S. 898 was introduced the Senate committee had by then benefited from feedback from its own bills as well as earlier House bills. Thus, much of the chaff of the debate had been swept aside by an emerging consensus, which served to refine and narrow the focus of the debate. With the shift to the Senate had also come the full flowering of the notion of deregulation. The title of S. 898 sought to convey unambiguously the committee's intention. Deregulation was thus set forth as a defining concept which focused the committee's efforts and helped to focus and structure the terms of the policy debate.

Deregulation had emerged as a phrase in the telecommunications policy debate as early as 1978 but obtained full form as a strategic concept after the 1980 election of President Ronald Reagan. Deregulation was an overarching strategy and theme of the first-term Reagan presidency. Degulation in effect became the overarching new policy theme, defining the major problem of government—too much regulation—and offering the solution—a major diminution of the federal regulatory role. The long-running debate over telecommunications policy fit well within this strategic and conceptual framework.

The Senate committee clearly felt that they were riding the crest of a new momentum with respect to deregulation. In his opening remarks, Senator Robert Packwood indicated that the committee intended to do everything to lessen the regulation of the communications industry. Other members of the committee were boastful of their past record of deregulation and eager to undertake the challenge of telecommunications deregulation. Senator Howard Cannon alluded to the committee's proud record of reducing federal regulation in virtually every field over which it had jurisdiction. The committee had deregulated railroads; it had deregulated trucking over the objections of the American Trucking Association and the Teamsters; and it had deregulated airlines over the objections of the Air Transport Association.[22] Telecommunications deregulation was seen as another challenge for the committee and an opportunity for it to take charge of a policy debate which had already dragged on for some five years.

Although the legislative initiative had apparently shifted to the U.S. Senate and much of the debate had been narrowed to a few questions of how best to implement competition, one thing which had not changed was the desire by members of congress to set telecommunications policy themselves and not leave this effort to the FCC or the courts. In a series of opening statements, several members of the committee spoke to this point. Senator Packwood held that without the enactment of a new congressional policy to guide the FCC in its efforts to cope with changing technology, a continuation of disruptive regulatory and court proceedings would not only delay the delivery of new services but would drive up their costs. Senator Barry Goldwater asserted that there was a clear consensus that Congress should pass a bill that was in the national interest and that "we cannot leave these matters to the FCC or the courts." Senator Harrison Schmitt expressed his concern that Congress should act lest "the FCC and the courts will continue to make policy without considering the broad social and policy implications for our nation."

Indeed, one of the findings in the introductory section of the bill was that "decisions of the Courts and the Commission (the FCC) have indicated a clear need for congressional guidance." However, there was substantial disagreement on whether Congress should take the lead. The hearings opened with strong references to the reluctance of the Reagan administration to take a position on S. 898, a reluctance attributed to the influence of the Department of Justice (DOJ). The DOJ took the position that Congress should take no action until the DOJ finished its longstanding antitrust suit against AT&T. Senator Goldwater pointed out (in comments to the chairman of the FCC) that the Secretary of Defense had asked DOJ to drop its suit against AT&T because of the harm which might come to the nation's defense as a result of the antitrust suit.[23] There had been suggestions that the Department of Defense (DOD) desired no changes in the structure of the telecommunications industry, as the DOD was dependent on the system which was in place and that system worked well in regard to supporting DOD needs. In testimony before the Senate committee, Undersecretary for Defense Richard D. DeLauer stated that the DOD strongly believed that Congress—and not the FCC and the courts— should establish the goals and guidelines for national telecommunications policy.[24] S. 898 was not original in its provisions. It mimicked both H.R. 6121 and *Computer II Decision* in its major provisions: The prohibitions of the *1956 Consent Decree* were set aside; regulated carriers could offer CPE and other telecommunications services through a fully separated subsidiary; resale of telecommunications services was deregulated; and the separations and settlement division of revenue system was replaced by a system of access charges. In the absence of new ideas, the Senate committee sought to alter the tone of the debate by explicitly placing the debate within the context of the broader policy theme (and Reagan administration strategy) of deregulation. The policy goals of S.898 were stated within the context of deregulation: to enhance existing competition and to encourage it where it did not exist; and to use the mechanism of deregulation to achieve the first goal. The bill provided for a planned and phased but definite transition to deregulation. For example, yellow pages revenue would be phased out of the local rate base over a four-year period; separate affiliates for the marketing and sale of CPE were required in two years and in four years for the manufacture of CPE. The central policy statement of the bill held that marketplace competition would be relied on wherever and whenever possible to provide all telecommunications services and thereby reduce and eliminate all unnecessary regulation.

Minimal regulation would be provided where there was no reasonably available alternative; this was a reluctant acknowledgment of a need to retain regulation to ensure the maintenance of a centrally integrated national telecommunications network. There was a continued commitment to the goal of universal service, but there was no a priori assumption that regulation was needed to maintain a goal which was widely held to have been achieved. The FCC was charged with determining what basic telecommunications services, as a matter of the public interest, should be universally available at reasonable charges, terms, or conditions. Absent a contrary showing, it was to be assumed that unregulated marketplace competition would universally provide such service. The burden would be on those petitioning for regulation to demonstrate clearly and convincingly that regulation was necessary to ensure universal availability at reasonable costs and conditions. However, the bill provided that prior to actual deregulation of basic telephone service in any market or area, the FCC was required to determine, i.e ensure, that basic telephone service would continue to be universally and reasonably available.

The FCC was further required to ensure that implementation of S. 898 did not result in unreasonable charges for basic telephone service and was authorized to use access charges to accomplish this end. Access charges were also to be assessed to ensure that all exchange carriers were compensated equitably for the costs of distributing interexchange telecommunications services. With regard to the maintenance of the universal service goal, the bill contained no explicit provisions for establishing a special fund, as had been the case in some earlier legislative proposals. However, S. 898 did make the Joint Board (comprised of FCC and state regulators) a statutory as opposed to voluntary entity with authority to determine the level of access charges. Some members of the committee would argue later that their making the Joint Board statutory was a reflection of the committee's explicit intention that long-distance rates would continue to subsidize residential and rural rates, with no increases in local rates as a result of competition and deregulation.

Although questions of the viability of universal service in a competitive, deregulated environment were raised, there was no significant debate on this issue. The bill did specify that nothing in its contents was meant to prohibit any state commission from allowing an exchange carrier to offer residential customers a basic lifeline service. However, there was no explicit provision or requirement for adoption of lifeline rates. There was also no significant consumer push for the adoption of lifeline rates. The only consumer organization testifying on S. 898, the Consumer Federation of America (CFA), held that lifeline rates should be determined by state commissions and priorities.[25] Yet another consumer organization emerged to offer some limited input into these hearings. The Conference of Consumer Organizations (COCO) did not send a representative to testify but submitted a statement for the record. COCO was defined as "a national umbrella organization of consumer groups, offices and individuals interested in consumer protection, consumer education, and resolution of marketplace issues as they affect consumers." The COCO statement raised questions about the impact of competition on universal service, the use of surcharges to support affordability, and whether under deregulation companies would be able to abandon service in unprofitable areas. It did not make a call for special lifeline rates.[26] However, the major failing of the COCO with regard to representation of consumer interests was their failure or inability to send a representative to testify in person at these hearings.

With regard to the position of the traditional industry participants in these hearings—AT&T, the independents, the new entrants, and other affected companies such as IBM—there had developed an amazing consensus. That consensus was essentially expressed as follows: "If there is to be competition, let's get on with it!" Although there were some concerns expressed about the continued dominance of AT&T even under competition and deregulation, each of the industry participants endorsed the thrust and objectives of S. 898.

SUMMARY

With acceptance of competition in the telecommunications industry as both inevitable and somewhat desirable, the policy debate began to narrow in terms of its broader contours while simultaneously becoming more complex in terms of some specifics. The policy debate narrowed to a question of balancing competition with the goal of universal service. The debate became more complex around the necessity of translating the idea of competition into operational policy. Particularly among new entrants, there was a recognition that given the historical structure of the industry, Congress was limited in its ability to facilitate competition. Thus, part of the challenge was how to implement competition using legislation as a fulcrum of sorts.

Although we have observed how the policy debate develops over time with the introduction of new legislative proposals and new ideas, we would not characterize this development as a linear process. Rather, the process is replete with redundancy and overlapping, incremental advances in the formulation of policy. Part of this is clearly attributable to efforts to make adjustments in response to feedback from the hearings on early legislative proposals. Yet much of it is also clearly due to the failure to set forth even a working definition of the problem being addressed, which would serve as a common frame of reference for the committee's deliberations and efforts to craft a sound policy. Indeed, the committees consistently refused to anchor their deliberations by setting forth even a common set of assumptions about the core issues they were attempting to address. The role and functions of the separations and settlement procedures within the Bell system were a prime example of this. The committee never made an explicit statement of the existence of this process, although in several proposals it implicitly sought to legislate for the consequences of terminating this arrangement.

One is also struck by the inefficacy of consumer input into this crucial policy debate. What little consumer input there was was disparate in its focus and of little or no effect in structuring the debate. No compelling arguments were made or forceful positions taken by consumer interests. Although the early legislative proposals did incorporate provisions for ensuring formal and substantive consumer input in regulatory and other decisionmaking activities, such provisions were dropped without debate in later policy proposals.

Throughout this phase of the debate on telecommunicatons policy, competition prevailed without challenge as the salient policy idea despite difficulties in defining the concept and despite doubts about its eventual realization. However, we observed the development of deregulation as a salient policy idea and as a corollary to the idea of competition. The policy idea of deregulation acquired saliency over time and was presumed to enhance and facilitate the policy debate on telecommunications due to its simultaneous emergence as the overarching policy theme of the Reagan administration. Although the saliency of the idea of deregulation also converged with the emergence of an apparent consensus with regard to rewriting telecommunications policy, the idea would not bear fruit by way of a congressional initiative in this policy area.

With regard to the overall telecommunications policy debate, all along there had been three separate sets of policy initiatives ongoing on three separate institutional tracts. Through a series of regulatory intitiatives, the FCC had embarked on a course to bring about competition in telecommunications and it successfully pursued that course despite intermittent efforts by Congress to forestall the FCC efforts. The DOJ had embarked on a course designed to end what it deemed were violations of the Sherman antitrust provisions and to force a restructuring of the Bell system. The DOJ pursued its course relentlessly; it, too, was largely undeterred by congressional action. A rather self-conscious Congress entered the policy fray belatedly and set out to seize the policy initiative by rewriting the 1934 Communications Act and preempting the efforts of the FCC and the DOJ. Although Congress had the advantage of statutory prerogative, in the end it was an institution without a clear, deliberate, and manageable goal. Prevailing policy initiative came from the DOJ with the January 1982 announcement of the proposed settlement of its antitrust case against AT&T.

NOTES

1. U.S. Congress. House. Committee on Interstate and Foreign Commerce. Subcommittee on Communications. *The Communications Act of 1978: Hearings on H.R. 13015.* 95th Cong., 2nd sess., 1978. Vol. II, pt. 1, p. 445. Testimony of J. Stephen Vanderwoude, Telecommunications Task Force of the Telephone Industry.

2. Ibid., Vol. II, pt. 2, pp. 82–83. Testimony of Honorable Charles Ferris, Chairman, Federal Communications Commission.

3. House. *The Communications Act of 1978.* Vol. I, pp. 499–507. Testimony of Richard A. Elkin, President, National Association of Regulatory Utility Commissioners.

4. Ibid. Vol. II, pt. 1, p. 301. Prepared statement of William M. Ellinghaus, Vice Chairman of the Board, AT&T.

5. Ibid., p. 263. Testimony of William M. Ellinghaus.

6. House. *The Communications Act of 1978.* Vol. II, pt. 1, p. 252. Testimony of William M. Ellilnghaus.

7. Ibid., pp. 409–414. Testimony of Philip M. Walker, Telenet Communications Corp.

8. House. *The Communications Act of 1978.* Vol. II, pt. 2, pp. 275–342. Testimonies and prepared statements of Orville Wright and Herbert N. Jasper, Ad Hoc Committee for Competition in Telecommunications.

9. Ibid., Vol. 1, p. 327. Testimony of Dean Burch, former chairman of the Federal Communications Commission.

10. House. *The Communications Act of 1978.* Vol. II, pt. 1, p. 415. Testimony of William McGowan, Chairman of MCI.

11. Ibid., pp. 64–65. Testimony of Paul Henson, Chairman of United Telecommunications, Inc.

12. U.S. Congress. House. Committee on Interstate and Foreign Commerce. Subcommittee on Communications. *Competition in the Telecommunications Industry: Hearings Exploring the Subject of Competition in the Domestic Communications Common Carrier Industry.* 94th Cong., 2nd sess., 1976, pp. 733–950. Testimony and material submitted for the record by the Honorable Richard E. Wiley, Chairman, Federal Communications Commission.

13. House. *The Communications Act of 1978.* Vol. I, pp. 520–527. Testimony of John M. Corman, National Rural Center.

14. Ibid., pp. 396–451. Testimony and material submitted for the record by Nicholas Johnson, National Citizens Communications Lobby.

15. House. The Communications Act of 1978. Vol. I, pp. 633–642. Testimony

of Thomas B. Cross, Communications Institute of Boulder.

16. See U.S. Congress. House. Committee on Interstate and Foreign Commerce. Subcommittee on Communications. *H.R. 3333, "The Communications Act of 1979" Section-by-Section Analysis.* 96th Cong., 1st sess., April 1979. Committee print 96-IFC 11.

17. Ibid.

18. U.S. Congress. House. Committee on Interstate and Foreign Commerce. *Telecommunications Act of 1980: Report to Accompany H.R. 6121.* 96th Cong., 2nd sess., August 25, 1980. Rept. 96-1252, pt. 1., pp. 70–71.

19. Ibid., pt. 1.

20. U.S. Congress. House. Committee on the Judiciary. *Telecommunications Act of 1980: Adverse Report to Accompany H. R. 6121.* 96th Cong., 2nd sess., October 8, 1980. Rept. 96–1251, pt. 2.

21. See Second Computer Inquiry, 77 F.C.C. 2d 384 (1980), *recon,* 84 F.C.C. 2d 50, *further recon,* 88 F.C.C. 2d 512 (1981), *aff'd sub nom* Computer and Communications Industry Association v. F.C.C., 693 F 2d 19 (D.C. Cir. 1982), Cert denied, 51 U.S.L.W. 3824 (May 17, 1983).

22. U.S. Congress. Senate. Committee on Commerce, Science, and Transportation. Subcommittee on Communications. *Telecommunications Competition and Deregulation Act of 1981: Hearings on S. 898.* 97th Cong., 1st sess. , 1981, pp. 1–6. Opening statement.

23. Ibid.

24. Senate. *Telecommunications Competition and Deregulation Act of 1981,* p. 133. Testimony of Honorable Richard D. Delauer, Undersecretary of Defense.

25. Ibid., pp. 228–232. Testimony and prepared statement of Lee Richardson, Consumer Federation of America.

26. Senate. *Telecommunications Competition and Deregulation Act of 1981,* pp. 582–584. Statement submitted for the record by Louis S. Meyer, Conference of Consumer Organizations.

Chapter 7

Divestiture and the Debate over Universal Service

THE PROPOSED SETTLEMENT

On January 8, 1982, the U.S. Department of Justice (DOJ) announced a proposed settlement of its long-running antitrust suit against AT&T. At the time, S. 898, the Telecommunications Competition and Deregulation Act of 1981, had passed the Senate by a vote of 90 to 4 and was pending in the House. Congress might well have been finally on the verge of enacting major telecommunications policy, but that opportunity had been usurped by the settlement worked out between the DOJ and AT&T. Competition would prevail in the telecommunications industry and the industry would be restructured, but primarily in accordance with initiatives taken by the FCC and the DOJ.

The DOJ had originally filed an antitrust suit against AT&T in 1949, charging AT&T with monopolizing the manufacture and distribution of telephone equipment in violation of the Sherman Antitrust Act. Part of the complaint was that the DOJ had at that time unsuccessfully sought the divestiture of Western Electric, the equipment manufacturing arm of AT&T. The 1949 suit was settled in a *1956 Consent Decree*, which restricted AT&T to engaging in "common carrier communications services" under governmental regulation. Although the Decree protected AT&T's monopoly position, it also effectively meant that AT&T would not be permitted to engage in the provision of competitive services. Under the Decree, Western Electric was restricted to manufacturing solely for use in the Bell system, and Bell was forced to license its patents to other manufacturers, who agreed to make their patents available to Bell. Thus, the restrictions sought to provide assurance that AT&T would not be in a position to subsidize competitive services with revenues derived from its regulated services. However, with the issuance of the *Computer II Decision* permitting traditional telcos (including AT&T) to sell certain enhanced services and certain equipment without regulation (through a fully separate subsidiary),

AT&T had sought and won in the New Jersey Federal District Court a new and more favorable interpretation of the 1956 Decree. The DOJ had appealed the district court's decision in this case and that appeal was pending up to the time the proposed settlement was announced. In 1974 the DOJ had filed a new antitrust suit against AT&T, Western Electric, and Bell Telephone Laboratories, charging the defendants with monopolizing telecommunications services and products. Again, the DOJ sought the divestiture of Western Electric as well as the divestiture of some or all of the Bell Operating Companies. Trial of the 1974 antitrust case had begun in January 1981, in the midst of congressional efforts to draft legislation to facilitate competition in telecommunications without requiring the breakup of the Bell system. The 1974 case had been pending at the time of the announcement of the proposed settlement.

The agreement worked out between the DOJ and AT&T in January 1982 had been filed as a modification to the 1956 Decree and later transferred to the jurisdiction of the Federal District Court in Washington, D.C. under Judge Harold Greene.[1] The original proposed settlement permitted AT&T to retain its intercity or long-distance services, its equipment manufacturer (Western Electric), and its research arm, Bell Laboratories. AT&T's long-distance services would continue to be regulated by the FCC, although the proposed settlement looked to the eventual deregulation of all long distance services. AT&T was forced to divest its twenty-two local operating companies under a reorganization structure to be submitted within 180 days to the court for approval and implemented over a period of eighteen months. Under the original proposal, the newly divested companies would be prohibited from manufacturing and marketing customer premise equipment, and from publishing the yellow pages. They would be required to provide, on a phased-in basis, equal access to the local exchanges to all intercity carriers on a nondiscriminatory basis. The divested BOCs would determine the level of access charges for these interconnections. Local exchange services would continue to be regulated by state regulators. Overall, the proposed settlement sought to separate the competitive aspects of the Bell system from the natural monopoly elements of local telephone services. Even the monopoly over the local loop would be broken up. Thus, the major barrier to competition in the telecommunications industry, the structure of the Bell system, finally was to be eliminated.

A proposal to settle a legal case by means of a consent judgment represents an agreement worked out by the defending party, in this case AT&T, and the DOJ, which has responsibility for enforcement of federal antitrust laws. It is an agreement which must be sanctioned by a federal district court. However, a consent judgment is not a private settlement of the type commonly associated with civil cases. Indeed, the Antitrust Procedures and Penalties Act of 1974 (P.L. 93-528), commonly called the Tunney Act, ensures that a consent decree emerges from a very public process. The congressional hearings record reveals that Judge Greene invoked the provisions of the Tunney Act over the initial objections of both the DOJ and AT&T. The Act sets aside a sixty-day public comment period which may be extended by the court. The Act requires that a consent proposal be published in the *Federal Register* and that copies of the proposal and determinative materials be otherwise made available to the public. The Act further requires preparation and publication by the DOJ of a competitive impact statement according to prescriptions of the Act. Public comments and responses by the government must be published in the *Federal Register*. Finally, the Tunney Act gives the court authority to determine if the proposed consent decree is in the public interest. In making that determination, the court may hear testimony of government officials and experts; appoint a special master and outside consultants; and request and obtain the views of parties as it deems appropriate, including participation *amicus curiae*.[2] Judge Greene held hearings and received extensive written comments on the consent proposal.

CONGRESS REACTS

Exercising prerogatives independent of the Tunney Act, both the U.S. House and the Senate convened hearings to explore the implications of the proposed settlement. Althoughthe proposed settlement would have resolved the question of competition in the telecommunications industry, it left unanswered, and made even more critical, questions of the fate of universal service. With the breakup of the Bell system would come the end of the separations and settlements and division of revenue arrangement, which (presumably) provided for national rate averaging and a subsidy for local rates. The proposed settlement did not address issues of pricing of telecommunications services. With legislation not yet having been enacted to provide for access charges to replace the separations and settlements, there were no measures in place to guarantee continued support for universal service. The FCC retained administrative authority to implement a new subsidy arrangement postdivestiture. However, members of the Senate committee viewed the FCC's authority in this area as most likely to be exercised in the elimination of subsidies. The Senate committee had therefore attempted to enact a bar against this possibility in S. 898 by making the Joint Board statutory and by establishing a regulatory standard of fair and reasonable rates. With the fate of S. 898 jeopardized by announcement of the forthcoming divestiture, the concerns of the committees in both houses of Congress suddenly narrowed substantially to a focus on the question of what would be the impact of divestiture on local rates.

Interestingly, there remained considerable disagreement and uncertainty among those formulating policy about whether the separations and settlements arrangement actually provided a subsidy for local rates. This was the case even though successive legislative proposals contained measures that were responsive to the assumption that such a subsidy existed. As part of a take cover attitude on the part of some members of the Senate Committee on Commerce, Science, and Transportation, and in light of an outpouring of public concerns over increases in local rates, Chairman Robert Packwood offered the following explanation and defense:

Let me explain to the audience once more, if I might, how the present system operates, so that if you're covering this or listening, you'll understand what we're driving at. There is a board known as the Joint Board, composed of some members of the Federal Communications Commission and some members of state public utility commissions. The Joint Board determines what's known today as "separations." Translated, that's simply the subsidy from long distance to local. And all of the local phone companies in this country, from General Telephone and Electric on down to the little companies, receive payments as subsidies for long distance. We simply changed the name of "separations" to an access charge in the bill that passed this committee, and again, this simply means the charge, in essence, that is going to be paid to tie into the local line. And we then said that the Joint Board would be statutory, and they will have an obligation to keep local phone rates reasonable, and that the local phone rates could not go up more than 10 percent above the national average in any year. And that's all statutory.[3]

Although the Packwood statement can be taken to mean that the Senate Committee had come to some resolution on the issue of the role of the separations and settlements process, there had been no similar resolution at the DOJ. In response to queries about a likely rise in local rates due to the post-divestiture demise of separations and settlements, William Baxter, Assistant Attorney General, Antitrust Division stated the following:

It is not at all clear to me that long lines' revenues presently perform any cross-subsidization function with respect to local rates. To insist that they do overlooks several important factors. At the present time the local operating companies pay what is called a license contract fee to the parent AT&T Co. This is a percentage fraction of their revenues that is conceived as having the purpose of reimbursing the AT&T co. for the value of research done by the Bell Laboratories, and for a variety of central corporate functions—pension fund management, payroll functions—performed by the general division of the AT&T Co. It is my view that the license contract fee is too large and that it has been a path through which the AT&T co. has siphoned out of the local operating companies revenues that ought to have stayed there.

The license contract fees will be halted by the decree. Those funds will stay with the local operating companies. So one must take that phenomenon into account in deciding whether, looking at the whole picture, AT&T and the long lines division has in any sense been subsidizing local telephone service.[4]

After six years of hearings and deliberations, key participants from the institutions most integrally involved in formulating major public policy in telecommunications had not acted to resolve basic questions about an issue which was central to crafting a policy of optimum benefit to residential telephone subscribers. Missing from the debate was any deliberate effort to bring clarity to the critical issue of the role and function of the Bell system separations and settlements. In effect, all parties continued to attempt to formulate policy based on assumptions which were never validated and which were continually disparaged.

In the congressional hearings initially convened to explore the implications of the proposed AT&T settlement, there were two key witnesses who appeared before committees in both houses. They were Charles Brown, Chairman of the Board of AT&T, and William J. Baxter, Assistant Attorney General, Antitrust Division, U.S. Department of Justice. Both were questioned intensively on the prospects of local rate increases. In response to the announced divestiture, officials of local Bell companies (speaking independently of AT&T) and members of state PUCs had publicly predicted that local rates would at least double and perhaps triple in a short period of time. Baxter and Brown were confronted with these claims. Both argued, in part, that local rates would not go up except   due to the ongoing pull of inflation. Both also gave other explanations of why local rates would not increase. Baxter's main line of reasoning was reflected in the foregoing quote. During the exploratory hearings of 1976 and 1977, AT&T had used the prospect of substantial local rate increases in the absence of the Bell system subsidies and the corresponding threat to universal service as major justifications for arguing against competition in the industry. As AT&T gradually lost the battle over competition, its position on the impact of competition on universal service changed. Brown now argued that the divestiture would have no major effects on local rates; that rates would go up due to inflation at a rate of about one dollar a year, and that regulators retained the mechanisms to continue to subsidize local rates.[5]

In a somewhat chilling depiction of a possible scenario of the future of universal service in telecommunications, Brown revealed his true sentiments:

I think the FCC and the other regulators need to be and are mindful of what is going on in the telecommunications industry. And it will not really be feasible to continue irrational kinds of pricing procedures in the face of competition. Let me suggest this: If access charges, which will under this decree be the substitute for the existing mechanism for subsidizing local rates—if those access charges are exceptionally high—as a matter of fact, if they are not reduced, the very simple economic and technological occurrence will be bound to happen. And that is technology will bypass the local plant. I"m talking about antennas to rooftops, I'm talking about cables or microwaves or cellular radio, which will go directly to customers and bypass the local plant if it costs too much to connect through it. These technological conditions are not going to wait for anyone. There is plenty of competition in the inter-city business, all of these competitors will move directly into the lowest cost means of reaching customers.

I know that both the FCC and the local regulators are fully aware that an irrational rate structure like this cannot be maintained forever under a competitive condition. It is one of the prices of competition and free choice in America, and I believe that it will be recognized over a period of time and cannot be legislated around.[6]

Although some members of the committee were apparently looking for some assurance that local rates would not increase in the postdivestiture world, such assurances were not forthcoming.

Congress appeared to have been caught off guard by the announcement of the proposed settlement of the AT&T antitrust case. Understandably, there had been much speculation that the trial proceedings could be delayed indefinitely, thus permitting time for consideration of other policy options. There is little doubt that the proposed settlement frustrated and complicated congressional efforts to craft a significant telecommunications policy and to assert a meaningful role for itself in the policymaking process. Immediately following the initial hearings held in response to the proposed settlement, the House Committee on Energy and Commerce opened hearings on H.R. 5158, the Telecommunications Act of 1982. H.R. 5158 was originally introduced on December 10, 1981 and had been reintroduced in the new session of Congress prior to the announcement of the proposed settlement. Thus, the situation within the telecommunications industry had been substantially altered from that which prevailed when H.R. 5158 was originally drafted. However, because the proposed settlement left many questions unanswered (such as the likely impact of divestiture on local rates), the committee also used the scheduled hearings on H.R. 5158 to hear testimony on the expected impact of the proposed settlement.

The Telecommunications Act of 1982 continued in the deregulatory trend of previous legislative proposals. It would have required that AT&T establish a fully separate subsidiary for the provision of any telecommunications service, product, or facility other than basic voice telecommunications; that local exchange companies provide nondiscriminatory interconnection access to all interexchange carriers; that interexchange carriers pay a cost-based access fee for interconnections in accord with a formula to be set by the Joint Board and regulated by state PUCs; that state PUC regulation be restricted to local exchange service (forcing them to relinquish to the FCC the regulation of intrastate toll service); and that there be equipment quotas that would require regulated and dominant carriers to purchase at least 8 percent of new equipment from nonaffiliated manufacturers. H.R. 5158 also provided for a National Telecommunications Fund (NTF) to assist high-cost, remote, and rural exchanges and to be supported by payments from interexchange carriers. Although the legislation firmly established access fees as cost based and not subsidy driven, the cost of funding the NTF was to be borne by interexchange carriers as well.

Although the committee made some changes in H.R. 5158 during the course of the hearings, the bill had been rendered effectively irrelevant by the announcement of the proposed settlement. There was no longer a question of what form competition in telecommunications would take or an apparent formal role for Congress in defining the structure of competition within this context. Yet the hearings on H.R. 5158 drew a large turnout of witnesses, who mainly ignored the bill at hand except to propose ways of changing it to address issues raised or left unanswered by the proposed settlement. Testimony in the hearings, which spanned twelve days, drew 144 witnesses, and generated 2701 pages of record, largely addressed the presumed implications of the proposed settlement. Different segments of the hearings addressed such topics as the impact of the impending consent decree on telecommunications users; the impact on competitors; the impact on labor and rural telcos; and the future of the BOCs.

The hearings were somewhat curious in that there were few certainties to assess. As a policy proposal, H.R. 5158 was largely irrelevant, yet the specifics of the consent decree had not been worked out. There was also some thinking that at the end of the sixty-day public comment period and after presentation of the detailed plan of divestiture, the court would not accept the proposed settlement. What was more important for the discussion here was the determination by Congress that it would play a significant role in shaping telecommunications policy.

Many of the issues raised in the hearings regarding the impact of divestiture were, in practical consideration, beyond the control of Congress and would be resolved as a part of the decree or via subsequent administrative actions by the FCC. Thus, in the midst of a sea change in telecommunications policy, Congress was left to focus primarily on a single issue—the future costs of basic telephone service—although there were several issues which would affect local rates (including the expected loss of cross-subsidies given the breakup of the Bell system; the possible loss of Yellow Pages revenues by the local companies; whether maintenance of inside wiring would be taken out of the local rate base; the financial health and viability of the divested BOCs; and whether the new access fees would be cost based or subsidy driven). None of these issues or other important ones were resolved at the time of these hearings. Although there was no presentation of facts as such which defined the projected rate of increases, there were assertions (some from reasonably informed sources, such as members of state PUCs) that local rates would increase from 98 percent to 200 percent. Members of the House Committee on Energy and Commerce reacted as if they accepted substantial increases in local rates as a certainty. Thus, the tone and the terms of the debate began to shift again, and dramatically so. Committee members began to make the case for legislative measures to mitigate the impact of rapid and substantial increases in local rates.

The announcement of the proposed settlement also provoked renewed concern about consumer participation and the representation of the interests of residential consumers in telecommunications policymaking. Thus, the hearings on H.R. 5158 were also used for what appeared to be a big push for establishing and institutionalizing a new and independent forum for consumer input into a broad range of policymaking activities by state and federal regulators. At the forefront of these efforts was the National Citizens Committee for Broadcasting (NCCB). NCCB was represented at these hearings by its Executive Director, Samuel Simon, who identified the organization as a telecommunications research and action center with over 8000 individual supporters and 120 group members. The work of the organization was described as promotion of a diverse and democratic communications system responsive to the public interest. Simon asserted that NCCB was the primary consumer advocacy group on telecommunications issues before the FCC. The chair of NCCB was Ralph Nader, a nationally known consumer advocate.[7]

NCCB opposed the proposed settlement and urged that Congress enact legislation to restructure the telecommunications industry. It argued that the decree as drafted put AT&T in the driver's seat and that the proposed decree raised compelling questions of DOJ expertise in telecommunications. NCCB also argued that the Tunney Act specifically authorized the court to obtain outside consultants and expert witnesses to assist in evaluating consent agreements. Thus, NCCB filed a petition to have Judge Greene appoint a consumer expert or panel to advise the court on whether and under what circumstances the settlement should be accepted. NCCB expressed a major concern that none of the consumer groups active in the sixty-day Tunney Act comment period would have the depth of resources or expertise to participate aggressively in the manner required by the circumstances. Simon also used the hearings on H.R. 5158 to express NCCB support for another piece of legislation for which the Committee had not scheduled hearings, H.R. 5421, the National Telecommunications Consumer Utility Board Act. H.R. 5421 had been introduced by Representative Ronald Mottl. The bill's core provision was the establishment of a National Telecommunications Consumer Utility Board.[8]

A more detailed discussion of the National Telecommunications Consumer Utility Board Act was given in later testimony by Ralph Nader, again within the context of hearings on H.R. 5158. Nader argued that NCCB and the Consumer Federation of America could not adequately represent consumers nationally in a policy debate which was so vast and complex. Thus, he offered a rationale for a new national organization to lobby the interests of residential users of telecommunications services before policymaking and regulatory bodies and to serve as a mechanism for educating the lay public about complex technologies and comlicated jargon.

The National Telecommunications Consumers Utility Board Act would authorize the creation of a not-for-profit, publicly supported corporation to represent residential telephone consumers. The corporation would not receive any tax revenues. Interexchange and intraexchange carriers would be required to include information about membership and impose a nominal annual fee in monthly billings to subscribers. Any administrative costs would be reimbursed to the carriers. The corporation would be governed by a democratically elected telecommunications consumer board of thirty members, elected from fifteen districts nationwide, plus five members to be elected by the board. Board members would be unpaid, except for expenses incurred in carrying out their board duties. The corporation board would hire a staff of economists, lawyers, etc., to represent consumers before policymaking and regulatory bodies. This, according to Ralph Nader, would give rise to an effective consumer movement which would give consumers real voice.[9]

The issue of consumer representation in regulatory policymaking was clearly a recurrent one in the protracted debate over telecommunications policy. The concern about consumer representation was generally expressed as a need for a specific sturcture for formal consumer input in the deliberations of regulatory bodies. As we have seen in earlier chapters, varied proposals for such input and representation were incorporated in different legislative proposals. Implicit in each proposal was the assertion that consumer interests were not forcefully articulated, not taken into account, and not well protected in the routine processes of regulatory policymaking. However frequently this assertion was made, it never gained a significant level of saliency in the policy debate. Thus, the proposal for a National Telecommunications Consumers Utility Board was never given a separate set of formal hearings. Furthermore, H.R. 5158, the Telecommunications Act of 1982, was not revised to respond to the announcement of the proposed settlement. Rather, the bill was withdrawn by the committee and there were no legislative proposals offered immediately as subsitutes or alternatives.

The settlement of the antitrust suit against AT&T via a consent decree was made final in July 1982, with an effective date of January 1, 1984. Judge Greene had been persuaded by the hearings and deliberations under the Tunney Act proceedings to exact some changes in the original proposed settlement. The Modified Final Judgment (MFJ) contained the following major provisions:

1. There was a requirement that AT&T divest all of its operating companies
2. There was a requirement that the divested operating companies (local exchange companies) provide equal access to all interexchange (long-distance) carriers.
3. AT&T retained its Long Lines (long-distance) Division; its manufacturing arm, Western Electric, and its research arm, Bell Laboratories.
4. There was a prohibition on AT&T's entry into electronic publishing (this restriction was not sought by the DOJ, but was imposed by Judge Greene).
5. The operating companies retained the right to sell or lease customer-premise equipment (excluding outstanding AT&T equipment) and the Yellow Pages. (This was a reversal by Judge Greene of provisions of the original proposal.)
6. The *1956 Consent Decree* was repealed, allowing AT&T to keep its patent and to provide unregulated enhanced services and related equipment. (This provision reaffirmed the provisions of the 1980 *Computer II Decision.)*
7. The Consent Decree permitted a system of access fees, to be implemented by the FCC, as a means of compensating local exchange companies for use of its acilities by interexchange carriers.[10]

THE ACCESS CHARGE DECISION AND THE DEBATE OVER UNIVERSAL SERVICE

The next major policy development following the MFJ was the December 12, 1982 announcement by the FCC of its access charge decision (Common Carrier Docket 78-72). The access charge decision was the primary means by which a major provision of the MFJ, equal access to the local exchange network, was to be accomplished. For competition to prevail, all long-distance carriers had to be granted equal access to the local exchange network. Similarly, local exchange companies had to be compensated for the costs of interconnecting to the local exchange. Moreover, the FCC had been concerned about the necessity of replacing the traditional Bell system of pooling and sharing of interstate toll revenues. The central issue was how to allocate costs for jointly used, embedded facilities (called subscriber plant costs) between the interstate and local rate bases. The access charge decision was the FCC's response to both of these problems. Under this plan, all interstate carriers would pay a usage-sensitive or volume-based subscriber line charge for interconnecting to the local exchange. Local residential and business subscribers would pay, too, for access to long-distance interexchanges. These fees would be set at a level designed to shift the burden of non-traffic-sensitive costs away from the interstate rate base and onto the local rate base. This shifting of costs would reverse a process begun in 1943 with a 3 percent allocation of subscriber plant costs to interstate rates. With subsequent adjustments, this allocation had reached a level of 26 percent in 1982. About 7.9 percent of total subscriber plant usage was actually devoted to long-distance service. Long-distance transmission had benefited from changes in computer and switching technologies. In 1982, much of the local loop still consisted of copper wiring, the material used since the early days of telephony.[11]

The access charges were set at $2 per month for residential subscribers, and $6 for each business line. The charges were set to begin on January 1, 1984 and were to be phased in and increased over a six-year period. By making access charges costbased and by shifting the cost burden over time to subscribers, the FCC expected that interstate carriers would make substantial reductions in long-distance rates. However, the access charge decision established an interesting principle, that local subscribers would pay a fee for having long-distance service available to them, separate from and independent of their actual usage of long-distance service. The access charge decision sparked a focused debate on universal service and prompted Congress to initiate further efforts at formulating some kind of telecommunications policy. On March 22, 1983, the House Committee on Energy and Commerce, Subcommittee on Telecommunications, Consumer Protection and Finance, held hearings on The prospects for universal service. There was no official legislation under consideration. Rather, the committee was hoping to obtain "hard data" on the impact of divestiture and recent FCC decisions on local telephone rates and universal service. The committee perceived a need to obtain more information on which to base some subsequent action. However, there was considerable ambivalence among its members as to both the nature and timing of its actions. Congressman Edward Markey of Massachusetts warned, in a statement submitted for the record, that the failure to ensure universal service could result in creation of an "information aristocracy" and an "information underclass," a division unacceptable to a free society. Congressman Albert Gore of Tennessee asserted in his submitted statement that "Congress simply cannot shirk its responsibility to insure that the goal of universal service is not sacrificed during the current restructuring of the telecommunications industry.[12]

Other members were less certain that the situation warranted congressional action, although they took care to articulate sentiments supportive of universal service. Congressman Tom Corcoran of Illinois asserted that it was imperative that rates be kept at reasonable levels to maintain universal service. He also added that it would be a serious mistake for Congress to consider legislation which would take specific steps to keep telephone rates at artificially low levels. Cocoran argued that it was impossible to identify the problems which might arise under competitive pricing; that it was irresponsible of persons to be screaming for immediate congressional intervention; and that it was impossible to know what might be needed to ensure universal telephone service.[13] Other members of Congress expressed similar views. Interestingly, in earlier stages of the policy debate Congress had been stymied by its status as an "uninformed interloper." It did not understand the intricacies of revenue flows within the telecommunications industry or the meaning and significance of the cumulative record of FCC administrative rulings and court interpretations of those rulings. Now Congress was stymied by uncertainty over whether it should act, an uncertainty apparently stemming from a concern that it would do the wrong thing.

Furthermore, after many years of efforts to assert a significant leadership role in formulating telecommunications policy, the sentiments of most members of the House Committee on Energy and Commerce was one of recognition that they had completely lost any opportunity for substantive policymaking. Their position was perhaps best summed up by Congressman Thomas Tauke of Iowa:

I believe that it is unfortunate that Congress last year failed in its attempt to address common carrier policy. As you, Mr. Chairman, noted on several occasions, it really has been the responsibility of Congress to attempt to bring some sort of direction to the policies that will govern the telecommunications common carrier policies in the future. But since Congress was unable to pass legislation in this area, it now falls to those who are testifying before us today, specifically the regulators and representatives of the telephone companies, and to the courts to make sure that consumers are protected and that the national interest is served.

We can prod. We can question. We can encourage. That is in part what we are going to be doing today, trying to make certain that the questions are asked, and that where necessary encouragement and prodding is offered in order to ensure that the public interest is protected and that the goal of universal service is obtained.[14]

If some members of the subcommittee were not yet convinced that Congress should act to protect universal service, that sentiment was not shared by most of the representatives of some half dozen state public utility commissions (PUCs) in attendance at the hearings. However, these representatives presented disparate levels of specificity about the components of coming rate increase which they felt would jeopardize universal service. Eric Schneidewind of the Michigan PUC provided testimony which captured the general sentiment of PUC regulators. Schneidewind stated that he foresaw a doubling of local rates by January 1984. He attributed these rate increases to FCC access charges mandating minimum flat fees and FCC changes in depreciation schedules which preempted state regulators' authority; the phaseout of interstate toll revenue; the higher cost of financing due to Moody's downgrading of all AT&T system bonds; and the loss of flexibility to spread costs over optional offerings such as CPE. These and other factors were expected to raise local rates and push one in ten people off the system.[15] Moreover, many states shared conditions similar to Michigan of multiple small telcos serving high-cost, low-income areas where any rate increases would have severe consequences for service providers and subscribers. Given that small telcos derived over 60 percent of their revenue from toll service, the impact of divestiture alone was expected to be severe.

Susan Leisner of the Florida PUC and chair of the NARUC committee on divestiture provided more specific details of a doubling of local rates in the state of Florida. Leisner reported that her PUC calculated that Southern Bell of Florida would have a shortfall of $270 million on January 1, 1984 (the effective date of divestiture and the start of implementation of the FCC *Access Charge Decision*. That would represent $8.50 per month for every residential and business subscriber in the state. These costs would be incurred due to divestiture alone. An additional $2 to $3 per month would be incurred from increases in depreciation for a total monthly charge of $25 to $30 a month for basic local service within a year or two of divestiture. Leisner predicted that for a transition period of five to ten years, it would be very difficult for many consumers to afford basic telephone service.[16]

The call for state PUCs to testify about specific impacts was not so readily answered by all representatives of state PUCs. A quote from Edythe Miller of the Colorado PUC captured the perennial problem plaguing Congress over the entire course of its deliberations:

In your letter of invitation, you asked us to present you with hard data, because hard data is what we need in order to make the decisions that are going to be necessary in the months to come. I would point out to you that hard data is exactly what we don't have.

I don't have any hard data. AT&T doesn't have any hard data. The FCC doesn't have any hard data. If anybody has any hard data, they are not letting on and they are not giving it out. Therefore, we seem to be embarking on a course with an unknown destination, uncertain as to exactly how we are going to get there.[17]

In response to direct questioning of all panelists at the start of the hearings with regard to their knowledge of any studies on the impact of divestiture, only one study had been mentioned. That was a study prepared by Lewis J. Perl of National Economic Research Associates, Inc. and submitted to the FCC. The Perl study had projected the impact on households of average monthly rate increases of 50 percent (an increase of $6.60), 100 percent ($13.20), and 200 percent ($26.40 monthly increase). Corresponding dropoff was projected to be 3.7 percent, 8.6 percent, and 22.5 percent, respectively. Slightly higher dropoff was projected in each case for blacks and the very poor. However, Perl had warned that if rates were not better aligned with costs, high volume business users would bypass the local telephone company, resulting in even higher rate increases for remaining subscribers with no place to go.[18] Such assessments would not appear to relieve the quandary in which the committee and the state regulators found themselves.

William McGowan, Chairman of the Board of MCI, made his familiar appearance at these hearings. He argued that congressional action would be premature before the dust settled on deregulation and divestiture and urged Congress and the regulators to resist the urge to finance the goal of universal service with price subsidies, which would interrupt the move to cost-based pricing. McGowan asserted that Congress could serve as a clearinghouse of information for all parties involved.[19] There were no indications from the record that any members of the committee were offended by McGowan's suggested role for them. In contrast, the committee expressed offense at the perceived deliberate absence of all CEOs of the BOCs at these hearings. Howard Trienens, General Counsel of AT&T, was questioned sharply by committee members about the CEO's "stonewalling" of the hearings. He assured the committee that there had been no orders from AT&T's upper management that CEOs of the BOCs not appear. At least one congressman, Albert Gore, threatened to subpoena the Bell CEOs.

Also appearing at the hearings was William R. Stump, Assistant Vice President of AT&T's District of Columbia offices. Stump was not viewed as a high-ranking executive in the AT&T system. He did, however appear as a representative of AT&T as a corporate entity, as opposed to merely representing the D.C. offices. Stump assured the committee that no one was more dedicated to preserving universal service than AT&T. After all, he stated, AT&T had spent 100 years achieving it. Then Stump proceeded to engage in a little "I told you so" type of prodding of the committee's collective memory. He reminded the committee that over a decade ago when Congress, regulators, and the courts were pressing for competition in the industry, AT&T had cautioned that along with the benefits of competition would come some consequences: a shifting of costs and major changes in the way service is provided. It was now time to assess those costs.

Stump asserted that AT&T had concluded that universal service at affordable rates could and would survive and that AT&T was dedicated to assuring the same. He cautioned that regulators had to adapt to a new environment; that the sky was not falling; that if rates doubled, few would leave the network; and that new depreciation rates and access charges were best viewed as guardians of universal service because they would ensure the financial health of the BOCs. Stump argued that subsidies were not needed, but rather what was needed were innovations in service and options in service prices; and that budget service and measured service could provide universal service at reasonable rates. What people needed, according to Stump, was dial tone, not unlimited calls.[20]

This position by AT&T was an attempt to redirect thinking with regard to a solution to the looming and intractable problem of significant drop-off from the telephone network. Stump attempted to make a counterargument to the inevitability of drop-off due to rate increases. He did so by arguing for a different kind of telephone usage for low-income consumers. He used the analogy of automobile drivers and their behavior in response to increases in the price of gasoline: Most do not cease driving, but they drive less or get smaller, more fuel efficient cars. They alter their usage. In Stump's analogy, the Honda was the measured service option many subscribers would switch to. Flat-rate service was the Cadillac which ate up a lot of gasoline for everybody.

The bottom line of Stump's argument was a warning not to overload access fees with subsidies because that would lead to bypass, especially since universal service could be retained through new service options.[21] Stump's argument was that overall, there was an economic solution to the problem of universal service as well as the threat of bypass. By offering low-cost service to the low-income public, the access fees could be kept low. With relatively low access fees and with a decision to shift the access fee burden to residential users over time, a positive signal would be sent to potential bypassers. Big-volume users would understand that bypass would not be economical because, in five years, as residential portions of access fees increased, they would have wasted their money. Thus, no legislation barring bypass would be required.[22]

The second part of Stump's argument was a revelation of still more subsidies of local telephone rates. Stump asserted that

on the average, local telephone service is about covering half of its cost. The other half must come from somewhere. . . Historically, what has happened, before we had competition, when we had a nice closed environment—regulators and companies were happy to go along with this because it kept the public happy—when you had a requirement for additional revenues, generally they would put those on vertical services like PBXs, like CPE, things like extension telephones, all kinds of services that were not basic.

We really held the basic rate down by collecting more than we needed from some of these. We took that extra money and put it where we needed it, namely, for the local service.[23]

The potency of the total argument put forth by the AT&T representative was not to be underestimated. The potential effect of Stump's argument was to undermine the near sanctity of the notion that local rates should be kept low, without a major change in the nature of basic service, and to discredit the corollary notion that competition and change in the telecommunications industry were taking place at the expense of the local ratepayer. However, the appeal of the proposed changes in local usage proffered by AT&T was not at all strong. Stump had indicated that in almost every recently filed rate case, Bell companies had offered a dial tone type of service at an extremely low price, much lower than the flat rate was before the most recently announced rate increases. These dial tone type of services were various budget service options and local measured service arrangements. Christine Hansen of the Iowa State Commerce Commission pointed out that low-cost dial tone services may be an option more available to Bell companies because the independents in Iowa (and in other states) did not have the technology that would enable them to measure services.[24] Eric Schneidewind of the Michigan PUC indicated that the state of Michigan already offered a low-cost, two-party measured service, but he argued that if too many subscribers opted for this subsidized service, Michigan Bell would go broke.[25]

Perhaps the most daunting response to the suggestion of locally measured service as a solution to the problem of retaining universal service was given by Susan Leisner of the Florida PUC:

Let me just point out an experience we had in Florida in the last rate case of Southern Bell, where the company introduced local measured service.

We had a half million petitions delivered to us in opposition to introducing optional measured service in the State of Florida. Consumers hate local measured service. They call it local long distance. The people who were protesting local measured service were the exact people that AT&T says it was designed to help. They were the elderly poor. They don't want to have to count their calls. They don't want to have to guess what their phone bill is going to be every month.[26]

Based on the counterarguments to the option of widespread use of low-cost basic service plans as a means of maintaining universal service, it did not appear that this option would be widely supported by state regulators.

In the closing minutes of the hearings on the prospects of universal service, the specific concept of lifeline telephone programs was raised. Telephone lifeline was emerging as a final resort service tether which could be used to retain the connection of low-income subscribers to the national telephone network. It was revealed that Michigan and California already had low-cost local service programs which were specifically identified as lifeline programs. In both states, lifeline service was available as an open plan, meaning that there were no requirements for verification of income. L. Reed Waters, Vice President for Regulatory Matters for Pacific Telephone (which covered parts of California), described the California lifeline service as costing $2.50 per month for thirty "free" calls. For the thirty-first call, an additional 10 cents per call was charged; and an additional 15 cents was charged for the forty-fifth call. California's measured service was offered for $3.75 with a $3.00 monthly usage allowance. The local calling zone was an average of eight miles from the place of residence, and each call was charged on a per-minute basis. It was pointed out that individuals on the measured service plan who had any considerable amount of telephone usage would incur costs equal to or greater than the monthly flat rate charge. The participation rate for California's lifeline service was 7 percent, and it was 3 percent for the measured service. It was estimated that a doubling of basic rates would result in a reduction of flat-rate participation from 90 percent to 80 percent.[27]

SPECIAL PUBLICS AND CONSUMER ADVOCATES

As the central issues of the policy debate shifted and narrowed from questions of the propriety and forms of competition in telecommunications to questions of the direct impacts of competition and divestiture on residential ratepayers, there was also an increase in the role and visibility of consumer groups in the policy debate. This became evident initially with the Nader group efforts discussed earlier. Participation of consumer groups increased when Congress shifted the debate to a specific focus on the plight of the elderly in the new competitive environment. In late June 1983, the House Select Committee on Aging held a day of hearings on The Telephone and the Elderly, with the stated purpose of assessing the impact of the entire restructuring of telecommunications on the elderly and organizations serving them. The holding of these hearings signaled an explicit effort on the part of Congress to broaden consumer input, especially that of special publics among the universe of consumers.

Congressman Timothy Wirth, who had played a major role on the House Committee on Energy and Commerce in processing legislative proposals for rewriting telecommunications policy, appeared as a witness before the House Select Committee on Aging. Congressman Wirth lauded the efforts of his committee in putting forth H.R. 5158 (The Telecommunications Act of 1982) and defended the thrust of that legislation while disparaging what he described as AT&T's multimillion-dollar lobbying effort to "disconnect" the bill. Wirth lamented that Congress had dropped the ball on telecommunications policy, but he still argued that there was a need for Congress to act, to give direction to the industry, and to ensure the universal availability of reliable and efficient telephone service in a competitive environment. However, Congressman Wirth also made a compelling admission: that congressional legislation could not prevent local phone companies from requesting inflated rate increases or the granting of such rate increases by state regulators. He asserted that Congress must focus on setting national policy and directing the actions of the FCC. He called on state regulators to exercise discipline and to grant only the amount of rate increases which were absolutely necessary.[28]

Appearing before the Committee on Aging on behalf of the FCC was Peter Pitsch, chief of the Office of Policy and Plans. He gave what was apparently becoming the standard FCC explanation and justification for its access charge decision and its decision permitting accelerated depreciation. His basic argument was that these regulatory actions would have few unique effects on the elderly and that the general shift to cost-based pricing would benefit the elderly along with everyone else. The FCC access decision was justified as a pragmatic balancing of three broad societal goals: universal service, nondiscrimination and efficiency in pricing of telephone services, and the avoidance of uneconomic bypass of local telecommunication facilities. Pitsch argued that the extent to which the phasing in of the access charge decision and the accompanying universal service fund did not adequately protect the interests of the elderly or the poor, the Congress should use general revenues to assure the goal of universal service. He further argued that low-cost service options such as dial tone plus a limited number of calls would meet the goals of universal service rather than the definition of universal service as unlimited, unmeasured flat-rate service.[29] We see here an interesting convergence of the AT&T position and that of the FCC.

AT&T's presentation before the House Select Committee on Aging, given by Charles R. Jones, Assistant Vice President for State Regulatory Activity, was brief and to the point. Jones asserted that universal service would remain a matter of national policy and a continuing objective of all players in the telecommunications industry. He further argued that the access charges would simply replace the old system of subsidies with no change in the total dollars available to support local service. Failure to implement the access charges would, Jones argued, result in uneconomic bypass of the conventional telecommunications network and would pose an even greater threat to universal service in the form of even higher local rates. Jones emphasized the position taken by AT&T representatives in earlier hearings, that the transition to competition in the telecommunications industry could be eased by offering services tailored to individual needs and by rate alternatives designed to mitigate the impacts of shifting to a competitive environment.[30]

The situation which confronted representatives of the elderly and other consumer advocates was now a relatively definitive one. Divestiture was occurring along with a restructuring of the pricing of telephone services. Access charges were to be imposed on all subcriber lines as a charge for access to long distance service independent of whether long distance service was ever used. Local rates were increasing by a significatnt amount even prior to the effective date of divestiture or the access charges. The key congressional committees had admitted their defeat and failure in efforts to enact policies which might have protected the interests of residential consumers in the dramatically changing environment of telecommunications. They had also stated forthrightly their inability to prevent the likely onslaught of future rate increases for local telephone service. The major industry service provider, AT&T, and the FCC were apparently agreed that the appropriate policy response to elderly and other low-income subcribers adversely affected by higher telephone costs was the offering of restricted use, low cost service options, primarily in the form of locally measured service.

The responses of consumer advocates was mixed but not particularly accepting of the policy response offered by AT&T and endorsed by the FCC. There was the continued insistence that Congress should act either to stave off the divestiture and the access charges or othervise intervene to protect consumer interests. Gene Kimmelman represented Public Citizens Congress Watch, the legislative arm of Public Citizen, a consumer research and advocacy group founded by Ralph Nader in 1971. Kimmelman argued that the solution to the problem faced by those most likely to be adversely affected was not lifeline, limited measured service or to "just wait and see." He reminded the committee that neither the divestiture nor access charges were yet in place, and thus time remained to pursue the question of why rate increases were already being implemented. He also reminded the committee that AT&T persisted in their contention that the breakup of the Bell system was not the cause of any rate increase. Kimmelman pointed out that a major repricing of residential telecommuncation services was taking place, resulting in subscribers having to pay for telephone installation; make a deposit to secure service; purchase telephones or pay a separate fee for rental; pay for wiring; pay for local service; and pay for access to interstate long distance. He argued that in the face of such enormous changes in pricing, Congress simply had to act.[31]

Jack Shreve testified on behalf of the National Association of State Utility Consumer Advocates, which he identified as an association of statutory representatives of utility consumers in approximately thirty states. Shreve voiced serious concern about the settlement as originally proposed and charged that the DOJ was either not viewing the settlement from the perspective of protecting the public interest or did not understand what was in the public interest. He also charged the FCC with intentional failure to ensure reasonable local phone rates in the postdivestiture world. Shreve argued that the FCC could not be relied upon to protect local ratepayers; thus the solution to their predictament rested with Congress and state representatives.[32]

Testifying for the American Association of Retired Persons (AARP) was president-elect Vita Ostrander. The AARP was identified as an organization of 14 million members. Ostrander reminded the committee that the telephone was particularly indispensable for the elderly because it provided an essential social link to the outside world as well as a link to emergency services. However, she informed the committee that AARP's legislative council had voted to oppose local measured service because it would adversely affect low- and moderate-income elderly by forcing them to restrict vital communications severely; to maintain a careful accounting of all calls made; or to incur costs beyond their ability to pay. The AARP recommendation was that the committee request the Congressional Research Service (CRS) to develop a model national rate structure to be used by all of the states. Ostrander was not forthcoming about the presumed benefits of a model rate structure in either her oral testimony or her written statement submitted for the record; nor did committee members query her on this issue. AARP pressed for more information regarding changes in telephone pricing to be made available to the elderly and urged that provisions be made for greater participation of the elderly in state ratemaking proceedings. In effect, the AARP position was one of acceptance of the changes taking place in telephone services and rejection of the key proposal being advanced as a means of mitigating the adverse impacts of these changes on the elderly.[33]

The most forceful position by a consumer group was taken by the National Council of Senior Citizens (SCSC), identified as a membership organization of over 4.5 million elderly citizens. NCSC took the position that local rates should be kept low and that a fee should be levied on bypassers. It also argued for a guarantee of some form of telephone lifeline service in each state and for federal legislation to mandate the establishment of citizen utility boards in each state. NCSC also urged that local telephone companies be made responsible for fully educating the public about service and rate changes to allow all consumers an opportunity to make informal decisions about their service.[34]

SUMMARY

Congress's long struggle to play a major role in rewriting telecommunications policy ended in preemption by the federal courts, the DOJ, and, of course,

AT&T. Major issues such as the nature and extent of competition and the restructuring of the telecommunications industry were settled by the Consent Decree. The policy debate then shifted and narrowed to the question of the impact of divestiture, and later to the impact of the access charge decision on local rates and the long-standing goal of universal service. In this sense, it was a debate which went nowhere.

In earlier phases of the debate, Congress had been stymied in determining what action it should take by its perceived role as an uninformed interventionist. For example, many members of the key congressional committees did not fully appreciate the meaning and significance of the cumulative record of FCC administrative rulings and court interpretations of these rulings. In the aftermath of the divestiture and the access charge decision, Congress was stymied by uncertainty over whether and how it should act to preserve universal service. It was apparently concerned that it might well do the wrong thing. This uncertainty contributed to Congress playing a major role as a prodder (of the FCC), not as an effective policy initiator.

The congressional role was made somewhat difficult by the way in which the debate over universal service was defined. The issue was defined as a choice between completing the move to rational, cost-based pricing and the enhancement of economic efficiency as a means of promoting universal service, or a return to uneconomic cross-subsidization of local rates by interstate rates, with a significant risk of imperiling universal service by encouraging bypass of the local exchange by high-volume users. That the debate did not become a rancorous standoff between these two perspectives is perhaps testimony to the fact that universal service was a well-institutionalized and widely supported social value. Neither industry participants nor government officials wished to bear the blame for having dismantled universal service. Thus, although the argument for cost-based pricing and economic efficiency was proffered as an important value and was heeded in policy formulation, the argument was not advanced in an effort to delegitimatize the policy goal of universal service. However, many service providers sought to redefine universal service. The MFJ was structured in a manner which permitted the FCC to play a key supporting policy role in imposing the access charge plan, a plan the FCC had been working on for some time. Thus, the FCC continued its pattern of making major public policy by accretion. Congress remained unable to check the FCC's initiative in this regard.

NOTES

1. For a good discussion of the background on the AT&T antitrust suit, see U.S. Congress. Senate. Committee on Commerce, Science, and Transportation. *AT&T Proposed Settlement: Hearings.* 97th Cong., 2nd sess., 1982, pt. 1, pp. 65–67 Prepared statement of William Baxter, Assistant Attorney General, Antitrust Division, Department of Justice.

2. *Amicus curiae* briefs, also called "friend of the court briefs" are comments and analyses filed in a case by knowledgeable and interested parties who are not legal

parties (plaintiffs or defendants) in the case. Such briefs in effect expand the range of viewpoints available to the judge(s) and are a means of lobbying the court.

3. Senate. *AT&T Proposed Settlement,* pt. 1, p. 5. Opening statement by Committee Chairman, Senator Robert Packwood.

4. Ibid pt. 1. Prepared statement of William Baxter.

5. Senate. *AT&T Proposed Settlement,* pt. 1, p. 7. Testimony of Charles Brown, Chairman, AT&T.

6. Ibid., p. 14.

7. U.S. Congress. House. Committee on Energy and Commerce. Subcommittee on Telecommunications, Consumer Protection, and Finance. *Telecommunications Act of 1982: Hearings on H.R. 5158.* 97th Cong., 2nd sess., pt. 1, pp. 491–495. Testimony of Samuel Simon, National Citizens Committee for Broadcasting.

8. Ibid.

9. Senate. *Telecommunications Act of 1982,* pt. 2, pp. 581–629. Testimony and prepared statement of Ralph Nader.

10. Citation for decree. See also Harry M. Shooshan III, "The Bell Breakup: Putting It in Perspective." In *Disconnecting Bell: The Impact of the AT&T Divestiture,* edited by Harry M. Shooshan III, pp. 8–22. New York: Pergamon Press, 1984.

11. For a discussion of the historical development of cost allocations in the telephone industry, see U.S. Congress. Congressional Budget Office. *The Changing Telephone Industry: Access Charges, Universal Service, and Local Rates.* Washington, D. C. June 1984. Chap. 2.

12. U.S. Congress. House. Committee on Energy and Commerce. Subcommittee on Telecommunications, Consumer Protection, and Finance. *Prospects for Universal Telephone Service: Hearing.* pp. 2–4. Written opening statements submitted for the record.

13. Ibid., p. 5. Opening statement of Congressman Tom Corcoran.

14. House. *Prospects for Universal Telephone Service,* p. 8. Testimony of Congressman Thomas Tauke.

15. Ibid., p. 9. Testimony of Eric Schneidewind, Public Utility Commission, Michigan.

16. House. *Prospects for Universal Telephone Service,* p. 103. Testimony of Susan Leisner, Public Utility Commission, Florida.

17. Ibid., p. 153. Testimony of Edythe Miller, Public Utility Commission, Colorado.

18. House. *Prospects for Universal Telephone Service,* pp. 81–82. Material submitted for the record by MCI Communications Corp. Letter dated January 8, 1983 from Lewis J. Perl.

19. Ibid., p. 43. Testimony of William McGowan, Chairman, MCI Communications Corporation.

20. House. *Prospects for Universal Telephone Service,* pp. 59–61. Testimony of William R. Stump, Assistant Vice President, AT&T.

21. Ibid., p. 91.

22. House. *Prospects for Universal Telephone Service,* p. 96. Testimony of William R. Stump.

23. Ibid.

24. House. *Prospects for Universal Telephone Service,* p. 93. Testimony of Christine Hansen, Commerce Commission, Iowa.

25. Ibid., p. 98. Testimony of Eric Schneidewind.

26. House. *Prospects for Universal Telephone Service*, p. 105. Testimony of Susan Leisner.

27. Ibid., p. 249. Testimony of L. Reed Waters, Pacific Telephone.

28. U.S. Congress. House. Select Committee on Aging. Subcommittee on Housing and Consumer Interests. *The Telephone and the Elderly: Hearing.* 98th Cong., 1st sess., pp. 7–9. Testimony of Congressman Timothy Wirth.

29. Ibid., pp. 44–45. Testimony of Peter Pitsch, Chief, Office of Policy and Plans, Federal Communications Commission.

30. House. *The Telephone and the Elderly*, p. 60. Testimony of Charles R. Jones, Assistant Vice President, AT&T.

31. Ibid., pp. 20–22. Testimony of Gene Kimmelman, Public Citizens Congress Watch.

32. House. *The Telephone and the Elderly*, pp. 64–67. Testimony of Jack Shreve, National Association of State Utility Consumer Advocates.

33. Ibid., pp. 26–31. Testimony of Vita Ostrander, American Association of Retired Persons.

34. House. *The Telephone and the Elderly*, pp. 33–34. Testimony of Joseph Rourke, National Council of Senior Citizens.

Chapter 8

Policy Responses by Administrative Rulings

CHALLENGING THE ACCESS CHARGE DECISION AND PROPOSING LIFELINE

Whether by pressures of the hearings held by the House Select Committee on Aging, direct pressures from their own constituents, or general frustration with their failure to execute a single telecommunications policy proposal, in July 1983 the key House and Senate committees (the House Energy and Commerce Committee and the Senate Committee on Commerce, Science, and Technology) took action to overturn the FCC *Access Charge Decision.* Members of both committees separately introduced legislation designed to protect universal service by shifting a major portion of local telephone service costs back onto the interstate rate base. Both bills (S. 1660 and H.R. 3621) carried the same name, The Universal Telephone Service Preservation Act of 1983.

The technical question addressed by both bills was how to replace the revenues lost to local telephone companies by the demise of the system of separations and settlements which had prevailed under the Bell System monopoly. Although consistently in dispute, the separations process was generally credited with having transferred substantial revenues generated in the long distance market to local telephone companies to constitute a subsidy which kept local rates artificially low. Moreover, Bell System representatives and some state PUC members also charged that tariffs for new telephone equipment and services had been inflated over actual costs as a means of keeping basic telephone rates low. Hence, with the divestiture and the unbundling of costs and repricing of services and equipment, the sheltering of local rates was no longer possible.

Yet there was no acknowledgment by many of the key players in the policy debate that anything had occurred or would occur which would provoke substantial increases in local rates. Despite its early contention that competition would be costly to local ratepayers, AT&T now took the position that local rates would rise only about $1 per year, and then largely due to inflation. Judge Greene had observed that nothing in the divestiture order provided a basis for significant local rate increases. The FCC argued that the initial phase of its six-year access charge plan required only a $2 charge to residential subscribers, hardly enough to explain the rash of filings for rate increases of 50 to 100 percent which were reported by state legislators across the country. Thus, the question of why local rates were increasing was compelling. Members of the two committees clearly felt compelled to attempt to protect local ratepayers. The committee members did not seek more discussion on why local rates were increasing. They simply pursued action to offset the need for substantial local rate increases by attempting to restore the flow of revenues from the interstate rate base to the local rate base. For many members of the committee, the issue was a philosophical one: Should local ratepayers have to pay disproportionately for maintaining a network from which multiple long-distance carriers would reap enormous profits? The Universal Telephone Service Preservation Act sought to address this issue.

Both the Senate and House versions of the Universal Telephone Service Preservation Act repealed the FCC access charge plan. Both bills established a system of exchange access charges to be paid to local telephone companies by interexchange long-distance carriers to cover interconnection costs. To guard against a loss of revenue due to the use of bypass systems, both bills imposed a system of payments on private systems providing telecommunications services without direct interconnection with local exchanges. Under both bills, residential ratepayers would not have to pay any access charges.

Both bills provided a two-pronged approach to preserving universal service. One, a universal service surcharge, was imposed on interstate or long distance carriers and private bypass systems to offset costs in high-cost rural and urban areas wherein local rates exceeded the national average by a specified percentage. The House bill was explicit in establishing a Universal Service Fund and a Universal Service Board to pool and distribute the universal service access surcharge revenues. The surcharge provision was offered as a reasonable substitute for national rate averaging, which had generally prevailed under the Bell system monopoly. Second, to offset the impact of major rate increases on the low income subscriber, both bills required the FCC and state regulatory authorities to take action to ensure that all persons have access to basic telephone lifeline service at discounted rates. Neither bill specified how lifeline telephone service was to be funded. (The measures designed to keep rates down in high cost areas—an attempt to retain general national rate averaging—were not measures designed to assist low-income ratepayers.) The House bill went one step further by authorizing state PUCs to require any local exchange carrier to lease and maintain at a discounted rate a basic one-line telephone to any subscriber unable to afford the cost of independently purchasing and maintaining a telephone instrument. This latter provision was defined as a "provider of last resort" provision.

In exempting residential ratepayers from access charges and by imposing both access charges and a special surcharge on interexchange carriers, both House and Senate versions of the Universal Telephone Service Preservation bills took strong stands in favor of placing the financial burden of universal service on the long-distance market. The concern for universal service as reflected in the two key committee bills was apparently widespread among members of Congress By the end of July 1983, a total of thirteen bills focusing on the issue of universal service had been introduced in Congress in response to the FCC *Access Charge Decision.*

On July 28, 1983, the House Energy and Commerce Committee and the Senate Committee on Commerce, Science, and Transportation took actions unprecedented in the debate on telecommunications by convening joint hearings on their two universal telephone service preservation bills (H.R. 4102 and S. 1660). At the opening of the hearings, the issue of universal service was characterized as an issue whose time had come. The atmosphere of the hearings was clearly charged by grave concerns over a wave of rate requests then being filed across the country. Congressman Mickey Leland of Texas reported that in June 1983 Southwest Bell had requested a rate increase for its Texas subscribers totaling $1.7 billion, raising basic one-party service from $10.75 to $34.35 per month. Senator John Danforth reported that in Missouri, Southwest Bell had requested an increase of $254,800,000, representing an increase in local rates of 99 to 164 percent depending on variation in population density throughout the state. Edward Hipp of the North Carolina PUC reported that a rate increase of 60 percent was pending from Southern Bell in North Carolina. Senator Wendell Ford of Kentucky stated that a national newscast of July 27, 1983 had reported a total of $4 billion in rate increases pending across the country. A survey conducted by the staff of the House Committee on Energy and Commerce during July 1983 was reported to have found a total of twenty-six rate requests pending, totaling $7 billion.[1]

In response to political pressures driven by this wave of rate increases, the FCC announced one day prior to the opening of hearings on the universal service bills that it was launching a comprehensive investigation of the facts surrounding the recent rash of proposed telephone rate increases in the states. The report from this investigation was promised by the end of 1983. The FCC had also announced that it was eliminating its end-user usage charge (the traffic-sensitive or volume usage charge) and reducing the flat-rate charge on residential subscribers from a minimum of $2 per month to a maximum of $2 per month in the first year.

These actions by the FCC were meant to blunt the determination by some members of Congress to overturn the access charge decision. They were also meant to ensure that the FCC did not bear the blame for the enormous rate increases taking place in the states. In his appearance at the joint hearings, FCC chairman Mark Fowler argued that the access fee decision was not the cause of rate hikes and that reversal of that decision would not cause rate increases to evaporate. He thus urged Congress to "stay its hands," at least until the receipt at

year's end of the FCC's special investigation. Fowler then attempted to cloak the
access charge decision within the fabric of a great strategy of economic growth.
He argued that the access charge plan would provide the foundation for the
country's growth in the information age; that it would create thousands of new
jobs, spawn countless new industries, and greatly improve national productivity
and the nation's position in international trade. Fowler then made a gesture of
political humility by asserting that he recognized that ultimately telecommunications policy was in the hands of Congress and not the FCC. He urged careful
consideration by Congress of whether any legislative remedy was warranted. He
pledged the services of the commission and its staff to the efforts of the
congressional committees.[2]

In his written statement submitted for the record, chairman Fowler detailed the
rationale for the FCC's access charge decision. First, he presented the familiar
argument of the need to shift the burden of fixed, non-traffic-sensitive costs of
the local loop, premises wiring, and terminal equipment away from the interstate
service base and to end the inequity of this arrangement, which had prevailed
under monopoly conditions. Fowler argued that the excessive burden on
interstate rates created both economic and technological inefficiencies by
encouraging large users to seek alternatives to conventional long-distance, such
as private lines that avoided usage-based charges for use of local facilities. New
long distance entrants were said to avoid usage costs similarly by masking their
service offerings as private line services. Fowler argued that, in sum, the
traditional use of usage-based charges to recover fixed non-traffic-sensitive costs
had the effect of inflating long-distance rates above the actual costs of providing
such services, thus effectively suppressing demand for interstate and foreign
services and creating inefficiencies in the use of the public switched telephone
network.

A second component of Fowler's rationale for the FCC decision was based on
pressure created by the modification of the Final Judgment (see Chapter 7).
Fowler referred to the requirement that the BOCs file non-discriminatory, cost-
justified tariffs for exchange access and the required termination of the
contractual-based separations and settlements and division of revenues. Thus, the
Modified Final Judgment was said to have created pressure for expeditious action
by the Commisison to move toward "cost-justified" pricing policies prior to the
January 1, 1984 implementation date.

The third component of chairman Fowler's rationale, the eminent threat of
bypass, was to emerge as a critical and persuasive issue in stymieing efforts to
return a larger share of non-traffic-sensitive costs to the interstate rate base.
Fowler made a strong argument that the efficiency and the continued viability of
the public network were threatened by the growing tendency of large users of
interstate services to bypass local exchange facilities to avoid usage based
charges for use of these facilities. Fowler explained that the means for bypass
had become available through the recent development of such technologies as
satellites, optical fiber, microwave radio, coaxial cable, cellular radio, and
traditional paired wire cables. He acknowledged that some of the bypass facilities

then constructed had not been efficient investments in that their costs exceeded the costs of the local exchange plant which could have been used, but he argued that such uneconomic investments were encouraged by distorted local exchange usage rates. Fowler proceeded to paint a picture of large users being driven to construct and use bypass facilities, thereby abandoning local exchange facilities and leaving residential and small business subscribers to pay even higher rates. Fowler identified an impressive list of major corporations and public and private organizations as already engaged in bypass, including Citicorp, Westinghouse, Boeing, Las Vegas casinos, and numerous state and local agencies. AT&T was identified as the largest potential bypasser of local exchange facilities. Thus, Fowler argued, the FCC was acting to eliminate built-in inequities and inefficiencies in the old pricing system which would be harmful to all consumers given new technologies and the realities of a competitive telecommunications marketplace. The thrust of Fowler's argument was that the FCC access charge decision sought to maximize economic efficiency, and that economic efficiency in pricing telecommunications services would best serve the goal of universal service.[3]

A panel of CEOs of telephone companies representing the seven regional BOCs gave testimony that reinforced Fowler's arguments regarding the threat of bypass and the ancillary threat to universal service. This panel, whose members indicated that they had coordinated their positions, voiced no support for the pending legislative proposals and expressed concern that the FCC had moved to modify its access charge decision. They argued that the docket which yielded the access charge decision had been underway for five years;that competition had been coming for a long time and it was too late to back down and that the new competitive marketplace needed certainty. They argued that the access charges as set forth by the FCC were absolutely necessary as a substitute for toll subsidies and as a preserver of universal service. The president of Bell of Pennsylvania, Raymond Smith, painted a dollars-and-cents picture of the threat of bypass. He explained that less than three percent of his company's customers contributed 50 percent of the revenues and all of the profits that just 200 customers made up all of business derived income; and that if the revenues provided by just the top 100 customers were lost, residential rates would rise by $4 per month. He further argued that because there was no specific method for identifying bypassers, telephone companies could not bill them for any fines imposed by Congress. Smith predicted that many bypassers would successfully petition Congress for exemption from bypass fines and that many others would pay the fines and still bypass.[4]

The Chairman and CEO of Pacific Telephone, Don Guinn, informed the committees about a study commissioned by his company from the accounting firm of Touche-Ross. The study was said to have revealed that of Pacific Telephone's 186 largest customers, one quarter of them already engaged in bypass, and another one quarter planned to utilize bypass technologies in the near future. Guinn painted a picture of bypass posing a threat of business revenue losses which would result in a $9 per month increase in residential rates.[5]   In sum, the panel of telephone executives argued that they were fully committed to universal service and that the way to ensure the continuation of universal service was to implement cost-based pricing. With regard to the issue of affordability for some subscribers, their solution was to offer an array of service options, including measured service, lifeline service, and premium (or wide area, unlimited calling) rate service.

AT&T was represented at these hearings by Charles L. Brown, Chairman of the Board. He seized the opportunity to remind the committees that AT&T had warned policymakers of the impact of introducing competition into a monopoly industry, that their warnings had been ignored, and that the result was now one of widespread panic. He expressed support for the FCC access charge decision as the appropriate way of dealing with a host of plaguing problems. Brown's argument was that the concern of state regulators about rising rates was a bit unseemly because they still retained complete control over local rates. He foresaw no threat to the impairment of universal service, but he pledged to work with the Congress in monitoring local rates.[6]

The positions of the independent telephone companies varied generally depending on their size, with the small, largely rural-based companies expressing support for the congressional counterproposals. The Independent Telephone Coalition, which represented the Association of Telephone Cooperatives and the Association of REA-supported Telephone Companies, expressed strong support for the pending legislation. It welcomed and urged congressional intervention and expressed fear that its 15 million rural customers would be left out of the emergent information revolution.[7] The dilemma faced by some small, rural-based, high-cost companies was vividly depicted in testimony provided by Rollie Nehring, president and majority stockholder of Arizona Telephone. Nehring's company served 1450 customers in a 5300-square-mile area, including 350 native Americans living in the village of Havasupai at the bottom of the Grand Canyon. Nehring testified that his company had an investment of $3,500 per line and monthly revenue requirements of $100 per line. Local revenues provided $11.70 per line, intrastate and interstate tolls provided $40.83 per line, and $47 per line came from subsidies provided under the Ozark settlements. Nehring believed that to shift all non-traffic-sensitive costs to local ratepayers would mean an immediate increase in local rates to $53 per month and the loss of much of the residential subscriber base for his company.[8] Thus, some of the independents, like Arizona Telephone, had compelling reasons for supporting congressional intervention.

The fact that not all of the independents were in similar financial situations or in agreement on emergent public policies was evident in the official positions of the United States Independent Telephone Association (USITA). USITA was represented by Robert H. Snedaker, Jr., First Vice President of USITA and President of United Telephone System, Inc. United Telephone was identified as the second largest independent telephone system in the United States, serving 3 million access lines in 3000 urban and rural communities, and generating $1.83 billion in local and long-distance revenues in 1982. Snedaker testified that

USITA's and United's position was that the FCC access charge plan was reasonable, workable, economically sound, and the best possible solution to a complex problem. According to Snedaker, cost-based pricing was imperative and did not pose a threat to universal service. He urged Congress not to intervene to set aside the FCC access charge plan.[9]

A nondefinitive position was taken by GTE. Theodore Brophy, Chairman and CEO of GTE, testified that he took no outright opposition to the pending legislation or offered any outright support for the FCC access charge plan. Brophy's position was that states could effectively address the needs of the poor by providing means-tested direct subsidies and by providing lifeline plans. Rival subscribers, he argued, would be taken care of by the Universal Service Fund provided for in the FCC plan for offsetting rates in high-cost areas. At this point, GTE was no longer just the largest independent local exchange telephone company in the United States and the somewhat noncommital position which Brophy articulated was no doubt reflective of the rapidly changing status of GTE as a major telecommunications corporation. Brophy informed the committees that GTE's Telenet subsidiary operated a nationwide public data communications network as a competitor in the enhanced services area; that GTE Satellite Corporation was building an advanced satellite system that would become opearational in 1984; that GTE had recently acquired GTE Sprint, the second largest non-Bell interexchange carrier, and GTE Spacenet, a domestic satellite carrier; and that GTE was a major manufacturer of telecommunications systems and equipment, lighting products, and precision materials.[10] Clearly, GTE had already become the conglomerate that other telephone companies would seek to become in the new telecommunications environment.

Perhaps the most interesting testimony was provided by William G. McGowan, Chairman and CEO of MCI. McGowan could easily be credited as the one individual who had played the most pivotal and aggressive role in bringing competition to the telecommunications industry. McGowan opposed S. 1660 and H.R. 3621 as hasty and unwise congressional action which would raise total charges for all customers; adversely impact competition; impede the development of new technologies; and encourage inefficiency on the part of local telephone companies. He then made the following assertion:

Let us look at some facts. In state after state, local telephone companies are blaming competition and divestiture for local rate increases. This is a smokescreen designed to obscure the fact that the bulk of the requested increases are for higher rates of return, faster depreciation, and—as you well know—a substantial amount that they put on top to compensate for what will be disallowed by the commission. Furthermore, these companies intend to load most of these revenue requirements on local telephone service. Some companies are actually proposing to reduce intrastate long distance rates, despite the fact that they will be left with the highest-cost toll plant, putting a further burden on local rates. . .

In any case, these rate cases should not have been filed now. Instead, they should wait until after divestiture when the various commissions and the operating companies themselves have actual experience operating in the new environment.

Nonetheless, telephone companies are using the uncertainty generated by the restructuring of the industy in an attempt to force monopoly ratepayers, local telephone users, into picking up an increased share of total revenue requirements while positioning themselves for anticipated intrastate competition.[11]

No one else appearing at these hearings had so unabashedly made such accusations of unjustifiable behavior by local telephone companies. However, McGowan believed that Congress should not act. He argued that state regulators had ample authority to deny unjustified or anticompetitive charges and to redirect any revenue requirements which were unjustified. He reminded the committees that state commissions historically had granted an average of only 25 to 40 percent of requested rate increases. McGowan was not convinced that local rate increases would pose a threat to universal service. The solution to such a situation would be mandated lifeline rates for certain groups paid for by a telephone company's other profitable services.[12]

Although Congress was clearly the target of considerable public angst over a changing telecommunications environment and rising telephone rates, it was state-level regulators who would be directly responsible for imposing higher rates on local subscribers. Only in the most technical sense did state regulators have "total control over local rates."   Although state PUCs held statutory authority to set rates charged by telephone companies and could deny rate requests found to be unjustified, they were also obligated to allow—indeed to guarantee—a reasonable rate of return on the investments made and costs incurred by local telephone companies. Thus, there were real limits to which state regulators could restrict increases in local rates when telephone companies could show evidence of the need for rate increases. The considerable cross-pressures felt by state regulators were reflected in testimony provided by the representative of NARUC.   Edward Hipp testified that NARUC wholeheartedly supported the philosophy contained in both the Senate and House bills. The reason given for NARUC's position was that state regulators foresaw turmoil coming in telecommunications which could constitute a crisis if left unabated. Hipp argued that universal service was in jeopardy due to a combination of factors, including a 100 percent increase in rates over the six-year phase-in period of access charges; the rapid rate of depreciation caused by new technologies which were aging present plants over a rapid period of time; and the shifting of costs onto residential ratepayers due to competition in the business sector. NARUC's position also included support for discounted lifeline rates.[13]

The consumer groups participating in the joint House and Senate hearings on the preservation of universal service included some familiar participants such as Congress Watch,[14] the Telecommunications Research and Action Center,[15] the American Association of Retired Persons,[16] and one new participant, Consumers Union.[17] Consumers Union was identified as a nonprofit organization established in 1936 to provide information, education, and counsel about consumer goods and services and the management of family income. Consumers Union's income was said to come solely from the sale of its magazine,

Consumer Reports, other publications, and films. The consumer groups were unanimous in support of the two bills under consideration by the House and Senate committees and unanimous in their support of a federally mandated lifeline policy as opposed to fifty-one (the fifty states plus the District of Columbia) different interpretations of minimum discounted service. They were also unanimous in their concern that lifeline policy not evolve into a welfare program with a cumbersome bureaucracy. There was continued concern about lifeline being defined as a restricted version of locally measured service. What was missing from the testimonies of the consumer representatives was the presentation of a compelling case for congressional or state-level action to preserve universal service. Rather, their appearances and testimonies at the hearings appeared to be somewhat perfunctory.

THE FCC YIELDS TO CONGRESS

At the end of the unprecedented joint hearings of July 1983, the committees departed to their respective chambers and returned to their respective internal rules for markup and further consideration. A review of reports prepared by both committees revealed that they considered a host of data generated by their staffs, the FCC, and state PUCs on local rate requests and awards, the costs of jointly used facilities, how costs would shift under various iterations of the FCC access charge plan, and the threat of bypass. The Senate committee gave particular attention to the bypass issue. The committee concluded that bypass was a matter of concern but not a clear threat. It based that conclusion on an FCC February 1983 survey of corporate communications managers, which reportedly revealed that corporate communications managers were skeptical of the reliability and durability of bypass technologies and were concerned about the security of messages on bypass systems. The Senate Committee also reviewed an article from *Bell Laboratories Record* which concluded that bypass posed no major threat to local rate bases. The *Bell Laboratories Record* article reportedly argued that local telephone companies had an edge in the ubiquitous local loop and in the fact that they would always have upgraded technology necessary to keep them competitive.

The committee acknowledged that it and the FCC still had incomplete information. However, the committee concluded that, contrary to the argument made by some industry spokespersons, bypassers could be identified. It reasoned that bypass systems making use of wireless or microwave radio facilities would need governmental approval to put those facilities in place. Wireless facilities would generally require right-of-way approval by state or local authorities, and microwave radio facilities would require licenses from the FCC. Thus, the committee concluded that the FCC and state and local regulators could develop a system for identifying bypassers.[18] The Senate committee favorably reported S.1660, with some amendments, but with the thrust of the original bill intact.

Under Rule XI of the Rules of the House of Representatives, the House Committee on Government Operations submitted a report of oversight findings to the House Committee on Energy and Commerce. The Government Operations Committee report was very critical of the FCC *Access Charge Decision*, concluding that it would lead to a doubling or tripling of phone rates in the next few years, with a severe impact on the elderly and the poor. The report also concluded that the access charge decision was not essential to or compelled by divestiture and that it unfairly expanded the federal role in setting telephone rates and diminished the role of state PUCs.[19]

The House committee's bill, H.R. 3621, was amended in committee markup and reintroduced as H.R. 4102 with the same title. On November 10, 1983, the House voted overwhelmingly to pass H.R. 4102, which in addition to its original provision regarding the FCC access charges, included an amendment to require the FCC to establish a national lifeline telephone service plan. This new provision replaced an original requirement that state PUCs establish lifeline programs.[20] In an apparent response to political pressures, on January 19, 1984, the FCC voted to postpone implementation of its access charge plan for one year, until 1985. The debate on universal service peaked in that all participants in the debate seem to have agreed that in the postdivestiture world of telecommunications, local telephone rates were rising dramatically. The issue of rate increases had achieved significant political saliency because of its obvious widespread effect on the millions of residential subscribers across the country. For policymakers, the critical question was what to do about the situation. By suspending its access charge plan for a year, the FCC had staved off a policy stampede by the Congress.

Efforts by Congress to craft a policy were now carried out within the context of efforts to obtain greater specificity about the extent and directions of cross-subsidization and the nature and extent of an expected problem of dropoff. Senator Barry Goldwater requested that the Congressional Budget Office (CBO) conduct an analysis of the impact of FCC actions on local telephone rates. In keeping with the CBO's mandate to provide objective and nonpartisan analysis, the report did not contain any recommendations for policy. Rather, the CBO analysis compared the approaches to the problem of cost recovery and jurisdictional cost allocations as represented in H.R. 4102, S. 1660, and the FCC access charge decision. The CBO also examined the nature of subscriber plant costs; historical patterns of allocating subscriber plant costs in relation to local and interstate toll usage; historical patterns of the relative decline in residentail telephone rates; telephone penetration rates by state; and the potential impact of changing telephone rates on different classes of residential subscribers. A major significance of the CBO report was because it came from a presumed neutral source, it helped to validate facts which otherwise might have been perceived as biased arguments on such issues as the historical contributions of the separations and settlements process.[21]

Also contributing greatly to clarity on the issue of pricing of telecommunications services and alternative means of cost allocation and recovery was a staff report from the Joint Economic Committee of the Congress, Subcommittee on Agriculture and Transportation. In October 1983 the Joint Economic Committee had held four days of hearings on the economic issues of a changing telecommunications industry. Those hearings had attracted over fifty witnesses and generated 500 pages of record. The Committee's staff report, "Public Policy Consideration of Pricing Telephone Services," was issued on March 1, 1984.

The staff report of the Joint Economic Committee was somewhat at variance with the arguments for cost allocations which underlay the FCC access charge decision. The report concluded that (1) the market structure problem of the telephone industry made determination of the true cost causer problematic in that virtually all users of telephone service-local, long distance, and WATS—shared common facilities; (2) the problem of large fixed costs not sensitive to use made marginal cost pricing elusive; (3) therefore, cost allocations in telephone services were not only difficult, but arbitrary; and (4) the characteristics of the industry did not match well with major prerequisites of a competitive market structure. The report expressed concerns about whether competition in long-distance markets was viable without critical regulatory supports. The report also concluded that universal service could be maintained in a newly competitive environment because the number of customers who would be particularly hurt by rising rates was relatively small, making financing of a universal service fund a manageable task. The Joint Economic Committee projected that a $1 per month, per-line fee would raise $1 billion annually and that a one cent charge per call would generate $3 billion annually.[22]

THE STATES RESIST THE CONGRESSIONAL LIFELINE INITIATIVE

As the time neared for the 1985 reinstatement of its access charge plan, the FCC began to yield on the issue of the impact of its decision on the poor. The original decision had included a provision allowing states to defer subscriber line charges (another name for access charges) on needy households at state expense. On December 19, 1984, the FCC adopted an optional plan for a total reduction of subscriber line charges for needy households with a 50-50 sharing of the costs between the FCC and the states. The FCC offered a 50 percent reduction in subscriber line charges. Participating states were required to implement an equal reduction in the local exchange rate for eligible households. Thus, the FCC action was an offer to meet the states halfway in shaving off an increment of the subscriber line charge and local exchange rates. The weakness of the FCC approach was that it was an optional plan. Low-income subscribers would be helped only if their states chose to participate in the program.

The FCC action did not satisfy many members of Congress, who still wanted a comprehensive, national telephone lifeline program. In January 1985, Congressman Mickey Leland (Texas) introduced H.R. 151, the Lifeline Telephone Services Act of 1985. Two years earlier, during the debate on H.R. 4102, the Universal Telephone Service Preservation Act, Leland had introduced an amendment to require the FCC to implement a national lifeline service plan. The amendment was passed by the subcommittee, the full committee, and by the full House. (H.R. 4102 was later tabled in the Senate.) Thus, Leland was confident that there was support in the House for a lifeline plan. His new bill shifted the institutional focus to state PUCs. H.R. 151 would require state PUCs to establish special lifeline rates for local exchange service at a discounted rate for low-income residential subscribers. Lifeline service was defined as basic service inclusive of a limited number of calls in the subscriber's local exchange area and additional charges for each extra call. Lifeline service was not to be defined as measured or budget service, which based charges on the duration of calls and restricted the subscriber's calling area. State PUCs would set eligibility criteria, taking into account the needs of the elderly, poor, handicapped, and unemployed. The lifeline plan would be subsidized up to 50 percent of costs by a surcharge on interstate long-distance service with a 50 percent matching contribution from state sources.[23]

With the shift in institutional focus to the state level came a substantial shift of the policy debate to the state level. The debate illuminated a host of practical and some philosophical obstacles to formulating a national policy which could be implemented readily at the state level. A month after Leland introduced his bill, the National Association of Regulatory Utility Commissions (NARUC) conducted a survey of state PUC reactions to H.R. 151. The basic response was one of opposition. A major reason for opposition was that establishing a lifeline program was a state prerogative and should not come as a mandate from Washington. A number of states indicated that they already had an equivalent service or had proposed a state lifeline program. Moreover, the response of many PUCs that administration of a lifeline program was a welfare function and/or beyond the acceptable functions for a regulatory agency was a telling one. Interestingly, the majority of states refused to estimate the number of subscribers likely to be eligible for a lifeline program and refused to estimate the costs of such a program. In a number of states, establishment of a lifeline program was beyond the statutory authority of the PUC (PUCs were generally prohibited from setting discriminatory rates) and would require legislative action. There were other questions as well, such as whether all telephone companies in a state should be subject to a lifeline program requirement (North Dakota had twenty-three telephone companies; Utah had fifteen; New Hampshire had thirteen; New Jersey had seven) or just the larger companies. The question of how states would fund their portion of costs for a lifeline plan was not an insignificant one. Possible options included state sales tax revenues, income taxes, excise taxes, gross receipts taxes on telephone companies, or spreading the cost over the remainder of the local rate base. Despite the persistent complaints from state regulators about the oncoming crisis of dramatically rising local telephone rates they offered little support for H.R. 151.[24]

THE FCC ADOPTS LIFELINE POLICIES

In announcing his lifeline bill, Congressman Leland had attempted to prod the FCC into taking action on "a responsible" national lifeline plan. Leland publicly stated that if in the next few months the FCC, NARUC, and Federal-State Joint Board were to act, congressional action would not be necessary. This was effectively the end of congressional efforts to formulate telecommunications policy. On March 20, 1985, the Federal-State Joint Board issued an order inviting comments on issues related to the development of measures designed to assist low-income households in affording telephone service. This began official FCC consideration of an explicit lifeline policy. This order and subsequent comments and hearings were known as Common Carrier Docket 80-286. The debate and the policy initiative now rested with the FCC. A review of some of the testimony filed in the lifeline docket reveals that the debate included a broader definition of universal service to include access or availability, relatively unrestricted usage, and affordable rates. This definition was more in keeping with the realities of the repricing of telephone services in that installation charges were increasing; deposits were required for first-time subscribers; and local measured service was undesirable and inadequate given standard usage patterns and given that the policy goal was to have rates for basic service within the economic reach of the low-income subscriber. Other issues in the debate included the relative price inelasticity of demand for telephone service and the resulting hardship endured by some subscribers to acquire and maintain basic service; the varying penetration levels among certain income groups and across geographic areas; and acceptable methods for measuring and predicting drop-off from the national network.[25]

On December 10, 1985, the FCC adopted a second and more expansive lifeline assistance plan. The plan provided for a total reduction in fixed charges for telephone service of twice the amount of the subscriber line charge. This would be achieved through a waiver of the full federal subscriber line charge up to the amount matched by state assistance. States were required to establish acceptable means tests subject to verification and to restrict participation to a single telephone line for a subscriber's principal residence. The state matching contribution could be in the form of reduced local telephone service rates, reduced connection charges, or reduced deposit requirements. There were no restrictions imposed on the source of funding for the state contribution.

In 1983 the FCC had committed itself to monitoring rates and reporting on rate increases to Congress in an effort to ensure that policy measures protective of universal service could be readily formulated. As a result of such monitoring, the FCC announced its third assistance plan on April 16, 1987. It was a two-part plan, "Link Up America," to connect low-income households to the telephone network. Under the first part, federal assistance would be provided to pay one half of the connection charges, up to a maximum of $30 in benefits for commencing telephone service. Under the second part, a local exchange company would be reimbursed for interest on a deferred payment plan in which the subscriber was charged no interest for up to one year for a maximum of $200 in costs for telephone installation and service commencement. Link Up America was to be a means-tested program designed to target those 2.9 million low-income households that were not connected to the public switched network.[26]

Thus, in a three-step process covering a period of three years, 1984 to 1987, the FCC established lifeline assistance programs to ensure that low-income subscribers would not drop off the telephone network and to assist low-income households without telephone service to obtain service. For each program, eligibility and (thus the level of participation) was determined at the state level. State programs had to be approved by state PUCs and certified by the FCC. As of July 1989, forty-two states, the District of Columbia, and Puerto Rico were participating in some type of lifeline assistance program (i.e., basic lifeline or Link Up America). However, partly because of varying eligibility criteria and partly because of varying outreach efforts across the states, the level of participation of eligible subscribers varied widely. As of January 1989, the highest level of participation of subscribers eligible for the basic lifeline plan was 66.43 percent in New Jersey, and the lowest level was in Ohio at 2.60 percent. Some of the poorest states (e.g. Alabama and Mississippi) did not participate in any federally assisted lifeline program. Because state participation was voluntary and states had total discretion in setting means-tested eligibility criteria, the so-called national lifeline program was considerably less than comprehensive in its coverage and impact. The argument for a program that targeted the needy rather than a blanket subsidy of local rates had been heeded in the FCC lifeline policy. However, the FCC had not taken action to ensure that lifeline programs were equitably extended to all needy subscribers.

In the end, things changed yet remained somewhat the same. Despite the debate over cross-subsidization of rates and a shift to cost-based pricing, the federal portion of lifeline programs was funded through charges paid by interstate ratepayers. Federal lifeline assistance was initially funded through the interstate carrier common line charge until April 1989. Subsequently, all three plans were funded through direct billing of the interexchange carriers by the National Exchange Carrier Association (NECA). The NECA served many of the functions previously carried out under the old arrangement of jurisdictional separations and settlements and division of revenues.[27] Similarly, despite the debate over the allocation of fixed, non-traffic-sensitive costs between the interstate and local rate bases, in the end the percentage allocation to the interstate base remained much the same.

In December 1983, the FCC adopted a long-term plan for cost allocation that utilized a new method, with implementation occurring in 1986 to 1988. The new method of allocation would not be related to measures of use. Instead, most companies would allocate 25 percent of local loop costs to the interstate jurisdiction and 75 percent to the intrastate jurisdiction. Under the old system, a high of 26 percent of local loop costs was allocated to the interstate base. Companies with local loop costs above the national average would recover their higher costs from the Universal Service Fund established in the access charge proceeding.[28]

SUMMARY

Despite protracted disagreement, in the end there emerged, almost ineluctably, agreement that universal service had been sustained by the separations and settlement arrangement of the old Bell system. Thus there emerged agreement that what was needed were replacement policies for these practices. In this context, a policy trade-off was made. Congress accepted the FCC's access charge plan once it became clear that the FCC would implement a national lifeline policy. The decision on some cross-subsidization of local rates in support of lifeline programs occurred with relative quiet. The FCC had made a strategic dodge, or perhaps a strategic genuflect, by articulating a formal acknowledgment of the superordinate role of Congress in policymaking initiatives. The states had not shown any such deference to congressional urgings and had resisted the imposition of a congressional mandate to establish state-level lifeline programs. Through its prodding, Congress succeeded in ensuring that the goal of universal service prevailed as an embodiment of the public interest in telecommunications policy. However, its operationalization as lifeline policy as established by the FCC was not a major triumph of the idea, and its actual implementation by the FCC was not conducted with great zeal. Nonetheless, the FCC persisted, effectively unabated, in its role as major policymaker in telecommunications by accretion.

NOTES

1. U.S. Congress. Senate. Committee on Commerce, Science, and Transportation; and House. Committee on Energy and Commerce. *Universal Telephone Service Preservation Act of 1983: Joint Hearings on S. 1660 and H.R. 3621.* 98th Cong., 1st sess., pp. 35–48. Opening statements.

2. Ibid., pp. 62–80. Testimony of Honorable Mark Fowler, Chairman, Federal Communications Commission.

3. Senate and House. *Universal Telephone Service Preservation Act of 1983,* pp.106–116. Prepared Statement of Honorable Mark Fowler.

4. Ibid., p. 187. Testimony of Raymond Smith, Bell of Pennsylvania.

5. Senate and House. *Universal Telephone Service Preservation Act of 1983,* pp. 89–190. Testimony of Don Guinn, Pacific Telephone.

6. Ibid., pp. 277–282. Testimony of Charles L. Brown, Chairman, AT&T.

7. Senate and House. *Universal Telephone Service Preservation Act of 1983,* p. 244–247. Testimony of Evan Copsey, the Independent Telephone Coalition.

8. Ibid., pp. 232–233. Testimony of Rollie Nehring, Arizona Telephone.

9. Senate and House. *Universal Telephone Service Preservation Act of 1983.* Testimony of Robert H. Snedaker, Jr., United States Independent Telephone Association.

10. Ibid., p. 284. Prepared statement of Theodore Brophy, Chairman and CEO, General Telephone and Electronics Corp.

11. Senate and House. *Universal Telephone Service Preservation Act of 1983,* pp. 290–291. Testimony of William McGowan, Chairman and CEO, MCI Communications Corp.

12. Ibid., p. 291.

13. Senate and House. *Universal Telephone Service Preservation Act of 1983,* pp. 118–123. Testimony and prepared statement of Edward Hipp, National Association of Regulatory Utility Commissions.

14. Ibid., pp. 370–376. Testimony and prepared statement of Gene Kimmelman, Congress Watch.

15. Senate and House. *Universal Telephone Service Preservation Act of 1983,* pp. 376–383. Testimony and prepared statement of Samuel Simon, Telecommunications Research and Action Center.

16. Ibid., pp. 383–388. Testimony and prepared statement of Vita Ostrander, American Association of Retired Persons.

17. Senate and House. *Universal Telephone Service Preservation Act of 1983,* pp. 361–370. Testimony and prepared statement of Robert Nichols, Consumers Union.

18. U.S. Congress. Senate. Committee on Commerce, Science, and Transportation. *Universal Telephone Service Preservation Act of 1983. Senate Report on S. 1660,* No. 90-270.

19. See: U.S. Congress. House. Committee on Energy and Commerce. *Universal Telephone Service Preservation Act of 1983. House Report on H.R. 4102,* No. 98-479.

20. Ibid.

21. U.S. Congress. Congressional Budget Office. *The Changing Telephone Industry: Access Charges, Universal Service, and Local Rates.* Washington, D.C. June 1984.

22. U.S. Congress. Joint Economic Committee. Subcommittee on Agriculture and Transportation. *Public Policy Considerations of Pricing Telephone Services: A Staff Study.* 98th Cong., 1st sess., 1984. Joint committee print 98-167.

23. Representative Micky Leland. Press release. *Regarding the Lifeline Telephone Services Act of 1985 (H.R. 151)* January 23, 1985.

24. National Association of Regulatory Utility Commissions. *Survey on State Lifeline Service.* Washington, D.C. 1985.

25. Consumer Federation of America. Report submitted in Common Carrier Docket 78-72 and Common Carrier Docket 80-286 before the Federal Communications Commission. Washington, D.C. March 29, 1985 (unpublished report).

26. Federal Communications Commission. Federal-State Joint Board. *Common Carrier Docket 87-339 Monitoring Report,* July 1989 (unpublished report).

27. Ibid.

28. Congressional Budget Office. *The Changing Telephone Industry: Access Charges, Universal Service, and Local Rates,* pp. 22–23.

Part IV

CONCLUSIONS

Chapter 9

Policy Ideas, the Policy Debate, and Policy Formulation

THE DEBATE ON ENERGY COSTS AND ENERGY POLICY

Before policy can be made, a problem must be identified and, implicitly or explicitly, defined. That is perhaps one of the simplest statements which can be made about poliycmaking. We have seen in all of the foregoing chapters that there is nothing simple about policymaking generally or problem definition specifically. We conclude from Chapters 2 through 4 that the policy debate lends itself to a ferreting out of issues in a process of problem definition. We might also conclude that the policy debate can yield multiple definitions of a single problem deemed appropriate for addressing in a policy response. Within the context of the debate on rising energy costs and utility rate reform, we observed that two major policy debates took place, which were carried out in three major phases. The two debates embraced two major conceptions or definitions of the core problem as well as several variants of the major problem definitions.

What evolved into a debate on electric utility rate reform began as an effort to seek solutions to a specific societal problem, that of the adverse impacts of rising energy prices on the elderly poor. This is the more conventional image held of policymaking activities—the search for a solution to a particular problem. The initial issue of rising energy costs might also be characterized as a relatively routine one. It involved an affected group, in this case elderly low-income citizens, which presented a list of grievances in making a case for justifiable government intervention on its behalf in regard to a particular problem. The initial phase of the debate was dominated by the argument that the elderly were particularly adversely affected by rising energy costs. The commodity at issue—energy for cooking, refrigeration, heating, and cooling—was one essential to sustaining life in modern society. Affected individuals were not in a position to alleviate hardships by substituting another commodity. Thus the elderly poor and their advocates apparently felt compelled to seek policy intervention.

The central thrust of the debate in this phase centered around an economic problem a problem of affordability. Thus having defined the problem as one of affordability for a life-sustaining commodity, the task was to identify an appropriate solution to the problem thus defined. Several solutions were put forth, including energy stamps, direct cash assistance to needy residents, direct payments to vendors on behalf of needy residents, and reduction of energy costs for needy residents through modification of the rates imposed for a basic amount of electric energy based on a policy of lifeline rates.

Even at the informal stage of the debate when a problem is being defined (prior to consideration of actual legislative proposals), we observed that the process of policy formulation cannot be fully separated from consideration of policy implementation. The participants in the debate appeared to understand that effective policy formulation required anticipation of implementation strategies. Thus, as each of the aforementioned policy solutions were advanced, the debate entailed some discussion of the likely problems and objections encountered in implementation. In keeping with implementation practices in assistance programs, eligibility criteria would have to be established and eligible recipients would have to be certified. Individuals eligible for energy assistance would not likely match that population certified as eligible for other assistance programs. In the case of an energy stamp program, systems would have to be established for production, distribution, and auditing of use. Direct payments to vendors would require certification of energy suppliers, validation of energy supplies actually provided to eligible recipients, and auditing for accountability. There was the implicit assumption that the aforementioned solutions would be funded out of general revenues, with some possible sharing of costs between the national government and state governments. Lifeline rates would require establishment of eligibility criteria, definition of what constituted a basic amount of essential energy, and certification of eligible households by the utility or some governmental agency. The idea of lifeline rates entailed an assumption that costs would be borne by the remaining rate base of residential, commercial, and industrial users. Although the problem might have been easily defined, implementation of any one of several proposed policy responses would involve a complex process.

We observed that from the earliest phase of the debate, different definitions of the problem were set forth as competing conceptions around which to formulate policy. One definition of the problem held that electric rates, specifically declining block rates, encouraged wasteful use of electric energy leading to higher consumption and higher costs for everyone. According to this explanation, the poor were simply penalized by declining block rates because they were disproportionately low energy consumers. The solution to the problem thus defined was to alter electric rates and reform the entire process of ratemaking.

Although this problem definition embraced economic concerns, it did not necessarily imply granting economic assistance to the low income.

Another definition of the problem focused on the alleged profligate practices of electric utilities and electric energy consumers and urged that strong energy conservation measures be imposed on both utilities and consumers. Strong conservation measures were seen as a means of stemming the rise in energy costs and as a means of curtailing major environmental damages incurred in constructing and operating more and more generating facilities to meet an ever-growing demand. The cost signal to consumers was seen as integral to this approach to formulating a policy response. Thus in its most pristine conception, this definition of the problem actually disdained the notion of providing assistance for meeting energy costs.

In the early phase of the debate, the plaintiffs, in this case were the low-income elderly and their advocates. The case had been brought initially before a select panel of policymakers, the Senate Special Committee on Aging. The issue network of participating individuals and groups with perceived substantive interests in the issue and likely policy responses was dominated by consumers-oriented interests. Among them were the National Council of Senior Citizens, the AARP and NRTA, the CFA, the OEO, a sympathetic governor, and the committee itself. The Ford Foundation was a major participant that advanced a more generalized approach to the issue, although it did not object to assistance for the lowincome. Utilizing what was comparatively an impressive array of data, a case had been made for justifying a policy response of economic assistance to the low income. It is interesting that the initial policy response to be adopted and implemented was that of home weatherization.

The policy response of home weatherization was the essence of policymaking as choice taking. There was no explanation discernible from the hearings record for why this particular policy response was adopted. Although the CSA had taken care to obtain what was considered valid technical input from the National Bureau of Standards on ideal specifications and standards for home weatherization, the argument had not been made that weatherization was the best solution to the problem. Logically, weatherization would improve comfort levels in some instances, but the argument had not been made that some elderly residents were freezing to death because of poorly insulated homes. Rather the argument had been made that many elderly could not afford to heat their homes due to rises in energy costs. Whether or not their homes were poorly insulated, the elderly had previously been able to heat them. Although there was some overlap between home insulation levels and energy costs, the administrator of the FEA admitted that energy conservation measures would offset only a very small portion of the energy costs of individual elderly consumers.

Why then did two major government agencies, the FEA and the CSA, not only champion the idea of home weatherization but engage in a struggle to dominate such activities when weatherization was actually a nonsolution to a serious problem? Perhaps the prior question is, Why did Congress engage in funding and otherwise supporting a nonsolution to a major problem? We might conclude that Congress felt strong political pressure to mount some kind of policy response and that weatherization was an easy policy response to execute. Given the way in which the CSA was organized, with branch affiliates in hundreds of local communities, it was an ideal agency for executing a policy response to large portions of the affected population across numerous congressional districts. The CSA was also an agency in need of a new mandate which was integral to an issue of national urgency. Involvement in energy policy was a solid means of serving the maintenance needs of this organization. Home weatherization activities also provided short-term economic gains at the local level to those directly involved in weatherization activities as well as to suppliers of weatherization materials. Home weatherization did not effectively address the problem of energy affordability; nor did it significantly affect the problem of energy conservation. Home weatherization did serve the idea of energy conservation long before that idea gained saliency in the policy debate. However, home weatherization was not a policy response supported by the problem definition which prevailed in the early phase of the policy debate.

The policy response of home weatherization provides insights into aspects of policymaking which are usually not given much consideration by analysts—that of policymaking via the the budget authorization process. We generally think of substantive policymaking as proceeding from the enactment of a new and distinct legislative statute. However, substantive policy is made by adjustments and additions to existing agency mandates in the budget authorization and appropriations processes. The initial policy response of home weatherization activities also provided insights into the ability of government to mount crisis-oriented responses, which require an escalation of the policy implementation process. A purposive course of action requires procedural and structural mechanisms for execution, generally referred to as the (public) administrative activities of policy implementation. The CSA provided a ready and ideal bureaucratic mechanism for implementing a broad scale home weatherization program.

At a later phase of the policy debate, when the focus had explicitly turned to direct cash assistance to the lowincome, we observed other dimensions of escalated policy implementation. Again the CSA was used as a mechanism for the appropriations of funds, which were then transferred to the HEW for actual disbursement. This arrangement permitted the most rapid policy response which the national government could mount. Even this response required a minimum of 120 days to identify the bulk of eligible recipients and to disburse checks to these recipients. This brings to mind the challenge of redirecting a supertanker which is traveling at full speed on the high seas. Its course cannot be redirected rapidly.

The second phase of the debate shifted to one focused around specific legislative proposals. These legislative proposals adopted various problem definitions, which continued the duality of the debate between economic assistance measures and utility rate reform measures. This phase of the debate considered comprehensive legislative proposals which combined electric rate reform and energy conservation via new load management technologies and economic assistance to the lowincome via special lifeline rates. The debate also considered single-purpose, dedicated lifeline proposals. The combined issues of rising energy costs, impact on the elderly, concerns about energy conservation, and growing environmental concerns made for a "hot" issue. Some fifteen bills were printed in full in the official hearing record, and an additional thirty-eight "identical, similar, and related bills" were cited has having been introduced. Moreover, a different and expanded issuenetwork was manifest in this phase of the debate, a network dominated by electric utilities and related groups such as NARUC, EEI, EPRI; state utility regulators; and representatives of federal agencies involved in energy policy issues. Consumer groups virtually dropped out of the second phase of the debate, and environmental groups exerted a strong and influential presence. Environmental groups supported rate reform as a means of advancing the goal of energy conservation and environmental preservation.

The second phase of the debate was dominated by the issue of electric utility rate reform. Again, this seemed to represent a form of choice taking by the congressional committee. Although the problem of utility ratemaking practices had been raised, there appeared to be a greater momentum in support of this problem definition than that which emerged from the earlier policy debate. Neither the state regulators nor utility interests held the view that ratemaking practices need reforming or that federal intervention was necessary for the adoption of energy conservation measures. Yet the congressional legislative committee appeared intent on enacting a policy of utility rate reform. We might conclude that the explanation derives in large part from the fact that congressional committees pursue their specific mandates. With the transferring of the policy debate from the Senate Special Committee on Aging to the House Subcommittee on Energy and Power, perhaps a difference in emphasis was bound to occur. The Special Committee had a social policy mandate. The latter subcommittee was one with a mandate for addressing energy policy issues. Despite obvious linkages between the two issue areas, convention and expertise no doubt structured something of a separation of concerns. We might also conclude that the public clamor over rising energy costs provided a window of opportunity for the Energy and Power Subcommittee to pursue a policy concern which had been on its informal agenda for some time.

During this second phase of the debate, the overall context for policymaking changed in a manner which effectively upstaged immediate concerns about energy costs. The idea of utilty rate reform was boosted by an enhanced definition of energy conservation incorporated in the idea of energy savings. The idea of energy savings gained considerable currency within the context of an overarching debate and focus on structuring a comprehensive national energy policy. Thus the first major policy response adopted via a comphensive legislative statute was PURPA, a rate reform and energy conservation measure which was enacted as part of a larger national energy policy. Perhaps it is not surprising that PURPA addressed two key sets of concerns. One set of PURPA standards required the adoption of various energy conservation measures incorporated in new rate structures. The other set of standards required the adoption of procedural reforms designed to make PUC ratemaking practices more open and accountable to lay consumers. The latter set of standards was responsive to the implicit assertion that if lay consumers were allowed to participate directly in PUC ratemaking procedures, PUCs would be more responsive to consumer concerns and less likely to raise rates. Moreover, the procedural reforms suggested that consumers were being empowered to affect ratemaking practices. Certainly the basis for a broad range of consumer complaints was alleviated.

Although the debate on rising energy costs and utility rate reform had continued to raise concerns about impacts on the low income, the argument for economic relief had not prevailed. The argument for economic relief had pivoted largely around the idea of lifeline rates. Alternative remedies such as energy stamps and payments to vendors, were perceived as carrying the stigma of a welfare program and as being too difficult to implement effectively. However, there were two arguments which vitiated the case for lifeline policy. One was the argument for rationalizing electric energy rates by abandoning declining block rates and shifting to marginal cost pricing. In making the case for marginal cost pricing in which each increment of electricity consumed would be priced to reflect the added cost of generation and transmission, the idea of structuring rates to subsidize even a relatively small component of usage was anathema. The second argument against lifeline policy was based on the primacy of the idea of energy conservation. The argument was made that the price signal was an ideal mechanism for advancing energy conservation, even among the poor. PURPA had included what was effectively an urging for voluntary consideration of experimental lifeline policies. The choice taking had been done by Congress. We might conclude that the argument for a lifeline policy did not garner the political force sufficient to overcome the objections lodged against it. On the other hand, we might conclude that Congress supported the alternative, which was advanced as the more rational policy course that would provide long-term benefits to all consumers. No doubt, Congress concluded that its actions best served the public interest.

The third phase of the debate became one of rising energy costs and national energy policy and involved a return to the original issue of the adverse impacts of energy costs on the lowincome. Six years after the issue was raised to the level of national concern, the issue of affordability had not been addressed. Just as early concerns for structuring a comprehensive national energy policy had helped to upstage concern for an energy lifeline policy within the context of utility rate reform, other aspects of structuring a national energy policy created a policy window for advancing the idea of economic assistance for high energy costs. President Carter's proposal for decontrolling domestic oil prices and taxing windfall profits which would accompany price decontrol resolved the question of how to pay for the initial stages of low-income energy assistance. However, resolving the funding issue was not so persuasive as to preclude a debate on the desirability of low-income energy assistance.

The third phase of the debate also gave rise to an issue network which differed somewhat from that which surrounded the earlier phases of the debate. In the third phase, on low-income energy assistance, energy suppliers such as the American Gas Association, the National Oil Jobbers Council, and EEI sought to exert strong influence. Although they clearly had a vested interest in any program designed to support the costs of energy for a sizeable clientele, this group made strong arguments on behalf of the poor when some other groups, such as environmental groups, did not. Moreover, at this stage of the debate, many of the advocates for the low income who had participated at the start of the policy debate in 1974–1975, had dropped out. The presence of the AARP and NRTA and the National Governors Association in this prolonged debate had been sporadic as well, but they reemerged for the final phase. The CFA was the most consistent consumer advocacy participant. A new but strong participant in the final debate phase was the League of Women Voters. Over the course of this debate, we observed manifestations of three different but overlapping issue networks. It appears that the structure of the participating issue network was determined by the definition of the problem which dominated the policy debate.

Only belatedly, and almost by chance, was the original issue of energy affordability addressed in a formal policy response. A debate with two faces had yielded two separate policy responses. This was the result of the separation of policy values, economic assistance for the poor, and energy conservation. Much of the debate was structured in such a manner that to promote one value was to preclude support for the other. This separation of values in the policy debate reflected a long-standing but specious convention in policymaking of not mixing concerns of social policy with policy concerns which can be defined otherwise.

In the case of utility rate reform and low-income energy assistance, Congress was in control of the policymaking process. The Senate Special Committee on Aging controlled the agenda-setting process which characterized the early hearings on rising energy costs. The House Subcommittee on Energy and Power essentially single-handedly redefined the problem, effectively structured the debate on utility rate reform and pursued a policy agenda of its choosing. In enacting PURPA, Congress assumed a role of policy initiator. Although the President played a key role in the Low-Income Home Energy Assistance Act, one cannot validly characterize the congressional role as that of follower. A more accurate characterization of the policymaking process in that case is that of Congress and the President as cosponsors of a policy response. Overall, we might conclude from this protracted policy debate that government is responsive to societal problems, in the long run.

THE TELECOMMUNICATIONS POLICY DEBATE

The policy debate on changing telecommunications policy was significantly different from the policy debate on rising energy costs and utility rate reform. The former debate did not involve a routine issue, and Congress was not being asked to respond to a societal problem as such. Rather, the debate on telecommunications policy opened with the world's largest corporation, AT&T, petitioning one institution of government, Congress, in a complaint about the policymaking activities of another institution of government, the FCC. This action by AT&T served to join Congress and the FCC in a struggle over the question of what constituted a legitimate policymaking role for the FCC as a regulatory agency. Thus the task for Congress was not so much one of problem definition. Instead, the initial task for Congress, as the debate was initially structured, was to decide two questions: (1) whether there should be competition in the telecommunications industry, and (2) whether the FCC could legitimately decide to implement competition in telecommunications or whether such authority legitimately rested with Congress alone. These were the questions around which the first phase of the telecommunications policy debate pivoted.

In a significant sense, the initial structuring of the debate was a specious one. In actuality, the FCC had already decided the question of competition in telecommunications in a series of administrative rulings spanning some twenty years, from *Hush-a-Phone* in 1953 to *Packet Communications* in 1973. Thus the exploratory hearings of phase one of the debate were little more than the result of AT&T demanding a public forum wherein Congress would be compelled to act decisively in validating or nullifying a policy determination already made by the FCC. Although this was a legitimate function for Congress, it was not an action which fit within the conventional conception of the congressional policymaking role.

The overall context for the questions the policy debate sought to address had been structured slowly over time by the force of new technologies. Not only had basic telephony been redefined, but new digital technologies had transformed telecommunications and vastly expanded the range of services to be offered in the industry. The FCC had issued a series of administrative rulings which had effectively followed the paths of emergent technologies. AT&T was seeking to suppress the expansion of the telecommunications industry, which was a natural outgrowth of the new business opportunities facilitated by the new technologies. However, AT&T's status as a regulated monopoly was still partially protected, though not without challenge, by public policy ensuing from the Communications Act of 1934. Thus there had developed over time a duality of interest and purpose in telecommunications policy, a duality that Congress was asked to resolve.

The second major factor which structured the dynamics of the telecommunications policy debate was that the operative policy statute, the Communications Act of 1934, was perceived as dated. After all, it had been written prior to the development of microwave, digital computing, fiber optics, and the like. Yet the Act provided the basis for the authority and existence of the FCC. The 1934 Act also incorporated two crucial public interest standards. One was tied to the FCC's role as gatekeeper and regulator of entry into the telecommunications industry and its role as regulator of the activities of companies engaged in voice communications. The second public interest standard incorporated the keystone public policy of domestic telecommunications, that of universal service. Support for universal service had been used as the rationale for numerous subsidiary policies internal to the industry, such as tariffs allocating costs between markets and services, as well as policies external to the industry, such as the REA loan program to support hundreds of independent telcos. As a policy concept and in its operationalization, universal service was so integrally tied to the Bell monopoly such that any threat to that monopoly was readily seen as a threat to universal service.

In addressing the question regading competition in telecommunications, the House Subcommittee on Communications assumed a posture akin to that of a court hearing arguments in a legal case. In the first phase of the debate, there was no legislative proposal of record around which the exploratory hearings were structured. Although a single bill had been introduced, in a unique and telling gesture the subcommittee did not print the Bell bill in the official record. Rather, the committee in effect summoned key components of the telecommunications issue network to present arguments. AT&T and the independent telcos draped their positions in the cloak of protector of universal service and the public interest. The new entrants argued their case within the context of the venerable American tradition of free enterprise. The FCC was forced to assume a posture of defending its decisions which, over the years, had laid the foundation for competition in the industry. This phase of the policy debate was high drama of a sort, involving profound questions of the public interest.

At the close of phase one of the debate, the subcommittee had answered the question of permitting competition in the telecommunications industry in the affirmative. However, the policy debate had not resolved the question of whether the FCC was the legitimate institution for structuring and facilitating competition. Thus it appears that the second phase of the debate, which considered specific legislative proposals, was driven by an assumption by Congress that it was obliged to enact distinct legislation which mandated and structured competition in telecommunications. The subcommittee sought to rewrite the whole of U. S. communications policy, "from basement to attic." Aside from the apparent reaction to the assertion that the FCC had usurped the congressional policymaking role, we might conclude from this action that there is much which is unknown and discomfiting in the statutory grant of authority by Congress to a regulatory agency. In other words, the boundaries of an agency's policymaking authority are not easily determined and cannot be fully anticipated by a statutory grant of authority.

We might also conclude from phase two of this debate that Congress is sometimes bound by a narrow view of what kind of activities are appropriate given its superordinate role in the policymaking process. Congress clearly felt compelled to formulate and enact new policy which mandated and facilitated competition. First, it was not clear that major new legislation was needed to facilitate competition. Second, Congress could have instructed the FCC to prepare and submit to Congress a detailed plan outlining the most appropriate purposive course of action, including recommendations for legislation as needed. Such instructions would have been in keeping with the congressional oversight role, a role which is laden with policy influence which potentially spans the reach of an agency's statutory mandate. Given the difficulties Congress experienced in formulating comprehensive communications policy, we might conclude that congress incurs a significant disadvantage in attempting to formulate comprehensive policy in an area in which its legislates on an infrequent basis. Such efforts appear to exceed easily the congressional institutional memory; and in an area affected by rapid technological change, such efforts appear to exceed easily the generalized expertise of the legislative commitees and their staff. We might also conclude from this phase of the debate that efforts to formulate comprehensive legislation in an area of mature regulatory policy require a level of strategic planning beyond that which accompanies the normal legislative process.

We are reminded by this policy debate of the distinction and distance between policy formulation and policy analysis. One is easily baffled by the fact that Congress never resolved definitively questions about the functions and impact of the Bell system separations and settlement arrangement. There were almost as many interpretations of the significance of this arrangement as there were participants in the debate. There were no indications in the hearings record that the legislative committees were troubled by the conflicting accounts of an arrangement which was presumably at the foundation of support for universal service. We might draw two conclusions from this situation. One conclusion is that at times Congress exhibits a willingness to legislate within a context of what one might characterize as an unreasonably high level of uncertainty. Second, it appears that Congress at times simply makes a choice about what it wishes to believe, with or without a reasonably definitive basis of facts.

The telecommunications policy debate revealed a degree of institutional competition among the FCC, the DOJ, and Congress in efforts to control the policymaking initiative. It also revealed the existence of somewhat separate institutional policy agendas. The DOJ appeared determined to complete execution of its antitrust litigation against AT&T. The antitrust suit was effectively a one time opportunity for the DOJ to play a major role in telecommunications policymaking. Thus the DOJ exhibited little interest in having its agenda compromised or mitigated in any way by actions of Congress. The FCC was clearly committed to a course of action in support of establishing competition in telecommunications. Interestingly, in the midst of congressional efforts to formulate comprehensive policy, the FCC issued its *Computer Inquiry II Decision* deregulating the telephone equipment market and furthering the inevitability of full-fledged competition in the telecommunications industry. In a policy tug of war, the FCC had the advantage of depth of expertise and constancy of involvement in the intricacies of the telecommunications regulation. Congress was not only intent on reasserting a lead role as policy initiator, but it apparently understood that it was the likely protector of last resort for the public interest standard and policy goal of universal service.

The second phase of the telecommunications policy debate on how to facilitate competition was ended by the announcement of the proposed settlement of the DOJ antitrust suit against AT&T. The third phase, on the question of how to preserve universal service, was begun by the FCC's announcement of its access charge decision. In an interesting manner, Congress was back to a key question from the earliest phase of the debate: how to preserve universal service in a competitive environment. Congress still had no answer to this question, and after numerous failures to formulate a comprehensive telecommunications policy, Congress had difficulty determining if it should attempt any action to preserve universal service.

The idea of lifeline rates as a means of preserving universal service had emerged at the outset of the debate but had been significantly upstaged by other issues in the debate. Moreover, the group which might have been the pivotal legitimater of a lifeline policy, the low-income elderly, considered such policies objectionable on the basis of their resemblance to a welfare program. The remainder of the poor were not only unorganized and unrepresented in the debate but were not as well regarded in the policy arena and thus could not compel policy concessions on their behalf. However, during the course of several efforts to enact specific legislation to preserve universal service, Congress was able to persuade the FCC to adopt a token lifeline policy by administrative ruling.

Congress never made new telecommunications policy despite numerous attempts over a seven-year period of debate. One explanation for this failure was that Congress was attempting to legislate in areas where it had already delegated significant authority and had thus "abdicated" the policymaking initiative. Congress had delegated to the DOJ (and other agencies) authority to enforce antitrust laws. Thus to a significant degree, some questions of competition in telecommunications were significantly beyond the immediate control of congress. Congress had similarly delegated to the FCC primary authority for implementing telecommunications policy and regulating the telecommunications industry. One might argue that Congress had not effectively exercised its oversight over the FCC over the years to have obtained insights into the implications of many FCC administrative rulings. However, one might also argue that Congress did not object to the goal of competition in telecommunications, and much of its struggle with the FCC and the DOJ was somewhat curious. Perhaps the most important conclusion which might be drawn from the debate on telecommunications policy is that the constitutionally superordinate position of Congress in the policymaking process can sometimes be irrelevant. Congress was not only unable to dominate the policymaking process, but Congress did not structure or control the terms of this debate.

POLICY IDEAS IN POLICY FORMULATION

We have observed that policy ideas can serve a useful function in the policy debate which undergirds the policy formulation process. Policy ideas help to structure the terms of the debate. However, their saliency and their ultimate fate appear to be a function of how the central problem of the debate is defined. This was much more clearly the case in the debate on energy costs and utility rate reform. The idea of electric lifeline rates emerged early in the debate and held considerable saliency when the problem to be addressed was defined as one of high energy costs and affordability. We also observed that other policy ideas such as energy stamps, emerged from this same problem definition. With the emergence of some policy ideas, the debate quickly shifts to anticipation of the policy implementation process. The focus on implementation can be used to generate a critique which becomes the basis for defeat of an idea.

Specific policy ideas must compete with other policy ideas and with overarching policy themes, which sometimes overtake and variably structure the underlying context of a protracted policy debate. In this regard, it appears that policy ideas are of at least two categories. It is important to make the distinction between the two categories. Some policy ideas seek specific solutions to problems by joining specific problems to policy responses in a way which implies a direct causal relationship. The idea of electricity lifeline rates (and energy stamps) falls into this category. If residential energy rates were too high for some residents to afford, the solution was to provide them a basic amount of electricity at sharply reduced rates,or provide them with energy stamps to pay their energy bills. These ideas held some currency because the facts substantiated the claims that increases in energy costs had outstripped the incomes of many residents who lived on low fixed incomes. However, once the problem was redefined by the policy debate, these ideas lost much of their currency.

Some policy ideas appear to be designed to serve broadly defined goals, which in turn may be served by numerous specific actions. I have referred to this second category as overarching policy themes. The idea of energy conservation falls into this category as an overarching policy theme. The argument for energy conservation was mainly that the nation should use less energy and use it more efficiently. Energy conservation was therefore a wise and prudent goal, buttressed by the fact that much of the nation's energy supply was imported, and buttressed by the claim (highly disputed in some quarters) that the world was running out of fossil fuels (coal, oil, and natural gas). Energy conservation was also linked to environmental preservation: The less extraction and use of energy fuels, the less damage to the environment. Although the argument was made that energy conservation would lead to an aggregate reduction in energy costs for the nation, the claim could not be made that energy conservation would directly address the specific issue of affordability at the level of the individual consumer. Energy conservation proved to be a much more potent theme in the policy debate than low-income energy assistance and prevailed in the initial policy resolution.

In the debate on telecommunications policy, the idea of lifeline rates emerged early as well. However, at the beginning of the debate the idea of lifeline rates was raised in anticipation of a problem of costs and affordability, which might accompany the eventual shift to competition in the telecommunications industry. In the early phase of the debate, lifeline was not linked to the central question which defined the policy debate. The central question of the debate on telecommunications policy was whether and how to facilitate competition in the telecommunications industry. Thus, for years, the idea of telephone lifeline rates was overwhelmed by the general debate on competition. Only in the final phase of the debate, when divestiture had ensured that competition would prevail, did the idea of telephone lifeline rates mesh logically with the definition of the problem which dominated the debate.

Policy ideas exert a more compelling hold on the policy debate when they embody values which reflect the dominant bias of the policy arena in which they compete. In both debates, the idea of lifeline rates was plagued by the criticism of irrationality. In both cases, the argument was made that rates should be structured to reflect real costs, and the structuring of rates to provide subsidies to one class of consumers made for an irrational rate structure. Of course it is not unusual, (or necessarily inappropriate) for public policies to be designed to serve political and social purposes instead of the goal of optimal economic efficiency. However, lifeline policies were perceived as issues of social welfare policy. Policymaking conventions generally dictate a separation between so-called technical issues and social welfare issues. Thus the idea of lifeline policy was lacking potency in policy arenas dominated by concerns about reforming electric energy rates to enhance energy conservation and rewriting telecommunications policy to enhance competition.

When afforded continuous presence in the policy debate, policy ideas can exert considerable influence on policy outcomes even in the absence of support by key participants in the debate. That is the primary lesson of the two debates presented in this book. In neither case was the idea of lifeline rates consistently at the center of the debate. In neither case was the idea of lifeline rates supported by major participants in the debate. However, in both cases the idea of lifeline rates retained a persistent presence in the debate, although not always a strong presence. Rather, in both debates the policy idea of lifeline rates embodied the issue of affordability of a vital utility service. Although the issue of affordability did not carry priority in the debates, it was an issue which carried considerable legitimacy. The policy ideas of lifeline rates succeeded in retaining the issues of affordability of basic energy supply and basic telecommunications service on the policy agenda until opportunities arose to translate these ideas into substantive public policy.

Selected Bibliography

Anderson, Douglas D. *Regulatory Politics and Electric Utilities.* Boston: Auburn House Publishing Co., 1981.

Anderson, James E. *Public Policymaking: An Introduction.* Boston: Houghton Mifflin, 1990.

Dobelstein, Andrew S. *Social Welfare Policy and Analysis.* Chicago: Nelson-Hall, 1990.

Gordon, Richard L. *Reforming the Regulation of Electric Utilities.* Lexington, Mass.: Lexington Books, 1982.

National Association of Regulatory Utility Commissions. *Survey of State Lifeline Service.* Washington, D.C.: National Association of regulatory Utility Commissions, 1985.

Reich, Robert, ed. *The Power of Public Ideas.* Boston: Ballinger Press, 1988.

Shooshan, Harry M., III, ed. *Disconnecting Bell: The Impact of the AT&T Divestiture.* New York: Pergamon Press. 1984.

U.S. Congress. House. Committee on Energy and Commerce. Subcommittee on Telecommunications, Consumer Protection, and Finance. *Prospects for Universal Telephone Service: Hearing.* 98th Cong., 1st sess., 1983.

U.S. Congress. House. Committee on Energy and Commerce. Subcommittee on Telecommunications, Consumer Protection, and Finance. *Telecommunications Act of 1982: Hearings on H.R. 5158.* 97th Cong., 2nd sess., 1982.

U.S. Congress. House. Committee on Energy and Commerce. *Universal Telephone Service Preservation Act of 1983. House Report on H.R. 4102.* 98th Cong., 1st sess., 1983.

U.S. Congress. Congressional Budget Office. *The Changing Telephone Industry: Access Charges, Universal Service, and Local Rates.* Washington, D.C.: U.S. Congress, 1984.

U.S. Congress. House. Committee on Interstate and Foreign Commerce. *Telecommunications Act of 1980: Report to Accompany H.R. 6121.* 96th Cong., 2nd sess., 1980.

U.S. Congress. House. Committee on Interstate and Foreign Commerce. Subcommittee on Communications. *The Communications Act of 1978: Hearings on H.R. 13015.* 95th Cong., 2nd sess., 1978.

U.S. Congress. House. Committee on Interstate and Foreign Commerce. Subcommittee on Communications. *Competition in the Telecommunications Industry: Hearings Exploring the Subject of Competition in the Domestic Communications Common Carrier Industry.* 94th Cong., 2nd sess., 1976.

U.S. Congress. House. Committee on Interstate and Foreign Commerce. Subcommittee on Communications. *H.R. 3333, "The Communications Act of 1979" Section-by-Section Analysis.* 96th Cong., 3rd sess., 1979.

U.S. Congress. House. Committee on Interstate and Foreign Commerce. Subcommittee on Energy and Power. *Domestic Crude Oil Decontrol, 1979. Hearings.* 96th Cong., 1st sess., 1979.

U.S. Congress. House. Committee on Interstate and Foreign Commerce. Subcommittee on Energy and Power. *Electric Utility Rate Reform and Regulatory Improvement: Hearings on H.R. 12461 and Related Bills.* 94th Cong., 2nd sess., 1976.

U.S. Congress. House. Committee on Ways and Means. *Windfall Profits Tax and Energy Trust Fund: Hearings.* 96th Cong., 1st sess., 1979.

U.S. Congress. House. Committee on Ways and Means. Subcommittee on Public Assistance and Unemployment compensation. *Administration's Low-Income Energy Assistance Program: Hearings.* 96th Cong., 1st sess., 1979.

U.S. Congress. House. Select Committee on Aging. Subcommittee on Housing and Consumer Interests. *The Telephone and The Elderly: Hearings.* 98th Cong., 1st sess., 1983.

U.S. Congress. Joint Economic Committee. Subcommittee on Agriculture and Transportation. *Public Policy Considerations of Pricing Telephone Services: A Staff Study.* 98th Cong., 1st sess., 1984.

U.S. Congress. Senate. Committee on Commerce, Science, and Transportation. *AT&T Proposed Settlement: Hearings.* 97th Cong., 2nd sess., 1982.

U.S. Congress. Senate. Committee on Commerce, Science, and Transportation. *Universal Telephone Service Preservation Act of 1983. Senate Report on S. 1660.* 98th Cong., 1st sess., 1983.

U.S. Congress. Senate. Committee on Commerce, Science, and Transportation; House. Committee on Energy and Commerce. *Universal Telephone Service Preservation Act of 1983: Joint Hearings on S. 1660 and H.R. 3621.* 98th Cong., 1st sess., 1983.

U.S. Congress. Senate. Committee on Commerce, Science, and Transportation. Subcommittee on Communications. *Domestic Telecommunications Common Carrier Policies: Hearings.* 95th Cong., 1st sess., 1977.

U.S. Congress. Senate. Committee on Commerce, Science, and Transportation. Subcommittee on Communications. *Telecommunications Competition and Deregulation Act of 1981: Hearings on S. 898.* 97th Cong., 1st sess., 1981.

U.S. Congress. Senate. Committee on Energy and Natural Resources. Subcomittee on Energy Conservation and Natural Resources. *Public Utility Rate Proposals of President Carter's Energy Program: Hearings on Part E of S. 1469 and Related Bills.* 95th Cong., 1st sess., 1977.

U.S. Congress. Senate. Committee on Labor and Human Resources. *Home Energy Assistance Act: Hearings on S. 1724 and Related Bills.* 96th Cong., 1st sess., 1979.

U.S. Congress. Senate. Special Committee on Aging. *Developments in Aging: 1973 and January-March 1974.* 93rd Cong., 2nd sess., 1974. S. Rept. 846.

U.S. Congress. Senate. Special Committee on Aging. *Energy Assistance Programs and Pricing Policies in the 50 States to Benefit Elderly, Disabled, or Low-Income Households.* 96th Cong., 1st sess., 1979.

U.S. Congress. Senate. Special Committee on Aging. *Hearings on the Impact of Rising Energy Costs on Older Americans.* 93rd Cong., 2nd sess., September 24, 1974.

U.S. Department of Energy. Economic Regulatory Administration. *Public Utility Regulatory Policies Act of 1978: Annual Report to Congress.* Washington, D.C.: GPO, 1981.

Index

About the Author

GEORGIA A. PERSONS is an Associate Professor in the School of Public Policy at the Georgia Institute of Technology in Atlanta. A graduate of Southern University in Louisiana and the Massachusetts Institute of Technology, she is the editor of *Dilemmas of Black Politics: Leadership, Strategy, and Issues* (1993).

ISBN 0-275-95039-5

HARDCOVER BAR CODE